Teaching Environments

Roman Bartosch / Sieglinde Grimm (eds.)

Teaching Environments

Ecocritical Encounters

Foreword by Greg Garrard

PETER LANG
EDITION

Bibliographic Information published by the Deutsche Nationalbibliothek
The Deutsche Nationalbibliothek lists this publication
in the Deutsche Nationalbibliografie; detailed bibliographic
data is available in the internet at http://dnb.d-nb.de.

Gefördert durch die Fritz Thyssen Stiftung

Fritz Thyssen Stiftung
für Wissenschaftsförderung

Umschlagabbildung
© Catrin Werntgen

Library of Congress Cataloging-in-Publication Data

Teaching environments : ecocritical encounters / Roman Bartosch, Sieglinde
Grimm (eds.) ; foreword by Greg Garrard.
    pages cm.
  ISBN 978-3-631-63850-7 -- ISBN 978-3-653-04008-1 (e-book) 1. Environ-
mental education. 2. Ecocriticism. 3. Ecology in literature--Study and teach-
ing. 4. English language--Study and teaching--German speakers. I. Bartosch,
Roman. II. Grimm, Sieglinde.
  GE70.T39 2014
  363.70071--dc23
                            2013043613

ISBN 978-3-631-63850-7 (Print)
E-ISBN 978-3-653-04008-1 (E-Book)
DOI 10.3726/978-3-653-04008-1

© Peter Lang GmbH
Internationaler Verlag der Wissenschaften
Frankfurt am Main 2014
All rights reserved.
Peter Lang Edition is an Imprint of Peter Lang GmbH.

Peter Lang – Frankfurt am Main · Bern · Bruxelles · New York ·
Oxford · Warszawa · Wien

www.peterlang.com

Contents

6   Contents

Foreword

Greg Garrard

Imagine for a moment that teaching were valued as highly as research in universities. Taking England as our example, we have to admit that, even after much of the direct funding was replaced by loans, there is a colossal amount of cash devoted to it: in 2012-13 HEFCE, the funding agency for England, will disburse £3.8 billion in teaching funds, but none will depend on teaching quality and only £19 million of it will be linked to pedagogical priorities. Efforts to find out if the money has been well spent are less than halfhearted. HEFCE does not advertise the cost of the National Student Survey, which is designed to ascertain students' 'satisfaction' with their education, but the *Daily Telegraph* claimed in 2010 that IPSOS Mori was paid "more than £2 million" to run it. Given that it would take me fifteen minutes to design an identical questionnaire on SurveyMonkey, this seems an absurdly large sum. Given the importance of the information collected, on the other hand, it seems suspiciously cheap.

The maxim of the neoliberal public sector is: "By their audit processes shall ye know them," though what ye shall know is less the activity itself than the political value attached to it. The Office for Standards in Education, Children's Services and Skills (OFSTED), the Big Brother of education in the UK, sends beady-eyed inspectors into every classroom and nursery and childminder's lounge in the land at a cost of £200 million every year. Higher education is barely glanced at by comparison: unlike its predecessor the Teaching Quality Assessment, which put assessors in lectures and seminars like a nascent OFSTED for HE, the Quality Assurance Agency spent £12 million in 2010-11 largely checking paperwork and talking to hand-picked students. Like the NSS, the cost is too high for what it does and far too little for what needs doing. Compare the miserly allocations for teaching enhancement in universities and the minute investment in gathering student feedback with the costs of assessing proposals for, and outcomes of, research funding. The Research Assessment Exercise,[1] which determines the distribution of around £1.5 billion in HEFCE funding, was considered good value by a Higher Education Policy Institute report because the process cost only £100 million over seven years, less than 1%

---

[1]   Now replaced by the Research Excellent Framework (REF), which is almost identical.

of the funds disbursed. The far more expensive peer review system employed by the research councils cost about £2 billion over the same period, or 10% of the grant. There is no exact analogy when it comes to teaching, but if we consider the NSS to be the primary means by which the effectiveness of HECFE's huge grant is assessed the cost of 'review' is just 0.0005%. In reality, it is even less than that, because the NSS includes questions about university administration and student's union facilities as well as teaching, assessment and feedback. Going (a fraction more than half-seriously) by the cost of review, audit and evaluation, the figures show research excellence is twenty-five times as important as institutional 'quality assurance', and 150 times as important as happy students.

No doubt priorities differ slightly between university systems. American universities, for example, take student evaluations into account when making decisions about tenure—but everyone knows a published monograph matters more. Many academics enjoy teaching and some of them excel at it (a fortuitous outcome since few have received any training in it whatsoever) but we all talk about "teaching load" whereas no one refers to their "research load." League tables such as the *Times Higher Education* World University Rankings include a score for teaching that is based on "reputation," as if anyone could make a meaningful judgment about the quality of teaching in a university where they neither studied nor taught. The Open University is renowned amongst serious pedagogues for its world-class teaching materials and innovative approaches to student learning, but somehow doesn't make the THE's Top 100. Where universities have feared to tread, the Internet has rushed in with the dreaded ratemyprofessors.com. Instead of a meaningful system of accountability and improvement for university teachers, the website collects scores for "easiness," "helpfulness," "clarity," and... "hotness." Not a mention of intellectual challenge, although many students do comment positively on such matters.

In ecocriticism, at least, the importance of teaching has long been acknowledged. In fact, one of the earliest textbooks in the field was aimed at teachers (Waage 1985), and there have since been quite a few publications on ecocritical pedagogy, most of them from the United States (Gaard and Murphy 1998, Murphy 1995, Crimmel 2003, Christensen, Long, and Waage 2008, Garrard 2012), including one specifically on secondary education (Matthewman 2010). There are at least two good reasons for this: environmental education is quite generally taken to imply a non-traditional approach to teaching, including outdoor learning and place-based education; and ecocriticism seeks social change as well as deeper understanding of literature. While we might dream that our research output will inspire people outside academia, it is much more likely to be our *teaching* that constitutes our best claim to environmental activism. So it is with especial pleasure that I recommend Roman Bartosch and Sieglinde Grimm's collection of essays. Not only is it the first new collection of essays on eco-pedagogy from continental Europe in this decade; it is also uniquely wide-ranging, taking in language teaching, children's literature and historicist modes of interpretation. Crucially, though, the editors ensure that the collection questions the moral mission of ecocriticism, rather than taking it for granted: they include both a critique of agenda-led teaching from Pamela Swanigan and a spirited debate sparked by critical comments from Andrew Major and Andrew McMurry, originally in the *Journal of Ecocriticism*. Eco-pedagogy, or eco-didactics as it is known in Germany, needs to question theory as energetically as it reconsiders the practice of the classroom. Can we be preachers as well as teachers? And does the urgency of environmental crisis rule out the slow processes of reflection and questioning the liberal tradition in education promotes? This collection presents articulate responses to these questions that we hope will inform your own.

Works Cited

Christensen, Laird, Mark C. Long, and Frederick O. Waage. *Teaching North American Environmental Literature, Modern Language Association of America Options for Teaching*. New York: Modern Language Association of America, 2008.

Crimmel, Hal. *Teaching in the Field: Working with Students in the Outdoor Classroom*. Salt Lake City: U of Utah P, 2003.

Gaard, Greta Claire, and Patrick D. Murphy. *Ecofeminist Literary Criticism: Theory, Interpretation, Pedagogy*. Urbana: U of Illinois P, 1998.

Garrard, Greg. *Teaching Ecocriticism and Green Cultural Studies*. Houndmills, Basingstoke, Hampshire; New York: Palgrave Macmillan, 2012.

Matthewman, Sasha. *Teaching Secondary English as if the Planet Matters*: Taylor & Francis, 2010.

Murphy, Patrick D. *Literature, Nature, and Other: Ecofeminist Critiques*. Albany: State University of New York Press, 1995.

Waage, Frederick O. *Teaching Environmental Literature: Materials, Methods, Resources*: Modern Language Association of America, 1985.

Introductions

Teaching Environments:
How 'Green' Can—and Should—a Classroom Be?

Roman Bartosch & Sieglinde Grimm (Cologne)

Although many reports and studies pessimistically agree that by far, not enough has been done to mitigate the looming environmental crisis, and that time is indeed running out, the recent years have seen a noteworthy change with regard to the role the humanities and arts have been assigned in these troubled times. Only six years after Sylvia Mayer and Graham Wilson's publication *Ecodidactic Perspectives on English Language, Literatures and Cultures*, the notion that "[t]he environmental crisis [...] is, in fact, a cultural crisis" (Mayer & Wilson 2006: 1; see also Buell 1995: 2 and Kerridge 1998: 4) seems to have become received opinion. Since the 1970s, UNESCO reports have been speaking of "environmental education" and, in contrast to a common understanding of such an educational objective in terms of an education aiming at scientific or engineering knowledge, the 2002 UNESCO report cited by Mayer and Wilson maintains that the "movement towards sustainable development depends more on the development of our moral sensitivities than on the growth of our scientific understanding" (cited in Mayer & Wilson 2006: 1).

Six years later, as we are writing this introduction, much more has changed. The recent report on education for sustainable development (UNESCO 2012) states even more clearly that education, a change of attitudes and, more generally, human ethical relationships with the biosphere and non-human others must precede any technological or scientific 'fix' of the crises ahead. Numerous studies and collections of essays, such as Greg Garrard's superb *Teaching Ecocriticism and Green Cultural Studies*, Sasha Matthewman's *Teaching Secondary English as if the Planet Matters* and Laird Christensen et al.'s *Teaching North American Environmental Literature* have underlined the relevance of the humanities and arts in this respect. However, there might be good reason in remaining skeptical. While the fact that the humanities and arts have joined endeavors at mitigating or adapting to environmental change and invest intellectual energy in questions of environmental justice and posthumanist ethics, the turn towards consciousness-raising and environmentalist agendas in education seems strangely at odds with the critical distance that many of us hold to be important. As Axel Goodbody has argued, a governmental and/or environmental agenda to foster ecological thinking "goes beyond the remit of the academic, and could be seen as coming dangerously close to attempts by industrial lobbies and political interest groups to manipulate public attitudes and behaviour by associating their aims with popular values" (Goodbody 2012: 14). This is why Goodbody, following the UK-based environmentalist report *Common Cause*, advocates the "moral obligation" for NGOs "to work transparently, inclusively, and reflexively" and, in short, "to 'democratise' the way cultural values are shaped" (14). We would like to second this claim and add that the academic enterprise of ecocriticism, just as much as the larger educational context of teaching English in what could be called an 'environmental classroom', should realize that it has the very same moral obligation.

It was therefore the aim of the conference "Teaching the Environment," from which many of the essays presented in this volume stem, to not only bring together scholars from diverse academic fields in order to engender multiple encounters—which we hope are still palpable in this book. That environmental crises require a truly inter- or transdisciplinary as well as a transnational framework is little more than a truism. We have, moreover, sought to bring together scholars with quite different approaches and notions about the question of what is to be done; scholars who, on the one hand, understand literary and cultural studies to be inextricably linked to the ethical questions with which ecocriticism became associated from its very start, as well as scholars who look critically at the naturalizing tendencies of environmentalist discourse, or at an often apocalyptic rhetoric that turns 'the environmental crisis' into something that inevitably restrains, for instance, democratic values and procedures, if only for the greater common good. We are happy to have been part of a conference where such debates had ample space while, at the same time, the general atmosphere was one of constructive collaboration, unbiased openness for dialog, yet also considerate concern about our main topic: the relevance of teaching in the context of environmental crises. In this context, Kylie Crane has pointed to the fact that "in the light of postcolonial studies and, more generally, postmodern thought, it has become increasingly difficult to consider identity, or text, as singular" (see her contribution in this volume) and that, if we want to seriously consider the multiple classrooms about which we are speaking, the title *Teaching Environments* might be more apt and more open for the polycentric attitude that Greg Garrard has identified at the core of ecocritical-pedagogical endeavors (see Garrard 2012: 2). We have, thus, gratefully accepted her suggestion.

The articles in this collection respond to our request to describe and discuss approaches of teaching in an environmentally or ecocritically oriented classroom, and they all add to the multi-faceted discussion of the place and *gestalt* of environmental pedagogy. We are convinced that such a debate cannot be limited to proposals for teaching specific topics (from animal ethics to climate change) or to apply certain teaching techniques and methods (from explorative, interdisciplinary studies to the outdoor practicum *in situ* discussed by Lawrence Buell (2008: 6-7)). Rather, we hope to have enabled a fruitful exchange of ideas, critique, and suggestions for the teaching practice at primary and secondary schools as well as the contexts of higher education. This is why the contributions in this volume, instead of being organized around specific topics and themes, follow a trajectory from primary education to the academic classroom and offer an increasing complexity of the contexts with which they are concerned. Starting with a programmatic discussion of the aims and ends of environmental pedagogy, **Uwe Küchler** discusses the role and potential of ecopedagogic teaching in the specific context of German classrooms where English is taught as a foreign language. While he is concerned with the specific situation of FLT on the one hand and the particularities of environmentalism in Germany on the other, his contribution also highlights the role of Foreign Language Education generally in fostering what he, following Mary Louise Pratt, calls "contact zones" that potentially engender "environmental literacy."

Opening the next section called "Beginnings: From Picture Books to Young Adult Fiction and Film," **Bettina Kümmerling-Meibauer** provides a thorough and highly interesting survey of insects in children's literature. While for many, insects are not associated with empathetic narrative accounts and thus do not seem to fit into the category of ecodidactic animal fiction, Kümmerling-Meibauer makes a strong claim for the commonness and relevance of children's literature that deals with "Ants, Bees, Bugs, and Spiders." **Roman Bartosch** tackles the question of empathy from a different angle, arguing that pedagogical engagements with animals have to take seriously the ambiguities and potential quandaries of anthropomorphisms. By drawing on the concept of a "poetics of failure," he offers a way of reading animals in picture books that do not aim at fully understanding animals but rather at engendering a sense of the fuzziness of the human/animal divide. **Janice Bland** discusses several picture books (by Van Allsburg, Martin, Browne, Rosen, Wiesner and Almond) as well and links their potential for what she calls "ecocritical sensitivity" and Lawrence Buell's well-known list of criteria that define an environmental text. By opening the definition in a way so as to include picture books and graphic novels, she stresses the literary potential of multimodal texts as well as their effectiveness in engaging "dialogically with nature as well as cultural phenomena." The last piece in this section, by **Kylie Crane**, moves to film and shows how by analyzing what she calls a "gentle" film such as *Babe*, students can be made to think through the most complex questions about (animal) ethics, materialities and the gaze. She claims that "a text such as *Babe* provides a non-threatening platform for discussing ideas such as the cyborg [...] and the pathways and meanings of meat and food."

The next two sessions are called "Transdisciplinary Encounters." In the first of these two, C.P. Snow's idea of the "two cultures"—at the same time strangely outdated yet highly relevant with regard to the interdisciplinary endeavors of ecocriticism—is the main point of interest. **Adrian Rainbow** argues that the dualism between the humanities and the sciences is counterproductive in the classromm because it is literary fiction and narratives that "ultimately contribute to a better understanding of scientific and ecological realities." In a discussion of the fiction of Margaret Atwood and Barbara Kingsolver, Rainbow explains how instead of pitting one against the other, both ecological and literary approaches can help to overcome reductionism and facilitate what Paulo Freire calls "conscientization." **Celestine Caruso** follows the same lead and in her essay outlines how "scientific encounters in literature" can be brought to bear on scientific understanding and vice versa. Drawing on a broad range of examples from science fiction and dystopian writing to the work of Paul Torday and Ian McEwan, Caruso makes a case for this scientific-literary cross-fertilization and maintains that ecocriticism may thus "eventually supersede the notorious distinction between literary and scientific cultures."

The second bit of the "Transdisciplinary Encounters" section engages in a project of historicizing environmental concerns and pedagogical objectives themselves: **Haiko Wandhoff** discusses medieval engagements with climate change—yet not from the scientific angle we are so used to today but in the context of a religious narrative of original sin and possible redemption. In reading Thomasin von Zerclære's epic poem "Der Welsche Gast" ("The Italian Guest"), he provides an uncommon but highly interesting perspective on debates about sustainability and the role of storytelling for the ecological imagination. **Dominik Ohrem** shows how concepts of nature are closely linked to ideas about manhood and national identity and in his paper discusses this relationship in the context of attempts at defining "Americanness" in 19th-century USA. "Ideological entanglements between nature and nation," he claims, "not only came to the forefront in a more distinct and insistent manner, they were also bound up with prevailing ideas about race and gender, the meaning of whiteness, and the bounds of national identity." **Sieglinde Grimm** turns to German literature and discusses the works of E.T.A. Hoffmann, Gottfried Keller, and W.G. Sebald with regard to their ecocritical potential. In the context of teaching literary texts, the ecocritical interest in the relation of word and world benefits the classroom experience since (young) readers expect the text to say something about their world and reality, and the changing conceptions of nature, environments and animals that can be found in the texts she discusses stand as stimulating examples of the relevance of cultural-ecological approaches.

The essays in this collection seek to bring together current developments in ecocriticism and the pedagogical practice of teaching English at all levels, from primary schools to Higher Education. They cover theoretical and practical discussions of the nexus between the sciences and the humanities and maintain that the notion of the two cultures be refused for good; they argue for the inclusion of particular texts or theoretical perspectives; and they suggest ways to teaching environments on different levels of language competence and in the context of historical and transdisciplinary encounters with ecology, nature, and animals. Despite this variety, they share some common threads and engage with questions that are highly relevant for teaching in general and have acquired even more relevance in our rapidly changing and posthumanist teaching environments: How do we raise consciousness without preaching? What kind of critical attitude is required for the empowerment of our pupils and students? How do we actually imagine encounters between the sciences and the (post)humanities, and which texts, what kind of texts, and which approaches will prove most fruitful?

While these questions and the discussions they entailed were pivotal during the conference, they can hardly be reprinted here in the same detail in which they were enthusiastically discussed during the talks or outside the venue, during dinner and in countless private conversations. Alas, this kind of debate seems lost in most cases once the proceedings are about to be processed into book format. This is why we are happy to be able to include another section, not featuring conference papers or essays but reactions *to* the conference from the academic world. In a preface to the *Journal of Ecocriticism*'s special issue "Ecocriticism—What Is It Good For?" (2012), **William Major and Andrew McMurry** put ecocriticism—as it has been practiced over the last years and developed into a diverse academic field of practice—to the test of its earlier ethical objectives of making a difference. Noting that "the course of global environmental health arcs steadily downward" (1), and that ecocritics ought to interrogate the *"quality and character of their ecological engagement"* (2, emphasis original), their conclusion is unambiguous: *"fewer words, more action"* (2). They claim that since "[o]ne of the unstated requisites for becoming a scholar of the literature is that you must, on a professional level, give up the notion that you are working in a biosphere," critics and literary scholars—even and especially ecocritics—are not "immune to the autopoietic pressures of the literary system, which programmatically shunts aside the real world" (2-3).

While we don't think this is true even for the most theory-laden disciplines (think of postcolonial studies and, yes, even deconstruction), we disagree even more with the idea that "fewer words, more action" can and should be the only option for critical, academic ecocriticism. True, there is all reason in the world to stop talking about one's own ecological footprint while still traveling to conferences via airplane; it is quite absurd to discuss environmental degradation and climate change over a generous serving of meat; and it seems ridiculous when people assert their commitment to saving animals (the Indian tiger, say) while in their own country, a single, drifting bear is being shot (as was the case in Germany in 2006). But is this enough for an academic enterprise to forfeit theory and professional caution altogether? And does this mean that we must do away with pedagogical principles that ask us to refrain from preaching and biased influencing, even for the good cause, even in times of urgent crisis? While we strongly believe that, especially in the context of education at schools, we as teachers have an obligation to remain cautious about the educational implementations of consciousness-raising, we pick the example of Major and McMurry particularly because in their piece, they quoted the Call for Papers for our conference, taking issue with the Call for Paper's explicit mention of caution and critical distance towards happy-go-lucky activism:

> We recently received a call for papers from an environmental humanities conference. Ostensibly, the conference should have been a dream come true for ecocritics like ourselves: "We are looking for contributors to a transdisciplinary symposium on the didactical implementations of ecocriticism, critical animal studies and green cultural studies. With a special emphasis on transdisciplinary perspectives, we would like to discuss how the tenets of these academic fields can be incorporated into the daily practice of teaching the humanities and arts—". So far so good. But here is the other side of that hyphen that sends this symposium off into the hallowed halls of humanist boosterism: "without either breaching the topics' complexity, falling into the mode of environmentalist propaganda or succumbing to warnings and claims to catastrophic urgency which are hard to reconcile with an ethos of critical and democratic pedagogy." In other words, the very thing that in the last 20 years has prompted many humanists to question humanism—i.e., the "catastrophic urgency" of our environmental moment—is dismissed out of hand (3)

The "Debate" section opens with **Greg Garrard and Roman Bartosch**'s response to Major and McMurry's piece, also originally published in the *Journal of Ecocriticism*. It then presents Major and McMurry's response to this short essay. And as the conference has been concerned with similar discussions as well, **Pamela Swanigan**, in a strikingly explicit and personal manifesto, makes a dedicated "Case Against Agenda," arguing that ecopedagogy needs to reflect more on the question whether environmental agendas should form a part of one's teaching practices at all. She goes on to suggest that ecocritics should be more than cautious about their own agendas, maintaining that an unreflected ecocritical bias in the classroom is "dishonorable, […] counterproductive, and it is unnecessary." In her response to the debate, **Sieglinde Grimm** tries to explain possible differences in German and US-American ideas about activism or activist scholarship. Commenting, on the one hand, on the historical dimension of applied knowledge versus what is called *Bildung* in Germany and, on the other, the different academic environments of Germany and the US, Grimm explains both some of the reasons why Major and McMury and Bartosch seemed to be at odds and moreover points to the specific situation of teaching literature at schools and undergraduate University programs in Germany: being cautious about political commitments is not necessarily a sign of "humanist boosterism" but a necessary move to ultimately establish ecocriticism as a discipline that is taken seriously.

Now that our cozy meeting in the hallowed halls of humanist boosterism is over, we see more clearly, anyway. It was not so much the debates which apparently "dismiss out of hand" the reality of environmental catastrophe (at the cost of the reality of the democratic, professional, and critical obligations of pedagogical practice) but the wording of the CfP that "struck a wrong note," as Major and McMurry claim (see their contribution to this volume)—thus underlining the point that the way we talk about things certainly influences whether such communication may be effective or not. And since one may very well call the practice of writing books about questions of the practical impact of humanist scholarship a formidable humanist enterprise, we are still very happy to have caused such a debate and to be able to offer it another forum in this book. This is why we added said special section—called 'Debate'—where these questions will be addressed in a manner that we hope does justice to Major and McMurry's relevant—and brilliantly written—intervention. We thank William Major and Andrew McMurry as well as Rebecca Raglon, general editor of the *Journal of Ecocriticism*, for the permission to reprint the pieces here and hope to encourage more ecocritics and scholars interested in environmental issues to join the debate.[1]

We also thank all the conference participants for a stimulating and constructive event as well as for the collaborative endeavors to publish this book without too much delay. We thank the Fritz-Thyssen foundation for their generous funding without which nothing of this could have happened. We also thank the University of Cologne for hosting the conference, in particular the English Department II, especially Professor Andreas Rohde and Dagmar Floßdorf, for every conceivable form of support, and Elizabeth Gilbert, Natascha Mizelle, and William Purcell for careful proofreading. It is a sad habit that student assistants and other friendly helpers are only mentioned at the end of such introductions; for without them, we would have had neither food nor drink nor technical support. Many thanks therefore to Kim Schick, Johanna Schnuch and Julia Kessel, who give "last but not least" a new significance.

We are most thankful, however, to those students and colleagues—and readers!—who are interested in the research we are pursuing, and who think

---

1   Readers interested in the original piece by Mayor and McMurry, from which the quotations are taken, are kindly referred to issue 4.2 of the *Journal of Ecocriticism* (2013). Alongside the introduction, a handful of essays deals with the (ostensible) conflict between imminent urgency or threat and 'lengthy' or 'ineffective' scholarship.

about, to use a phrase by Matthewman, ways of "teaching as if the planet matters". Which it does, certainly, for most of us.

Works Cited

Buell, Lawrence. *The Environmental Imagination. Thoreau, Nature Writing and the Formation of American Culture*. Cambridge (MA): Harvard UP, 1995.
— . *The Future of Environmental Criticism. Environmental Crisis and Literary Imagination*. Malden/Oxford/Victoria: Blackwell Publishing, 2008.
Christensen, Laird; Mark C. Long & Fred Waage (eds.). *Teaching North American Environmental Literature*. New York: Modern Language Association, 2008.
Garrard, Greg (ed.). *Teaching Ecocriticism and Green Cultural Studies*. Basingstoke & New York: palgrave Macmillan, 2012.
Goodbody, Axel. "Frame Analysis and the Literature of Climate Change." *Literature, Ecology, Ethics. Recent Trends in Ecocriticism*. Eds. Timo Müller & Michael Sauter. Heidelberg: Winter, 2012. 15-33.
Kerridge, Richard. "Introduction". *Writing the Environment. Ecocriticism and Literature*. Eds. Richard Kerridge & Neil Sammells. New York: Zed Books, 1998. 1-9.
Major, William & Andrew McMurry. "Introduction: The Function of Ecocriticism; or, Ecocriticism, What Is It Good For?". *Journal of Ecocriticism* 4.2 (2012). 1-7.
Mayer, Sylvia & Graham Wilson, "Ecodidactic Perspectives on English Language, Literatures and Cultures: An Introduction." *Ecodidactic Perspectives on English Languages, Literatures and Cultures*. Eds. Sylvia Mayer & Graham Wilson. Trier: Wissenschaftlicher Verlag, 2006.
Matthewman, Sasha. *Teaching Secondary English as if the Planet Matters*. London & New York: Routledge, 2011.
UNESCO. *Shaping the Education of Tomorrow*. Paris: United Nations Educational, Scientific and Cultural Organization, 2012.

Where Foreign Language Education Meets, Clashes and Grapples with the Environment

Uwe Küchler (Bonn)

Introduction

The past few years have seen a newly awakened interest in the topic of the environment with regards to foreign language education, yet only a small number of specialized journals for teaching foreign languages have published issues that take ecology as their point of reference if not subject.[1] Even so publishers have put extra learning materials on the market that answer to medial and societal needs to engage with the environment and thus address ways of living.[2] At the same time, it can be observed with some astonishment that foreign language education—defining itself as a discipline open to all matters of contemporary, inter/transcultural, and communicative affairs—has *not* followed suit in providing this subject with a theoretical and methodological framework for teaching and learning. The question thus needs to be posed: can foreign language education be a fruitful area—a contact zone—where learners encounter and engage with different concepts of nature, the environment, or sustainability? And can the learning about environmental issues further the understanding of foreign languages, cultures, or literatures?[3]

---

1   See, for example, an issue on 'Nature and Environment' in *Praxis Englisch* 2011 (3); with restrictions see also the issue on 'Water, the precious element' in *Praxis Englisch* 2013 (1).

2   For EFL learning materials on the environment see, for example the following task books: *Our Environment: A State of Emergency?* (Speight 2009), *The Day After Tomorrow: A Film Study* (Diehr & Rohlmann-Reineke 2011), *Saving the Planet: The Environmental Debate* (Sammon 1995). Further environmental topics are featured in materials focusing on globalization/global village, utopia/dystopia or urban vs. rural spaces to name just a few.

3   I will frequently talk of English as a Foreign Language (EFL) because this is the subject that I am working with and researching. At the same time, I often use the broader field of Foreign Language Education also because many of the discussed features are

Since the 1970s, many academic disciplines and school subjects have adopted ecological topics in their own right. For the past decades, English (EFL) textbooks in Germany have also used the environment as a topic for tasks or texts. They have attempted to raise awareness about problems and imminent dangers. Yet, in stark contrast to other fields of study and its related disciplines, foreign language education has been reluctant to tackle these issues in a more encompassing fashion that would provide the field with a *theoretical* framework for engaging with the topic while learning foreign languages. Furthermore, it has neglected to critically evaluate findings of the related disciplines and their ecological specializations. Thus it remains to be asked: How can the learning of a foreign language and its primary teaching objective of intercultural communicative competence be related to concerns about nature, environment, or sustainability?

In the following, I will introduce the rationale and the cornerstones of a research project that tackles the theoretical concerns of working with ecological and environmental questions in the field of foreign language education.

Point of Departure: Germany and the Environment

Germany is often regarded—and most certainly regards itself—as an ecological vanguard. This impression is based on important political and technological successes. Engineering feats, such as the nationwide recycling system, ecological design,[4] or the success of the renewable energy branches, can serve as an example. And so can the early development of Germany's Green Party (today *Bündnis 90/Die Grünen*) and its constantly growing political force and influence since January 1980. Therefore, it may not be surprising that the German population seems to have a solid, fundamental knowledge of environmental

---

probably transferable to the learning and teaching of other foreign language. The terminology particularly popular in Germany—*Fachdidaktik*—seems out of place in an English text and might lead to more confusion than clarification. Thus, I avoid the German terms altogether.

4   Ecological design or sustainable design tries to combine the effective use of resources with principles of sustainability as well as fair trade and production conditions, see for example low energy consumption houses, development of cars with low fuel consumption and exhaust gas emission triggered by Greenpeace's SmILE car, the avoidance of ozone-depleting refrigeration technology in *GreenFreeze* . Furthermore, it has become a trend to produce fashionable consumer products that persistently reuse worn-out materials (cf. furniture made of used cardboard; bags made of plastic sheeting, scaffolding or covers of sports equipment). More recently, efforts to implement the cradle-to-cradle concept, the cyclical (re)use of resources, have attracted attention.

issues. Interestingly, the kind of knowledge the majority has—about climate change, for instance—is mostly restricted to all those issues that make headlines in mass media. A cross-check shows that the topics less covered by the media also hardly feature in the awareness of the public. Germans are aware of recycling, solar energy and, most importantly, of climate change. But the knowledge or mentioning of the serious loss in biodiversity is rarely found (for a comprehensive overview of Germany's environmental awareness cf. Kuckartz 2010, 147; Kuckartz & Rheingans-Heintze 2006).

These findings by educator Udo Kuckartz indicate some of the difficulties encountered when arguing for more knowledge about environmental issues. The assumption that by adding environmental topics to a teaching situation the awareness for certain societal or environmental issues may proportionally rise is misleading. This seems to be particularly so if the hope for an increased awareness is bound to demands for a broad, societal bettering of individual behavior. Instead, it needs to be asked what (kind of) knowledge is promoted in a teaching situation and to what environmental scenario the chosen knowledge relates. Are we talking about global or regional, about national or transnational, possibly even transcultural knowledge? For whose benefit has this knowledge been constructed and whose interest does it promote? Most importantly, with regards to aspired learning outcomes, the question needs to be posed how chosen information relates to an individual's needs and behavior. Alas, many educational endeavors and also the 'Decade of Sustainable Education', rely too heavily on the fragile assumption that an increase in knowledge makes a difference in people's behavior. Furthermore, the approach of shock and awe is expected to inspire different or preferably better moral standards and more sustainable lifestyles (Kuckartz 2010).

The results of Kuckartz's national survey titled 'Trends in Ecological Consciousness'[5] (Kuckartz & Rheingans-Heintze 2006) offer a picture quite different from the obliging perception of German environmentalism. Although, in the European average, certain activities are practiced in Germany more often than in other countries on the continent (such as separating waste, reducing the energy consumption of one's house or reducing a household's water use), Germany does hold not a single top position in *any* of those activities. Thus, Germans cannot claim to be the vanguard of environmental awareness or behavior, but fall prey to a rather complacent auto-stereotype:

> Alle [...] genannten Verhaltensweisen werden in Deutschland zwar häufiger praktiziert als im europäischen Durchschnitt, doch belegen die Deutschen in keinem einzigen Fall den Spitzenplatz. Offenbar geht dies mit einer gewissen Selbstzufriedenheit einher, denn in

---

5   Original title in German: *Trends im Umweltbewusstsein: Umweltgerechtigkeit, Lebensqualität und persönliches Engagement.*

kaum einem anderen Land sind so viele der Meinung, dass der Bürger doch schon genug tue (150).[6]

Kuckartz provocatively concludes that Germany's environmental consciousness can best be described with three slogans: 'Not here', 'Not now', 'Not me'. 'Not here' refers to the people's knowledge about the favorable geographic position of Central Europe and the assumption that environmental disaster will (probably) strike far away before it comes here. Daily news programs mostly prove the expectations right and—in correspondence with their knowledge about Central Europe's stable geography and temperate climate—reinforce the smug feeling of security. People have become more afraid of the future than of present dangers: 'Not now'. They do worry about the deteriorating living and health conditions for their children and grandchildren, but feel comparatively safe with respect to their own well-being and the present moment. There is a general feeling of 'seize the day' rather than, say, postpone travel plans to the future. In consequence, an increasing growth rate can be observed for long-distance voyages such as to the Caribbean, Mauritius, or the Seychelles in spite of the tourists' environmental awareness. Finally, individuals do not feel that they can make much of a difference: 'Not me'. Instead, people expect the state to take control and impose legal constraints that are mandatory for everyone. Until the government introduces political measures, individuals continue to seize the moment (Kuckartz 2010). This leads to the conclusion that the personal willingness to change one's lifestyle seems not very distinct.

Kuckartz' findings are astonishing for another reason, too: for about 30 years, ecology and the environment have been taught as relevant topics in some school subjects. It seems that the growth in knowledge and awareness does not necessarily equate with the aspired outcome in environmental behavior. Possibly, it may even come at the expense of behavioral changes and not necessarily lead to more 'eco-friendly' activities. The attitude of 'not here, not now, not me' seems to gain at least part of its strength from knowledge. Thus, the knowledge about ecology and environment has to be scrutinized: What kind of knowledge is to be taught at school?

---

6 "Although all […] mentioned behaviors are practiced in Germany more often than in the European average, in no single instance do the Germans hold the lead. Apparently, this coincides with a certain contentedness with oneself; in no other country are so many people of the opinion that the citizens are already doing enough" (150; my translation).

Environmental Behavior and Socio-Ecological Research

Germany's Federal Ministry of Education and Research (*Bundesministerium für Bildung und Forschung, BMBF*) has identified a need to foster investigations in the field of societal and ecological living. In an initiative on climate change research, the *BMBF* added the warning: This publication alerts researchers and the public to the expectation that without radical changes in lifestyles, patterns of consumption, and forms of urbanization, it will not be possible to bridge the gap between diagnosis of environmental crises and strategies for prevailing over them.[7] Those formulations, if not the entire outlook of society and its environment, come across as rather gloomily moralistic. The Ministry defines the research priority for this endeavor mainly in the field of socio-ecological projects. Interestingly, it invokes a complex system of interrelations[8] and tries to answer the isolation of disciplinary knowledge areas[9] for the benefit of interdisciplinary research particularly in the broader area of ecology. As the research aims to bring about changes in lifestyles and behaviors, *BMBF* claims that projects need to be substantiated by an analysis of cultural phenomena. And yet, the focus of the socio-ecological research promoted by the Ministry and the Federal Government is clearly on technical, economic, and fiscal aspects.[10]

It is somewhat mind boggling to find such a broad societal endeavor defined without the mere mentioning of the humanities, in spite of the cultural focus. Is the expertise of the humanities not needed? This can hardly be the case, as it is the primary goal and singular expertise of the diverse humanities research areas to interpret or understand the world and to help in finding orientation particularly in times of uncertainty and rapid change. With regards to the role of the humanities, Harald Welzer, Hans-Georg Soeffner and Dana Giesecke assert that:

---

7   The original passage in German reads: "Ohne einschneidende Veränderungen von Lebensweisen, Konsummustern und Urbanisierungsformen [...] wird es nicht möglich sein, die Kluft zwischen der Krisendiagnose und Strategien zu ihrer Überwindung auch nur annähend zu schließen" (BMBF 2008: 3).

8   In the German original: "komplexe Systemzusammenhänge" (BMBF 2008: 3).

9   In the German original: "isolierte Wissensstände" (BMBF 2008: 3).

10 It is stated in the report, that the German *Bundesregierung* reacts to the phenomena of climate change with a high-tech strategy and describes its agenda as follows: "In consideration of academic, technological, economic and fiscal aspects, [the *Bundesregierung*] predetermines the political research program regarding climate for the years to come" (my translation). The original quotation in German reads: "Unter Berücksichtigung von wissenschaftlichen, technologischen, ökonomischen und finanzwirtschaftlichen Aspekten gibt sie die forschungspolitischen Leitlinien zum Klimaschutz für die kommenden Jahre vor" (BMBF 2008: 6).

Die Expertise betrifft den historischen Erfahrungshaushalt in Bezug auf antizipierte, gefühlte und erlebte Katastrophen genauso wie die dazugehörigen Deutungsrahmen. Sie bezieht sich ebenso auf die kulturellen Praktiken und Sinnkontexte, die zur Verursachung anthropogenen Klimawandels geführt haben, wie auch auf das weite Feld seiner gesellschaftlichen, politischen, psychologischen und juristischen Bearbeitung. Nicht zuletzt fordert sie das menschliche Deutungs- und Sinngebungspotential heraus: die philosophische Bearbeitung von Aspekten der Gerechtigkeit und Verantwortung sowie die philologische beziehungsweise literarische Sprachkritik und die wissenssoziologische Analyse kollektiver Deutungsfiguren. (Welzer, Soeffner & Giesecke 2010: 13)[11]

If the role of the humanities is as essential to make sense of present developments as Welzer, Soeffner and Giesecke claim, then the humanities are needed for engendering unusual thinking and interconnections between disparate fields of knowledge and experience, for the exploration and productive use of possibilities, chances, and challenges. It is in the humanities where hermeneutic, qualitative, and anthropological methodologies of cultural analysis are developed and where probing into the intricate fabric of cultural and inter/transcultural connections has its home; in other words, for the work in and with cultural, societal, disciplinary and human/non-human contact zones.

If the goal is a broader societal participation in all the efforts aimed at sustaining the ecological basis for our living, it seems indispensable to clarify the contribution the humanities can make to the environmental debate and to the development or invention of more sustainable life styles. After all, the natural sciences and the inventiveness of engineers—not incidentally the backbone of this country—have not managed to bring the crises to a halt. There is no technological fix that inspires behavioral change large enough to counterbalance the rebound effect: technological progress, while saving energy or resources, also creates new needs or desires that outweigh the savings in the long run. As a consequence, all advances in environmental awareness are quickly swallowed up by far more encompassing technological advances, gadgets and subsequent consumption of resources and energy needs.

Considering the socio-psychological findings (Ernst 2010; Kuckartz 2010; Welzer, Soeffner & Giesecke 2010) and the rebound effect, it seems that the singular reliance on technological solutions does not solve, but in the long run

---

11   "The expertise [of the humanities] touches upon the historical economy of experience with regard to the anticipated, felt or experienced catastrophes as much as the corresponding interpretative framework. It refers to the cultural practices and contexts of meaning leading up to the causing of anthropogenic climate change as much as to the broad field of its societal, political, psychological and judicial handling. Not least of all, it challenges the human potential to interpret and make meaning: the philosophical processing of the aspects justice and responsibility as well as the philological or literary language critique and the sociological-epistemiological analysis of collective patterns of interpretation" (Welzer, Soeffner & Giesecke 2010: 13; my translation).

perpetuates the crisis of humans with their non-human environment. By ignoring the uniqueness of climate change and the encompassing, formative nature it will have for life in the 21st century, Harald Welzer, Hans-Georg Soeffner and Dana Giesecke argue that the Humanities and particularly the Social Sciences and Cultural Studies neglect to understand the deeply heuristic value they could bring to the debate:

> Die systematische kulturwissenschaftliche Unterbelichtung eines Phänomens, das die Lebenskonditionen des 21. Jahrhunderts in vielfacher Hinsicht mitbestimmen wird, ist nicht nur deshalb fatal, weil sich die Sozial-, Geistes- und Kulturwissenschaften mit ihrer Indolenz gegenüber der Konsequenzerstmaligkeit des Klimawandels selbst um einen Gegenstand von tiefem heuristischem Wert bringen. (Welzer, Soeffner & Giesecke 2010: 15)[12]

Yet I would argue that not only the signature topic of climate change, but the relationship between humanity and the non-human environment in general constitutes an important and fruitful pillar of humanities research.

Behavior, in general, and environmental behavior in particular are not isolated from other factors, but are embedded in a quite material, yet also physical and social context, as ecopsychologist Andreas Ernst claims (2010). In accordance with the belief in individualism, Western societies seem to overestimate the self-determination and independence of an individual's action and behavior. Ernst claims that concrete, situated behavior is codetermined by the structures that a society creates:

> Verhalten steht nicht alleine, solipsistisch im Raum, sondern es ist immer eingebettet in einen Verhaltenskontext. Dieser Verhaltenskontext hat sowohl materielle und physische, als auch soziale Aspekte. Wir überschätzen im täglichen Leben bei Weitem, wie viel wir von unserem Verhalten eigenständig entscheiden. Tatsächlich ist die überwiegende Mehrzahl unserer täglichen Verhaltensweisen durch architektonische, physikalische, geografische, organische und schließlich soziale und institutionelle Dinge so bestimmt, dass wir sie auf eine bestimmte Weise ausführen und nicht anders. (Ernst 2010: 137)[13]

---

12   "This phenomenon, which for multiple reasons will codetermine the living conditions of the 21st century, is systematically underexposed by cultural studies. This is fatal not only because, with their indolence towards consequential uniqueness of climate change, the humanities, social studies and cultural studies are robbing themselves of a research object of deep heuristic value" (Welzer, Soeffner & Giesecke 2010: 15; my translation).

13   "Behavior is not put forward alone, solipsistically, but is always embedded within a behavioral context. This behavioral context has material and physical as well as social aspects. In our everyday lives, we greatly overestimate our behavioral independece. In actual fact, the predominant majority of our daily behaviors is determined by architectural, physical, geographic, organic, and, finally, social and institutional matters in such a manner that we carry them out in a certain way and not in any other (Ernst 2010: 137; my translation).

As the majority of our daily routines are governed by those superimposed structures, the given contexts can be said to lead us to behave in one way and not another. To a certain extent the societal context determines in advance which behavioral options an individual is likely to take and which ones seem too removed from her habits or comfort zones as to be (easily) adopted. As those realizations suggest, the grappling with humankind's relationship to its non-human environment needs a lot more than mere information and production of knowledge. It seems promising to focus instead on the reconceptualization of many, if not all, details of our daily lives, from architectural structures to linguistic and narrative patterns. Working with vocabulary, metaphors or narratives from an intercultural and transcultural perspective, therefore, promises to be a good starting point. Language and narratives provide needed insights into perceptions of ourselves and of the world around us.

Contact Zones and the Greening of Foreign Language Education

The argument above underlines that the expertise of the humanities is urgently needed in the debate on ecology and environment. Foreign language education can contribute to this larger undertaking by

- probing the interface between one's own and other languages with regards to their idiosyncratic ways of 'pre-structuring' our perception, fostering linguistic, textual and cultural awareness across languages, literatures and cultures or;
- by perusing the findings of related ecological disciplines, and critically processing and adapting them for teaching and learning processes.

The role of nature, environment, and sustainability in foreign language education still needs to be determined. Furthermore, the concept of 'environmental literacy' has to be applied to the humanities as much as to foreign language classrooms.

US-American foreign language educator and linguist Mary Louise Pratt coined the term 'contact zone' as an area where "cultures meet, clash and grapple with each other" (Pratt 1991: 3). She found those areas particularly fruitful in terms of cultural production, hybridization and transculturation. The process of creative and productive intermingling, the grappling with difference and the creative integration of diversity into prior patterns has particularly inspired the field of intercultural communication and learning. In the title for this article, I use and adapt Pratt's famous motto and agenda to fit the field of foreign language education. Pratt refers to physical border regions and to people speaking different languages and working under quite unequal power relations. I take this quote metaphorically to also refer to academic territories bordering on each other. Often, those knowledge areas function as territories indeed and as sacrosanct home turfs. Fields of knowledge, even when engendering interdisciplinary topics, are often perceived under unequal power relations with regards to educational and commercial policies. Thus, I consider contact zones a metaphor for all those aspects that find their interface in foreign language education. The teaching of other languages is a specialized knowledge area

- where interdisciplinary academic theory (related disciplines) meets, clashes and grapples with classroom practice and actual teaching scenarios,
- where knowledge generated by university research meets, clashes and grapples with experiential, empirical knowledge created in schools and by action research of teachers, teaching trainees, students, pupils, and administrators,
- where people as well as language, culture, literature and other media of the diverse English-speaking diaspora meet, clash and grapple with their influence and impact on the rest of the world, their impact on other and on our own culture(s), on other and on our own language(s),
- where, last but not least, the multidimensional goals of foreign language education meet, clash and grapple with each other: foreign language learning aspires to provide knowledge about language (as well as culture and literature). At the same time, it wants to train the foundation for communicative skills (the instrumental, functional dimension of language learning). Yet, also, out of historical traditions of the philologies, learners are to understand their languages, cultures and literatures in an intercultural and transcultural context of their use (the language and culture awareness dimension of language learning).

Thus, I have set out to explore those contact zones and to find out how those intersections of conditions, interests, and disciplines influence the perception of and the everyday work with languages, cultures, and the environment.

Providing a Theoretical Framework

The significance of ecology and the environment for all fields of education has been pointed out by Germany's renown education specialist Wolfgang Klafki

(1991). He demands that ecology, as a characteristic key issue of our era—in German "*epochaltypisches Schlüsselproblem*" (Klafki 1991: 50-1)—be made part of every educational endeavor. Currently, the topic 'environment' is more often than not framed within expressions and associations of a perceived threat and of predominant catastrophes. It is presented as difficult, menacing, possibly unsolvable and in any case indicative of the moral misconduct of people. Particularly the focus of many current textbooks on an environment fraught with problems poses the question: are we seriously expecting school children to set the world right? Taking a look at current EFL teaching and learning materials creates this lasting impression.

With regards to foreign language education, an interesting paradox can be observed: although environmental topics are frequently approached by all media and, thus, promise to provide up-to-date and authentic material for language learning, teachers and pupils frequently seem frustrated with these issues. Upon first glance, it seems that certain topics are overused across the board of several school subjects and the issues presented leave little possibility for exploration and inquiry but fall mostly under the rubric of moralistic behavioral reprimand and all-too-transparent social desirability. Furthermore, the research in foreign language education has only tentatively touched upon ecological issues. This becomes apparent particularly in contradistinction to other topics that have triggered a radically new perception since the 1970s and, subsequently, new theoretical conceptualization and the rewriting of materials, such as the issues race, class, gender, multicultural society, or inter/transcultural learning. As of today, the ecological and environmental impetus has left almost no considerable mark on foreign language education.

Establishing a well-reasoned approach to teaching ecological issues within foreign language education asks for a theoretical framework that takes the complex array of factors for teaching English and the premises of foreign language education (Edmondson/House 2006: 25) as its starting point and explores all the related disciplines that provide knowledge and arguments for specialized teaching. What innovative impulses, theoretical concepts and models, what fresh topics and ideas can related disciplines bring to the teaching of foreign languages? The number of related disciplines, which foreign language education relies on, already indicates that a vast amount of knowledge has to be considered in this endeavor.

Most of the related disciplines have established very productive and innovative research branches with an ecological focus. Those new interdisciplinary knowledge fields address themselves to ecological questions within the framework of their disciplines and consider the relationship between mankind and the non-human environment. With environmental education, ecolinguistics, ecocriticism and cultural ecology, environmental psychology and ecosociology, a rich texture of research findings closely related to foreign language learning and teaching can be found. Alas, the findings of those branches have hardly been considered by foreign language educators or by publishers who produce teaching materials. Articles that go beyond the instrumental adoption of environmental topics for the classroom or a rather fuzzy global, transnational perspective on these issues are hard to find.

Because ecological issues have not generated a larger extent of research in foreign language education, it seems imperative to empirically scrutinize the current state of development with regards to language learning as much as ecological thought in the EFL classroom. Data should be acquired and analyzed with the help of an exploratory, qualitative and interpretative research design. First and foremost, a 'thick description' in the sense Clifford Geertz defined for qualitative (anthropological) research is needed. This could be achieved by scrutinizing many different perspectives with the help of interviews, derived from individuals of different stakeholder groups:

- What are current teaching practices in EFL classrooms with regards to ecological and environmental issues?
- What are individual's perspectives in connections with the linking of foreign language learning and environmental education?
- What role is ascribed to ecology with reference to the large pool of possible topics for EFL classes? What would be a desirable measure for ecology in EFL teaching and what goals would actually be pursued concerning both: learning English and learning about the environment?
- Which images, metaphors, narratives or conceptualizations of ecology and environment are used in EFL materials?
- Which curricular support is offered to teachers? How are ecological issues taken up by the curriculum in different *Bundesländer* and by transnational curricular guidelines?
- How do the materials for teaching English as a foreign language represent the contact zones of the related disciplines, of interdisciplinary research and transnational nature of the topics?

To find answers to these questions, an empirical exploration of the field is needed. The results of such an empirical study allow for more concrete and better argued work with ecological topics in the classroom and they invite for better founded, theoretically reasoned use of a diversity of topics rather than an unwanted (but to this day dominant) focus on catastrophes and gloomy perspectives.

Works Cited

BMBF, Bundesministerium für Bildung und Forschung. 2008. *Klimaschutz erfordert Handeln: Beiträge der Sozial-ökologischen Forschung*. Bonn, Berlin. http://www.bmbf.de (19 Nov. 2011).

Diehr, Christina & Cordula Rohlmann-Reineke (eds.). *The Day After Tomorrow: A Film Study (Schwerpunktthema Abitur Englisch)*. Berlin: Cornelsen, 2011.

Edmondson, Willis J. & Juliane House (eds.). *Einführung in die Sprachlehrforschung*. Tübingen, Basel: A. Francke, 2006.

Ernst, Andreas. "Individuelles Umweltverhalten—Probleme, Chancen, Vielfalt." *KlimaKulturen: Soziale Wirklichkeiten im Klimawandel*. Eds. Harald Welzer, Hans-Georg Soeffner & Dana Giesecke. Frankfurt am Main: Campus Verlag, 2010. 128-43.

Klafki, Wolfgang. *Neue Studien zur Bildungstheorie und Didaktik: Zeitgemäße Allgemeinbildung und kritisch-konstruktive Didaktik*. Weinheim, Basel: Beltz, 1991.

Kuckartz, Udo. "Nicht hier, nicht jetzt, nicht ich—Über die symbolische Bearbeitung eines ernsten Problems." *KlimaKulturen: Soziale Wirklichkeiten im Klimawandel*. Eds. Harald Welzer, Hans-Georg Soeffner & Dana Giesecke. Frankfurt am Main: Campus Verlag, 2010. 144-60.

Kuckartz, Udo & Anke Rheingans-Heintze. *Trends im Umweltbewusstsein: Umweltgerechtigkeit, Lebensqualität und persönliches Engagement*. Wiesbaden: VS Verlag für Sozialwissenschaften, 2006.

Pratt, Mary Louise. "Arts of the Contact Zone." *Profession* 91 (1991). 33-41.

Sammon, Geoff (ed.). *Saving the Planet: The Environmental Debate (Textsammlung für den Englischunterricht)*. Berlin: Cornelsen, 1995.

Speight, Stephen (ed.). *Our Environment: A State of Emergency?* Braunschweig, Paderborn, Darmstadt: Bildungshaus Schulbuchverlage Westermann Schroedel Diesterweg Schöningh Winklers GmbH, 2009.

Welzer, Harald, Hans-Georg Soeffner & Dana Giesecke. "KlimaKulturen." *KlimaKulturen: Soziale Wirklichkeiten im Klimawandel*. Eds. Harald Welzer, Hans-Georg Soeffner & Dana Giesecke. Frankfurt am Main: Campus Verlag, 2010. 7-19.

Beginnings: From Picture Books to Young Adult Fiction and Film

Ants, Bees, Bugs, and Spiders
Insects in Children's Literature

Bettina Kümmerling-Meibauer (Tübingen)

In Lewis Carroll's famous classic *Alice Through the Looking-Glass and What Alice Found There* (1871), Alice is sitting in a train carriage in company of an elderly man in a white suit, a goat, and, maybe surprisingly, a gigantic gnat about the size of a chicken. During the train ride, the following conversation between Alice and the gnat takes place:

> '—then you don't like all insects?' the Gnat went on, as quietly as if nothing had happened. 'I like them when they can talk,' Alice said. 'None of them ever talk, where I come from.' 'What sort of insects do you rejoice in, where you come from?' the Gnat inquired. 'I don't rejoice in insects at all,' Alice explained, 'because I'm rather afraid of them— at least the large kinds. But I can tell you the names of some of them.' (Carroll 1999: 43).

Being afraid, even horrified of insects seems to be a quite popular attitude among people, whether children or adults. Insects can sting, suck people's blood, make holes into clothes, touch food, and often look ugly and abhorrent, if one considers wasps, mosquitoes, moths, cockroaches, spiders, maggots, and worms as representatives of this species. It is no wonder, then, that the toy industry exploits children's, especially boys', interest in insects, which is often characterized by an imbalance between fathomless disgust and inexplicable fascination. This fascination was certainly the main reason for the incredible success of the "Hamilton's Invaders," released by the US-American toy maker Remco in 1964, and inspired by the 'giant insect' film genre as a subspecies of horror films. Hamilton Invaders were conceived as a series of giant plastic insects, such as the horrible Hamilton Spider, which could be moved via pull-string motors. As advertisements run on TV and in newspapers showed, the popularity of these insect monsters also originated from the prospect to frighten mothers, sisters, and female teachers. Another favored product was the activity toy "Creepy Crawler," first produced by Mattel in 1964. This toy consists of a series of die-cast metal molds resembling various bug-like creatures, into which a liquid chemical substance called Plastigoop is poured, which comes in assorted colors. The Creepy Crawler or "Thingmaker" line was aimed at both boys and girls, sold worldwide in the 1960s, and was prominently advertised as a method for children to become little scientists, investigating the diverse forms of insects. This product is still available, but the idea to spread knowledge about insects did not remain. Contrariwise, the contemporary Creepy Crawler series apparently intends to give other people a fit. Even more shocking is a parodist version of the classic "Easy Bake Oven," a toy for girls who learn cooking. Instead, the "Queasy Bake Oven" by Hasbro is aimed at boys and lets them create gross edibles such as "Mud'n Crud Cake," dips and cookies that resemble insects and worms, not to mention "Fright Candies" and "Scream Rollers." Admittingly, children's toys, at least in the US, are quite creative when it comes to insects and other nauseating things that cause goose bumps and make people jump.

Animal Stories for Children

After this telling insight into a branch of modern children's toys, let us turn to children's books. Intuitively, people and even scholars working in the realm of children's literature would assume that insects do not play a significant role in children's literature. Insects might appear in non-fiction books informing the reader about bugs, butterflies, bees, spiders, and ants, but what about insects as main protagonists in fictional stories for children? At a first glance, this seems to be quite an unusual topic. Although animal stories as a subgenre of children's literature are still popular among children, these stories usually focus on pets, farm animals, and wild animals, such as bears, beavers, foxes, lions, rabbits, wolves, and dolphins (Blount 1974; Duan 1996; McCrindle and Odendaal 1994; Rayner 1979). Adults certainly will remember the famed animals that accompanied their childhood: the brave collie Lassie, the funny dolphin Flipper, and the intelligent horse Fury, to name just a few. What is the difference, then, between these animals and insects?

One major difference consists in size: insects are tiny, therefore often invisible to humans.[1] Another difference consists in their appearance. Pets, farm animals, and wild animals are either cute or impressive; insects are generally neither cute nor impressive. A further important issue that determines the majority of animal stories is the concept of friendship between animal and child. Generally, the difficulty of thinking oneself into an insect, which can be seen as the prerequisite for human-insect friendship, presents a significant obstacle as far as the presence of insects in animal stories is concerned. How, then, can children establish a friendly relationship with a bee, bug, caterpillar, flea, or

---

1   Hollingway (2011) indicates that children are especially attracted by depictions of miniature worlds.

spider? This idea seems quite ridiculous because a friendship between a child and an animal relies on the opportunity of caring, on the one hand, but also on the possibility to build up a more or less intimate relation with the animal, on the other. To touch, even caress insects, to talk with them, and to expect some friendly reactions, appears to be somewhat weird. Another seminal feature that characterizes the common child-animal friendship is eye contact. To have eye contact with insects is quite impossible, and—as is indicated in the conversation between Alice and the gnat—to have empathy with insects, or even identify with them, is quite unusual. This survey might lead to the conclusion that insects virtually do not appear in fictional children's stories, at least not as main characters.

However, as a look at international children's classics reveals, there exist more books that focus on insects than one might assume at first glance. A case in point is *Die Biene Maja und ihre Abenteuer* (1912) ("The Adventures of Maya the Bee") by German author Waldemar Bonsels, a novel inspired by Neo-Romanticism that illustrates, in the style of a "Bildungsroman," the life of a young bee. This novel, which celebrated its hundredth anniversary in 2012, is still popular, above all, thanks to the Japanese anime released in the 1980s that apparently contributed to its worldwide success in the second half of the 20th century. Other countries have classical children's books about insects as well: the most prominent picturebook with an insect as main character certainly is *The Very Hungry Caterpillar* (1969) by Eric Carle. One of the best-known Czech children's classics focusses on the adventures of an ant called Ferdinand. Ondrej Sekora's *Ferda Mravenec* (Ferdinand, the Ant, 1936) has been released as animated film and comic, and a selection of Sekora's original drawings for this book are exhibited in the National Gallery in Prague. Russian author Kornej Cukovskij wrote a satiric poem about a giant cockroach, *Tarakanishhe* (The Giant Cockroach, 1935), which frightens all animals and establishes a sort of dictatorship. This famed poem was regarded as a pamphlet against Stalin and therefore banished by censors until Stalin's death in 1957. Finally, one has to keep in mind the sophisticated children's novel *Charlotte's Web* (1952) by US-American author E.B. White. The main protagonist is a spider called Charlotte, who saves the life of the pig Wilbur by weaving advertising slogans into her webs. In any case, these five children's classics clearly indicate that children's books about insects do exist, and that indeed some authors obviously believe that insects might be interesting and fascinating main characters.[2]

---

2   For further information on these children's classics, cf. Kümmerling-Meibauer (1999).

Insects in Children's Books: A Short Survey

In the following sections, I will firstly give a short overview of the representation of insects in international children's literature from the late 18th century until the present. It will be shown that the increasing interest in insects is strongly connected with Charles Darwin's study *The Descent of Man, and the Selection in Relation to Sex* (1871), which contains chapters on the emotional and social life of insects. Secondly, based on recent studies in ecocriticism and animal studies, a thorough analysis of some recently published picturebooks and children's novels will demonstrate that insects have multiple functions in these works. One function consists in enticing the child's awareness of ecological topics,[3] another one in building up a relationship between insect(s) and children, thus stimulating the child's empathy.

To begin with, insects appear in children's books both as groups, either conceived as swarm (in a more negative sense) or as society, and as individuals. The concept of the insect society especially played a crucial role in cultural discourse since antiquity, emanating from diverse philosophical and literary sources. This prospect apparently influenced the depiction of insects in children's books. Insect societies have been regarded as miniature worlds, mirroring different aspects of human societies. In this regard, particularly the beehive and the anthill serve as metaphors for human behavior (Hollingsworth 2001: xii). The stunning construction and the social life of the beehive and the anthill present an image of "order" that reflects power relations on the one hand, and the relationship between individuals and society on the other. Although hive and hill are equally regarded as metaphors for the city, philosophers and writers such as Plato, Homer, and Vergil, already made a distinction concerning the social "behavior" of bees and ants. They claimed that the hive is a symbol of harmony, home, and the ideal state, while the anthill stands for struggle and even war (Hollingsworth 2001: 48). Moreover, the higher esteem of bees as opposed to ants has been justified by contrasting their color (gold versus red), type of movement (flight versus crawl), construction of building (hive versus hill), and location of building (sky versus earth). This distinction led to the development of a culturally determined hierarchy among insects, with bees and ants on the top, and flees, worms, and maggots on the bottom of the ladder. Surprisingly, this hierarchical model has persisted until modern times and influenced many literary works written for adults and children alike. Whereas only beehive and anthill—in a more restricted sense—are regarded as positive counterparts to human societies, other insects that live in societies, such as wasps and bumblebees, or crop up in huge groups, such as grasshoppers and

---

3   Cf. Lesnik-Oberstein (1998) and Lindenpütz (1998) on the impact of ecological topics on children's literature focusing on nature, animals, and the environment.

flies, are negatively connoted with the notion "swarm." Although these swarms show a stupendous capacity for high-level-organization, they are considered as a possible threat for humans, who place these insects on the same level with parasites.

Besides this tradition, insects also appear as single characters in ancient texts, above all in Aesop's fables, where animals are considered as representatives of human character traits. The most prominent fable with insects is, without doubt, "The Grasshopper and the Ants," followed by "The Eagle and the Dung Beetle," and "Jupiter and the Bees." Since selected fables have been considered suitable reading matter for children since antiquity, most of them have featured in anthologies and illustrated books for children until today.

These two streams of reception—the perception of the insect as individual being that stands for a specific human behavior, and the perception of insect groups that represent either typical features of human societies or are regarded as negative images of chaos and threat—also emerge in children's books. However, in comparison to literature targeted at an adult audience, the insect as main character turned up relatively late, at the beginning of the 19th century, with William Roscoe's poem *The Butterfly's Ball and the Grasshopper's Feast* (1807), illustrated by William Mulready. The beginning asks some imaginative children to join in a festivity arranged by insects: "Come take up your hats and away let us haste/To the Butterfly's Ball and the Grasshopper's Feast." This amusing poem about insects gathering for an evening of innocent entertainment was divested of any overt moralizing or didacticism. The book was an immediate success, with more than 40,000 copies sold in 1807; and it was at once treated as a "nursery classic" and spawned numerous imitators, such as *The Butterfly's Birthday* (1808) by the same author, Catherine Dorset's *The Peacock "At Home": A Sequel to the Butterfly's Ball* (1807), and J.L.B.'s *The Butterfly's Funeral* (1808), among others.[4] These playful accounts, lavishly illustrated by Mulready, focus on the adventures of anthropomorphized insects living in gardens and fields, inviting the child audience to recognize the insects' beauty—focusing on butterflies, grasshoppers, bugs, dragonflies, bees, and spiders. The illustrations were so popular that they elicited a sort of media convergence, displaying the illustrations on handkerchiefs and card games (Kümmerling-Meibauer 1999: 926). Since butterflies take center stage in the majority of these illustrated poems, the new subgenre established by Roscoe was called "papillonade" (derived from French "papillon" = butterfly), an early attestation for the re-emergence of fantasy in England in the beginning of the 19th century (O'Malley 2003: 135).

Another early children's book that focuses on insects is the fictional autobiography *The Curious Adventures of a Field Cricket* (1878) by Ernest

---

4   This famous poem has been analyzed by several scholars, for instance Muir (1954), Jackson (1989), and Styles (1997).

Charles Candèze, translated into English by N. D'Anvers. This text mainly serves a didactic purpose, since it focuses on children's cruelty towards insects. The drastic examples depicted in this book intend to show children the imprudent consequences of their behavior quite plainly. The field cricket has lost her complete family due to children's mindless curiosity and brutality. Her "autobiography" therefore is an appeal to consider insects not as vermin but as valuable and pitiable animals on a par with pets and farm animals (Coslett 2006).

This small book, which ascribes feelings to insects and appeals to the reader's empathy, was published seven years after Charles Darwin's study on evolutionary theory *The Descent of Man, and Selection in Relation to Sex* (1871), whose tenth and eleventh chapter focus on insects, especially butterflies and moths. In this book, which is a follow-up to Darwin's famous *The Origin of the Species* (1859), Darwin concedes higher mental processes to animals. Indeed, he concludes in the third chapter that "even insects express anger, terror, jealousy, and love" (69). Later on, he states that "bees express certain emotions, as of anger, by the tone of their humming" (293). The initial point for this argumentation is Darwin's contention that the relationship between animals and humans might be described by notions such as "love" and "attachment." Even if he restricts these feelings to higher order animals, such as apes and dogs, he believes that all animals are gradually able to express emotions, including birds, reptiles, fish, and insects. However, he also concedes that the behavior of these species is often not intentional, but guided by instincts. Considering these innovative ideas, it does not seem to be incidental that since the end of the 1870s, an increasing number of animal stories appeared that focus on animal emotions and their relationship with humans, whether children or adults. While the majority of animal stories focus on pets and farm animals, with a preference for mammals, other species, such as birds and insects, crop up as well.

The Depiction of Insects in Children's Literature: A Classification

Although the number of children's books with insects as main characters is quite manageable, they can be classified in different respects, considering theme, relationship with humans, biotope, educational purposes, and their underlying image of childhood. Although there exists a great number of non-fiction books about insects, I will concentrate on fictional stories with insects as main characters. Concerning the depiction of insects, at least four different types can be distinguished. First and second, there are books with talking insects and books where insects do not talk at all. In addition, there are stories that display an insect world, sometimes populated by other animals, such as mice, birds, and frogs, without contact to humans, while other books present a relationship between insects and children, which is mostly characterized by friendly feelings and even leads to unusual friendships. What is more, these four types might overlap, as in *The Adventures of Maya the Bee*, which depicts an insect world with talking insects, but without direct communication with humans.

Garrard's (2011) classification of the representation of animals in fiction serves as a model for the analysis of the depiction of insects in children's literature, complemented by Finzsch's (1999) and Hollingwood's (2001) studies on the depiction of animals and insects in literature and film. Garrard distinguishes two main issues that characterize the relationship between humans and animals. This relationship is either determined by "likeness," often leading to anthropomorphism and zoomorphism, or by "otherness," stressing the superiority of animals (allomorphism) or the animal's inferiority (mechanomorphism) (2011: 154). Looking at children's books with insects as main characters, the preference for anthropomorphism catches the eye. Comparable to the presentation of pets, farm animals, and wild animals in children's books, insects can talk, wear clothes, own flats with furniture, and often have a family with parents, grandparents, and children. Moreover, they are depicted as individuals with proper names, specific bodily features, and "human" properties. Hence, they are intelligent, emotional, and social, and even show empathy for each other. These anthropomorphized insects usually live in an insect or animal community; they do not have relations with humans, not to mention children. Whenever humans are involved, they are regarded as a menace, since they deliberately destroy their biotope or unknowingly kill them because of their tiny size. Most often, as is the case with *Maya the Bee*, humans are regarded as superior to all animal species because of their ability to get in close contact with God and nature—an evident allusion to Romantic thinking—, and to conquer and govern the whole world, thus highlighting the insects' inferiority. Only a few contemporary children's books prompt the reader to consider insects' possible superiority because of their sheer number and their ability to stunningly adapt even to inhospitable life conditions where humans struggle to survive.

Concerning genre classification, the stories shift between fantasy, adventure story, realistic story, and story of initiation. Besides picturebooks focusing on insects there even exist detective stories with insects as main characters, such as Paul Shipton's *Bug Muldoon and the Garden of Fear* (1997), with the sequel *Bug Muldoon and the Killer in the Rain* (2003). Both novels are located in a garden populated by numerous insects, which are horrified by abominable crimes. Due to the ingenious detective Bug Muldoon's flashes of inspiration, the criminals are always debunked in the end. Bug Muldoon's outfit, inconvenient behavior, and sappy slogans are apparently influenced by Humphrey Bogart, the famous actor in several detective films from the 1940s, thus contributing to the novels' humorous effects.

Another genre which shows a tendency to include insects is dystopian fantasy, such as Suzan Collins' *Underland Chronicles* (2003-2007). Collins, who became famous for her *Hunger Games*-trilogy (2008-2010), received prestigious awards for this bestselling series as well. The five volumes tell the story of eleven-year-old orphan Gregor, who accidentally falls through a vent in the basement of their flat with his two-year-old sister Boots. Both find themselves in a strange world called Underland, which is hidden beneath New York City. This world is inhabited by humans who live in the stone city of Regalia along with giant creatures, such as bats, ants, bugs, spiders, and cockroaches. Gregor is at once identified as Gregor the Overlander, the warrior of the prophecy, who shall free Underland from the Rat King Bane. Together with his sister, who is worshipped by the cockroaches, Gregor takes part in the war between Regalia and the rats. Because of his translucent skin and his capacity of echolocation, Gregor is able to walk and fight in absolute darkness. Supported by the inhabitants of Regalia and the giant insects, he finally defeats the rat army and finds his lost father among the prisoners. The remarkable quality of the *Underland Chronicles* consists in the combination of an enthralling dystopian fantasy with ecological and political topics, such as biological warfare, military intelligence, and genocide. Rat King Bane, for instance, is a charismatic speaker whose political opinions and rhetoric devices obviously refer to Hitler. In addition, Bane uses poison gas to kill his enemies and to diminish the mice population. Although the insects are minor characters, their huge size (for instance, bugs are described as being as big as buses), inscrutable behavior, and gluttony contribute to the menacing and nightmarish atmosphere. The insects support Gregor and his human army, but their relationship is sober and diplomatic. Since humans and insects are depicted as very different species, they are not able to build up empathic, or even amicable, relations.

Although it might be promising to continue this synopsis of children's literature focusing on insects, in the following, I will rather focus on four children's books; two picturebooks and two children's novels. This selection is not random; my analyses will show that the representation of insects in modern children's literature is quite multi-faceted and displays an astonishing variety concerning the relationship between children and insects.

Insects as Representation of "Otherness"

The title of the picturebook *Alien Invaders* (2010), written by Lynn Huggins-Cooper and illustrated by Bonnie Leick, alludes to the science fiction genre, thus evoking the expectation that the story deals with aliens from outer space. However, the book cover shows five huge insect heads depicted against a night sky with a shining full moon. The insects are staring at the viewer and their oversized eyes, tentacles, and upper limbs cause a feeling of unease. This impression is intensified by the image on the back cover, which displays two fat caterpillars on a branch whose faces are turned towards a little boy with a helmet, oversized glasses, and a cape. The boy stares with open mouth at the caterpillars, while his facial expression and posture express fear and curiosity alike.

fig. 1: Cover Illustration of the book *Alien Invaders*.
Reprinted with kind permission © Raven Tree Press (www.raventreepress.com).

The picturebook story starts with the little boy, who watches a film on aliens on TV. Fascinated by the description of aliens and the prospect that they probably have already invaded Earth, he begins to look for aliens in his surroundings. He is startled by the vast number of insects in his parents' garden, and compares them to the images of aliens shown on TV. He is surprised to discover that the insects have tentacles, robot legs, wear tiny helmets and shiny suits, and watch everything with camera-like eyes, just like aliens. In addition, they whisper in strange languages, slither, leave clues everywhere, build cities underground, perform strange dances, construct dangerous traps, and even sneak into the house. He sums up: "There are many more of them than us" (n.p.). This statement is accompanied by an illustration depicting the boy and a girl sitting on a bench in the garden. They have turned their backs on the viewer and are eating drumsticks and chips. Next to the table, a big barbecue is fired up. In the foreground, however, a row of countless ants is engaged in carrying away cucumber, cheese, peanuts, meat, bread, and other food.

On the subsequent double spread the text performs a shift in point of view when the boy's mother assures him that the creatures the boy is afraid of are "only" bugs. The boy, however, cannot calm down completely. On the contrary, he confirms that he attempts to befriend the insects, just in case. Therefore, he disguises himself as an insect, with a sieve as helmet, big sunglasses, dark boots, and an old blind as wings. In this outfit, he stands on the lawn with two plants in full blossom in both hands, thus attracting bees, butterflies and other insects. On the last double spread the boy blatantly confirms that "they sure look like aliens to me!" (n.p.). The illustration once again depicts the boy sitting in the dining room and watching TV. The screen reveals that he is watching another sci-fi film, showing a child that is chased by giant insect-like creatures. In order to conceal his fear, he offers his popcorn to three insects that are sitting nearby. Despite the humorous effects of the illustrations and the boy's comments, the repeated comparison of insects to space invaders and the allusion to the vast number of creepy crawlers disclose an ambivalent feeling. Seen from the boy's angle, the insects are weird creatures that seem to be present everywhere, in the garden, but also in the boy's bedroom, the kitchen, and the dining room. Because of their unusual compound eyes, the boy gets the impression of being permanently watched by the insects. While his parents are not alarmed at all, the boy believes that the insects have already started to conquer the human world.[5]

---

5   This picturebook clearly supports the thesis that the depiction of animals always reveals
     underlying attitudes of humans towards animals. Cf. Manning and Serpell (1994).

fig. 2: Illustration from the book *Alien Invaders*.
Reprinted with kind permission © Raven Tree Press (www.raventreepress.com).

It is a well-known fact that insects surpass mankind by their sheer number. Moreover, some scholars even claim that insects are much better adapted to changing life conditions and that they are better conditioned to survive life-threatening situations. This idea is staged, for instance, in Andrew Stanton's animation film *Wall-E* (2008). In this film, mankind was forced to leave a devastated and polluted earth in order to live in a huge space ship. The only living creatures on earth are the robot Wall-E and his friend, a cockroach. Obviously, *Alien Invaders* also alludes to a dystopian scenario discussed in the context of climate change discourse by presenting a worldview where insects are the secret rulers of the world. In the boy's imagination, which is evidently influenced by sci-fi films, insects are "alien invaders," although they ironically do not come from outer space. Whereas adults usually consider insects as harmless but sometimes annoying animals, often ignoring them due to their tiny size, they appear strange and mysterious from the boy's perspective. The viewer is attracted by the lavishly crafted illustrations, whose subtle tones and a broad range of hues and depth were created through the use of pencils. The images were then manipulated on the computer to add radiance and a luminous glow that emanates from the pages and amplifies the mysterious atmosphere. Pictures and text emphasize that insects are fascinating animals with stupendous capacities.

However, while the boy starts several futile attempts to get in contact with them, the insects show an indifferent behavior. They are just attracted by the food and flowers offered by the boy. He feigns affection to outwit the insects which have already invaded his home and garden. By shifting points of view, the illustrations highlight the boy's increasing feeling of inferiority. In all illustrations, the ants, bugs, and spiders are presented as giant creatures in comparison to the small boy. But on closer consideration, it is obvious that these images depict the boy's perspective. He is overwhelmed by his discovery, which he is not able to communicate to adults. Since the insects talk in strange languages the boy cannot manage to understand, any direct communication is impossible. Hence, the idea of building up a friendship with insects is a failure from the beginning. The oddity of this prospect is additionally stressed by the insects' facial expression and body language, which express indifference and insensibility towards the boy's advances. That their behavior is determined by instincts is obvious to the viewer but not to the little boy, who is gradually disappointed by the adults' lack of understanding. Left alone with his imagination and feelings, he increasingly dives into his own imaginative world, which correlates real insects with gigantic monster insects from sci-fi films. In this regard, the insects present "the other" from the boy's perspective (Hollingsworth 2001: 120). While adults may fear the invasion of aliens from outer space, the boy acknowledges that the earth has already been invaded by countless insects that populate all places where people live. *Alien Invaders* is marked by this ambivalent attitude, thus balancing humorous and creepy effects, and provoking the reader to (re-)consider the close relation between environment and the imagination.

Friendship between Children and Insects

While the boy's multiple attempts to befriend the insects are somewhat unidirectional, the children's novel *Masterpiece* (2008) by Elise Broach is based on a developing friendship between an eleven-year-old boy and a bug. James lives with his mother, stepfather, and baby brother in New York City, while the beetle Marvin lives with his family under the kitchen sink in the family's apartment. James is suffering from his parents' divorce, and he is an outsider at school. His father Karl, an artist, gives him art paper, an ink bottle, and a fountain pen for his birthday, hoping that James will follow in his footsteps. But James is disappointed about the present and the unpleasant birthday party arranged by his mother. In the night, Marvin detects the art things on James's desk. Fascinated by the tiny pen, he draws a miniature replica of the winter scene outside. Absorbed in his art work, Marvin does not notice that he is observed by James, who marvels at the beetle's artistry. Although they cannot talk to each other, this encounter is the beginning of an unusual friendship. By rapid movements and changing directions, Marvin is able to communicate with James, who is sensible enough to accept that bugs might have feelings and intelligence. The beautiful drawing evokes the admiration of his parents, and James is considered a promising artist. When Karl takes his son (with Marvin riding along in his pocket) to the Metropolitan Museum of Art, a curator chances to see the drawing and compares it to Albrecht Dürer's work. Since James cannot confess that his masterpiece has been created by a beetle, he gets into trouble. The curator, Christina, suggests that James should help the museum to carry out a plan: the museum hosts an invaluable drawing of Dürer that belongs to a picture cycle presenting four virtues. However, three of these drawings have been stolen from different museums during the course of several years, and rumor goes that the last drawing might be stolen as well. In collaboration with the FBI and the director of the museum, James is asked to create a forgery of Dürer's drawing that is to be exhibited instead of the original work.

With the help of Marvin, James succeeds in this endeavor, but despite this ingenious scheme, the thief manages to steal the original. Dürer's drawing would have been gone forever had Marvin not been hiding in the office where the drawing was locked. It turns out that the main curator, Denny, had organized the theft – not for money, but out of a passion for Dürer's art. He is also in possession of the other stolen drawings, which have been kept hidden in the curator's apartment. The way Marvin manages to inform James about his discovery is quite thrilling and seems to be inspired by hard-boiled detective novels. Just like Sherlock Holmes and Doctor Watson, James and Marvin uncover the culprit and return the stolen Dürer drawings to the museum. Despite all complications, the adults' mistrustful questions, and the police questioning, James manages to keep Marvin's involvement a secret. He even finds a solution to avoid his mother's request to draw more "masterpieces" in order to sell them to art connoisseurs. He purposely falls down the staircase and breaks his arm. Since his hand is severely damaged, the doctor claims that James will not be able to draw such elaborated pictures anymore. While James is content with his new role as successful detective, Marvin keeps on refining his drawing skills, admired by his beetle family.

Masterpiece is a quite unusual novel, combining different genres, such as animal story, detective story, and coming of age story, dealing with art heist, forgery, and a secret friendship between a boy and a beetle. The relationship between James and Marvin refers to a well-known pattern of animal stories for children: how an emotionally neglected or even traumatized child gains self-confidence by caring for a weak, sometimes even despised animal.[6] In contrast to cute or impressive animals, such as rabbits, cats, and dogs, a tiny beetle as friend seems to be completely nonsensical. Nevertheless, Broach succeeds in drawing the readership into this suspenseful story. Although the novel is built upon some fantastic preconditions—that animals can talk with each other, that a beetle is able to draw pictures, to read human writing, and to think and behave in a quite rational manner—, the reader accepts the exceptional liaison between James and Marvin in the long run. From the start, the author makes clear that their friendship is put to the test several times. Marvin has to defend his relationship with James as his family disapproves of any contact with humans; and James has always to be alert not to betray his beetle friend. Consequently, their relationship is defined by concern and empathy. Marvin takes pity on James, who is neglected by his mother and stepfather, whereas James consistently attempts to discover feelings in the beetle's face and body language. In this regard, James is sometimes skeptical whether Marvin is really able to express emotions in a way comparable to humans, especially when he tries to scrutinize Marvin's face for emotional cues.[7] He is not even sure whether the beetle is a boy or a girl, but assumes that he must be a boy because of his frantic movements and self-assured behavior. Since they cannot talk to each other, James never finds out that his new friend is called Marvin by his family.

James and Marvin's friendship is challenged in even more ways. For instance, James has to hide Marvin from his intrusive mother, and at one point, he loses Marvin in the museum's office. Marvin, on the other hand, argues with his parents, who do not understand why their son ventures into dangerous, even life-threatening situations in order to help James. They rightly emphasize that they all will get in trouble should James's parents detect their hidden home under the kitchen sink, due to Marvin's frequent crossings of the kitchen floor. However, in the end they accept this unusual friendship and Marvin's artistic career, thus acknowledging their son's maturation. Just as James struggles with the

---

6   See Burt (2001: 177ff.) and Melson (2005: 105ff.).

7   The importance of eye contact with animals as a precondition for the emergence of empathy has been stressed by John Berger in his seminal essay "Why look at animals?": "And so, when he [i.e. the human, BKM] is being seen by the animal, he is being seen as his surroundings are seen by him. His recognition of this is what makes the look of the animal familiar" (2009: 5). Derrida (2008) picked up this thread, arguing that animals might observe humans, thus establishing an "animal gaze." This change in perception is necessary to have compassion and pity with animals (34). Paton (2009) and Wiedmann (2012) even claim that the depiction of friendships between children and animals in films establish an own subgenre, characterized as "animal rescue film" (Paton 2009: 30) or "Tierfreundschaftsfilm" (Wiedmann 2012: 148). On the animal gaze in film and cultural studies, see also Kylie Crane's and Sieglinde Grimm's contribution to this volume.

devastating family conditions, Marvin must assert himself against his family's restrictive worldview.

Masterpiece is not only an animal-friendship story, but it is also a story about the coming of age of *both* protagonists. While Marvin detects his artistic skills and becomes a devoted artist, James is able to emancipate himself from his parents' ambitions to turn him into a famed *wunderkind* and to accept his new patchwork family. Thus, in the end, both gain their respective families' respect. As this comparison makes clear James and Marvin can both be seen as "round" characters with their own identity. Thus, the narrative explores imaginative avenues for thinking about the emotional equality of insects and humans. Besides, the comparison of Dürer's exceptional craft to Marvin's artistic skills has a share in the novel's humorous atmosphere. Prima facie, equating Marvin's drawings and Dürer's famous copperplate engravings seems quite ridiculous. However, the subtle irony consists in the apprehension of Dürer's remarkable capacity to draw such fine lines and hatchings, while other artists are not able to imitate this paragon artist. Ironically, the exception to the rule is a beetle with tiny legs. Marvin is the ideal copyist who succeeds in drawing an almost perfect copy of Dürer's famous virtue cycle. Notably, Marvin never depicts imaginary scenes but always draws what he can perceive with his goggle eyes. In the end, his two "masterpieces," the view from the window and the forgery of Dürer's drawing, are framed and displayed in James's bedroom, reminding the two friends of their shared adventure.

As far as I can say, *Masterpiece* is as yet the only children's novel that presents a friendship between a child and an insect in a convincing manner. It demonstrates that insects not only embody traits of "otherness," but that they might be considered animal species with feelings and emotions as well. During the course of the novel, the reader is gradually dragged into the beetle's emotional conflict of being torn between concerns for his beetle family and his new human friend. Thus, the reader is enticed to accept that insects—in this case: beetles—have feelings comparable to those of humans, and that they might also be able to think strategically.

Kafka's *Metamorphosis* as Intertext

The depiction of such a friendship between humans and insects might seem quite provocative to some readers. How might these readers react to children's books that present the metamorphosis of a child into an insect? Proficient readers are certainly reminded of Franz Kafka's famous novella *Die Verwandlung* (*The Metamorphosis*, 1912), which displays the inexplicable transformation of the main protagonist Gregor Samsa into a giant beetle. As a result of this transformation, Gregor is subdued to appalling trials that finally lead to his death. Repudiated by his parents and beloved sister, smiled at by the lodgers, and despised by the cleaning lady, Gregor suffers from horrible humiliations. Deprived of his voice, he is unable to express his emotional state. Since Kafka demanded that the original edition should not be illustrated at all, it is left to the reader to decide whether the metamorphosis really happened or whether it is only subject to the protagonist's imagination. Be that as it may, at least two children's books picked up this topic, focusing on the metamorphosis of a boy into an insect. Unsurprisingly, both works intertextually refer to Kafka's novella. Lawrence David's picturebook *Beetleboy* (1999), with illustrations by Delphine Durand, describes one day in the life of ten-year-old Gregor Samsa. The first sentence is a literal adoption of Kafka's text. After this, the story takes a different turn. Gregor is still able to dress himself and to leave his bedroom. However, his family does not acknowledge that he has transformed into a beetle. His parents and sister laugh at him when he claims that he has turned into a beetle, comparing this assertion with Gregor's previous contentions to be an astronaut and an explorer. Even at school nobody seems to discern the change, except for his best friend Michael. Although Gregor has some advantages because of his new body, such as being able to play soccer with six legs instead of two, he dearly wishes to become a human boy again. When the teacher scolds him for his repeated claims to be a beetle, Gregor is desperate. He hides in his bedroom and climbs to the ceiling, where he stays for several hours. Finally, his family accepts that Gregor has turned into a beetle, but, contrary to Kafka's story, the parents appreciate Gregor nevertheless, confessing their love and concern. In conclusion, Gregor can approve of his new existence. However, when he awakens the next morning, he realizes that he has changed into his old self and is relieved that the "beetle day" is over.

Although the pictures show from the beginning that Gregor has really turned into a beetle, the text is somewhat ambivalent. It remains open whether Gregor only thinks of himself as a beetle, or whether the metamorphosis actually happens. Since Gregor is an imaginative child, changing between diverse roles and pretending to be another person, the attentive reader might be skeptical about Gregor's transformation. Perhaps the boy just decided to have a "beetle day" instead of an "astronaut day," thus checking how his family, teacher, and schoolmates might react to his strange behavior. The parents' and teacher's comments on Gregor's fanciful stories and exaggerated movements might alert the reader that the metamorphosis takes place only on a metaphorical level. Gregor's depiction as beetle in the picturebook's illustrations then take on the boy's perspective, while other people just perceive him as a ten-year-old boy. Michael is the first character that accepts Gregor's transformation, but it is not clear whether he just affirms his best friend's imaginary world, or whether he really notices Gregor's metamorphosis.

Dirk Walbrecker's novel *Greg. Eine rätselhafte Verwandlung* (*Greg. A Mysterious Metamorphosis*, 1999) goes a step further. The story openly addresses the problems of the main protagonist, who is on the verge of despair after having turned into a giant caterpillar. Comparable to Kafka's novella and Lawrence's picturebook, 16-year-old Greg awakens in the morning with a feeling of unease. He gradually acknowledges that his body has been transformed into a huge caterpillar. Consequently, he develops a great appetite, devouring even the books on the shelves and the clothes spread on the floor. The various members of his family react differently: while his mother still believes that the huge caterpillar is her son Greg, his father is horrified about the insect, and his older brother is both fascinated and disgusted. Only his grandfather, who is seriously ill, accepts Greg as he is and tells him the story of Kafka's Gregor Samsa in order to encourage Greg to make the most of the situation. Whereas the family ponders over possible reasons for the metamorphosis and blames either Greg's greedy watching of animal films or genetically modified food, Greg starts to explore the house and the garden, staggered about his newly acquired capacities, such as climbing high walls and ceilings without effort, looking in different directions at the same time because of his goggle eyes, and the possibility to defend himself with his poisonous horns.

During the course of the novel Greg struggles with his hybrid existence. He behaves like a caterpillar, on the one hand, but feels and thinks like a human, on the other. When his family "sells" him to a TV show, Greg appears to capitulate, only devoting himself to his greedy appetite. But the recollection of his grandfather's encouragement and the secret love for the neighbor's daughter Sara prevent him from a total transformation into an animal. Although everyone praises the paradise-like conditions at the TV studio, Greg gradually gets the impression to be living in hell. Tormented by nightmares and the inability to communicate his feelings, he ultimately is at the mercy of a ruthless scientist who has the ambition to receive the Nobel Prize for the discovery of a new species. The scientist stops at nothing and plans to kill Greg before he can skin for the last time. This is foreclosed by his family and Sara. With their help, Greg is set free. He finds himself on a garbage dump—a clear allusion to the dishonorable death of Kafka's Gregor Samsa. Greg manages to crawl away and finally settles in a gingko tree in Sara's garden. There he starts to weave a cocoon and falls asleep. The next morning Sara discovers Greg in the tree top and asks him whether she should climb up or whether he would prefer to climb down. The last sentences indicate that Greg has turned into a human again, now ready to confess his love to Sara.

The author's decision to metamorphose Greg into a caterpillar instead of a beetle demands an explanation. The main difference consists in the caterpillar's several molts before he turns into a butterfly. Greg also experiences three molts, every time changing into an even bigger caterpillar that frightens other people. But with every molt Greg notices an inner change that he can hardly communicate to his surroundings. Since he cannot speak, he develops a body language to disclose his feelings. Interestingly, only women (his mother, Sara, the keeper) are able to recognize Greg's efforts to express his demands. Therefore, they play an important role in his act of liberation. The allusions to Greg's shyness and sensibility in his former existence reveal the ambiguous message of his metamorphosis. Being on the threshold between adolescence and adulthood, Greg has to accept his body and its peculiarities before being able to gain a complete identity. Like the caterpillar, Greg must experience several metaphorical "molts" in order to become a matured young adult who overcomes all obstacles.

Conclusion

As this article has shown, insects have appeared as main characters in international children's literature since the beginning of the 19th century. However, they do not play such a prominent role as pets and farm animals, who dominate animal stories for children to this day. Despite the increasing amount of studies in the realm of animal studies, which also touch upon the depiction of animals in diverse media for children, there is little research on the representation of insects in fictional children's books. One finding is that the fascination for insects is brought about by their tiny size. In relation to humans they are very small and present a world scaled differently, thus enticing the reader to imagine what the world is like "down there." Moreover, the relationship between insects and children, as it is presented in books such as *Masterpiece* and *Alien Invaders*, evidently discloses power relations and mirrors the child's experiences with powerful adults.

The anthropological difference between humans and animals in general, and humans and insects in particular, has been investigated by numerous philosophers and scientists. Charles Darwin played a prominent role in this respect, since he first advocated that insects have emotions and can express feelings as well. Thereby, he paved the way for a change in perspective: to perceive animals not only as objects, but also as subjects. Consequently, Darwin and his followers fostered a sense of connectedness with other creatures, which includes insects as well. Since then, the number of children's books about and with animals, including insects, has been increasing gradually. Although the relationship between children and insects faces several obstacles—the insects' tiny size, the lack of cuteness, and the difficulty to have eye contact—some authors have created stories for children that successfully engage with this unusual topic. Notwithstanding the fact that humans and insects are entirely different—as far as their size, communication, and appearance are concerned—, the preoccupation with insects in the children's books analyzed here shows astonishing similarities: most importantly, the attempt to get in contact with insects, and the first eye contact between child and insect, play an important role, as they show that it is possible to feel empathy with insects and to acknowledge their life conditions by temporarily adopting an insect's perspective. Surely, this demands strenuous efforts and is not always successful, as Briony Tallis, the main protagonist in Ian McEwan's novel *Atonement* (2001), acknowledges: "How could anyone presume to know the world through the eyes of an insect?" (149). But children's books do so, and they do so successfully.

Works Cited

Primary Sources

Bonsels, Waldemar. *Die Biene Maja und ihre Abenteuer*. Berlin: Schuster & Loeffler, 1912.
Broach, Elise. *Masterpiece*. Illustrated by Kelly Murphy. New York: Henry Holt and Company, 2008.
Candèze, Ernest Charles. *The Curious Adventures of a Field Cricket*. Trans. N. D'Anvers. London: Sampson, Low, Marston, Searle and Rivington, 1878.
Carle, Eric. *The Very Hungry Caterpillar*. New York: Penguin, 2007 (first American edition 1969).
Carroll, Lewis. *Through the Looking-Glass and What Alice Found There*. Illustrated by John Tenniel. Oxford: Oxford UP, 1999 (first British edition 1871).
Collins, Suzanne. *Underland Chronicles*. 5 vols. New York: Scholastic, 2003-2007.
Cukovskij, Kornej. *Tarakanishhe*. Moscow: Malysh, 1977 (first Russian edition 1935).
David, Lawrence. *Beetleboy*. Illustrated by Delphine Durand. New York: Random House, 1999.
Huggins-Cooper, Lynn. *Alien Invaders*. Illustrated by Bonnie Leick. McHenry, Ill: Raven Tree Press, 2010.
McEwan, Ian. *Atonement*. London: Jonathan Cape, 2001.
Roscoe, William. *The Butterfly's Ball and the Grasshopper's Feast*. Illustrated by William Mulready. New York: McGraw Hill, 1967 (first British edition 1807).
Shipton, Paul. *Bug Muldoon and the Garden of Fear*. Oxford: Oxford UP, 1997.
Shipton, Paul. *Bug Muldoon and the Killer in the Rain*. Oxford: Oxford UP, 2003.
Sekora, Ondrej. *Ferda mravenec*. Illustrated by the author. Prag: Artia 1965 (first Czech edition 1936).
Walbrecker, Dirk. *Greg. Eine rätselhafte Verwandlung*. München: Bertelsmann, 1999.
White, E.B. *Charlotte's Web*. Illustrated by Leonard Weisgard. New York: HarperCollins, 2006 (first American edition 1952).

Secondary Sources

Berger, John. *About Looking*. London: Bloomsbury, 2009 [1980].
Blount, Margaret J. *Animal Land: The Creatures of Children's Fiction*. New York: Morrow, 1974.
Burt, Jonathan. *Animals in Film*. London: Reaktion Books, 2002.
Cosslett, Tess. *Talking Animals in British Children's Fiction, 1786-1914*. Aldershot: Ashgate, 2006.
Crist, Eileen. *Images of Animals: Anthropomorphism and Animal Mind. Animals, Culture, and Society*. Philadelphia: Temple UP, 1999.
Cross, Gary. *The Cute and the Cool. Wondrous Innocence and Modern American Children's Culture*. Oxford: Oxford UP, 2004.
Darwin, Charles. *The Descent of Man, and Selection in Relation to Sex*. London: Murray 1875.
Derrida, Jaques. *The Animal that Therefore I Am*. Trans. David Wills. New York: Fordham UP, 2008 (first French edition 1997).

Duan, Shu-jy. "A Tale of Animals: A Study of Animal Fantasy for Children from Aesop's Fables through 1986". *Other Worlds, Other Lives*. Eds. Myrna Machet et al. Vol. 2. Pretoria: UNISA Press, 1996. 149-69.

Dwyer, June. "A Non-companion Species Manifesto: Humans, Wild Animals, and 'The Pain of Anthropomorphism'." *South Atlantic Review* 72 (2008): 73-89.

Finzsch, Norbert: "'I don't rejoice in insects at all'. Soziale Insekten in der westeuropäischen Kulturgeschichte und im Science Fiction Film". *Tiere im Film. Eine Menschheitsgeschichte der Moderne*. Eds. Maren Möhring; Massimo Perinelli & Olaf Stieglitz. Köln & Wien: Böhlau, 1999. 163-76.

Garrard, Greg. *Ecocriticism*. New York: Routledge, 2011.

Hollingsworth, Christopher. *Poetics of the Hive. The Insect Metaphor in Literature*. Iowa City: U of Iowa P, 2001.

Holloway, Marguerite: "'In Amongst the Green Blades'." *The Lion and the Unicorn* 25.2. (2011). 132-45.

Jackson, M.V. *Engines of Instruction, Mischief and Magic*. Nebraska: U of Nebraska P, 1989.

Kümmerling-Meibauer, Bettina. *Klassiker der Kinder- und Jugendliteratur. Ein internationales Lexikon*. 2 vols. Stuttgart & Weimar: Metzler, 1999.

Lesnik-Oberstein, Karin. "Children's Literature and the Environment." *Writing the Environment. Ecocriticism and Literature*. Eds. Rchard Kerridge & Neil Sammells London: Zed Books, 1998.

Lindenpütz, Dagmar. *Das Kinderbuch als Medium ökologischer Bildung. Untersuchungen zur Konzeption von Natur und Umwelt in der erzählenden Kinderliteratur seit 1970*. Essen: Die Blaue Eule, 1998.

Manning, Audrey & James Serpell (eds.). *Animals and Human Society: Changing Perspectives*. London & New York: Routledge, 1994.

McCrindle, Cheryl & Johannes Odendaal. "Animals in books used for preschool children." *Anthrozoos* 7.2 (1994). 135-46.

Muir, Percy. *English Children's Books*. London: Patsford, 1954.

O'Malley, Andrew. *The Making of the Modern Child. Children's Literature and Childhood in the Late Eighteenth Century*. New York: Routledge, 2003.

Melson, Gail F. *Why the Wild Things Are. Animals in the Lives of Children*. Cambridge & London: Harvard UP, 2005.

Paton, Priscilla. "Furry Soul Mates, Aloof Birds, Pesky Rodents: Liminality, Animal Rescue Films, and Sarah Orne Jewett." *Of Mice and Men: Animals in Human Culture*. Eds. Batra Nandita & Vartan Messier. Newcastle: Cambridge Scholars Publishing, 2009. 28-41.

Rayner, Mary. "Some Thoughts on Animals in Children's Books." *Signal* 28 (1979). 81-7.

Ritvo, Harriet. "Learning from Animals: Natural History for Children in the Eighteenth and Nineteenth Century." *Children's Literature* 13 (1985). 72-93.

Styles, Morag. *From the Garden to the Street. Three Hundred Years of Poetry for Children*. London: Cassell, 1997.

Wiedmann, Natália. "'I looked at him and I saw myself.' Über den Tierfreundschaftsfilm." *Von wilden Kerlen und wilden Hühnern. Perspektiven des modernen Kinderfilms*. Eds. Christian Exner & Bettina Kümmerling-Meibauer. Marburg: Schüren, 2012. 148-70.

Teaching a Poetics of Failure?
The Benefit of *Not*-Understanding the Other, Posthumanism, and the Works of Shaun Tan and Wolf Erlbruch

Roman Bartosch (Cologne)

Animals and the representation of animals are important issues in ecocritical studies. Similarly, since pupils, especially younger ones, seem to like reading and talking about animals, animals also play a crucial role in the general pedagogical context of teaching English language and literatures. And since ecocriticism, as Greg Garrard maintains, "has been preoccupied with pedagogy since its inception" (2012: 1), my contribution seeks to bring into fruitful tension the interest both educational areas have in animal others. That is to say, I want to call into question the idea that by virtue of their popularity in the classroom, animals can serve ecocritical educational ideas in a straightforward manner. It is, indeed, likely that "animals may be the first point of contact with 'nature'" (Matthewman 2011: 63), but that does not—and should not—mean that animals can serve a metonymic function of inevitably 'greening' the classroom.

Even *if* animals provided such an 'easy access' to ecocritical thinking, the case of *literary* animals complicates matters further: Since literary texts rely to a great extent on anthropomorphisms if they engage with animals, and since anthropomorphism is "a term of reproach, both intellectual and moral" (Daston & Mitman 2005: 2) and, thus, the "core problem" of modern representation of animals (cf. Ingensiep & Baranzke 2008: 52-6), the role and benefit of literary texts in this context is far from clear. Indeed, in the context of the demands of Education for Sustainability, for instance (see UNESCO 2012), a focus on literary tales of animal consciousness at the cost of precious curriculum space better reserved for systemic and science-based teaching units on ecology, for instance, may seem like a provocation. And it is—but for good reasons, as I will claim in this essay.

In the following, I wish to challenge the idea of "presenting animals to students in the sense of making them *present* in literal, literary, bioregional and scientific terms" (Welling & Kapel 105),[1] and I will, first of all, explain my doubts about the merits of such representations. Secondly, I will show why I think literary texts can do other things and achieve other objectives better, and I hope to arrive at a point where we can read the animal by deliberately not trying to 'read' it at all—maybe a reading that highlights the degree of not-understanding will be to more avail to ecocritical education than meets the science-oriented eye.

*****

In Greg Garrard's recent publication *Teaching Ecocriticism and Green Cultural Studies*, Bart Welling and Scottie Kapel propose an interesting pedagogical approach to teaching animals in literature and culture with a specific emphasis on what they call response-ability. To be response-able means to negotiate a position that neither "[defers] to biology for purely objective [...] explanations" nor "[overestimates] the role that anthropocentrism and anthropodenial have played in science's approaches to animals" (Welling & Kapel 2012: 112). For someone wary of scientific reductionism and conscious of the narrativity of facts and truths, this is a very good starting point but, at the same time, I find myself in an epistemological and ontological dilemma, delineated already by their chapter's title: "The Return of the Animal." Who returns? Where? Through whom? Welling and Kapel are of course keenly aware of these questions and the paradox that a return of the animal in a classroom entails when they ask how, "[o]n a practical note," one may be teaching animals or even "'teach like an animal' in a classroom from which non-human beings have been deliberately excluded" (Welling & Kapel 112) and within an institution that is certainly anthropocentric—what else could it be? In other words: the return of the animal suggests a possibility of presence that is made impossible by the very institutional, contextual and not least the material limitations of the whole enterprise of teaching, in particular, literary texts. And unless one starts teaching on a farm—or, for that matter, in a factory farm—there are no animals returning. But while such a return must be bound to fail eventually, there are ways to connect with animals and approach animality that are likewise promising.

Sasha Matthewman, for instance, offers an interesting perspective on animals that are present only via literary mediation when she suggests focusing on the tension that animals are at the same time 'other' and 'like us' (2011: 63). The ambiguous nature of animal being, "so like us, so unlike us" (Diamond 2006: 61), is the very basis for emotional responses in general and, in the field of

---

1   This does not mean that I do not think that it is a worthy enterprise. Indeed, I am
     convinced that this is one of the central achievements of ecocriticism: rediscovering that
     nature and animals in texts refer to *real* environments and animals, and that there is a
     real world, and not only signifying practices, that matters.

literary production, it is the backbone of fables and animal narratives in particular. This is why Matthewman, instead of dismissing anthropomorphism as a pathetic fallacy, discusses its potential. Since "animals are ubiquitous in children's fiction," she goes on to argue, and since "one of the ways in which children begin to understand themselves as human is through comparison and contrasts with animals" (2011: 63), she suggests teaching anthropomorphization as well as what she describes as 'categories of anthropomorphism'. Humans, she explains, can be described as animalistic; humans may actually be transformed into animals and vice versa, writers may seek to depict animals 'realistically', or scientific description and close observation may replace interpretations of mental states—all in all, she suggests seven categories of anthropomorphism and claims that "[r]ecognizing that there are different degrees and intentions to anthropomorphism can be a strong starting point for the comparison and evaluation of texts which feature animals as important" (64). While I agree with her contention that a reflection on forms and functions of anthropomorphization is a pivotal task in any ecocritical or environmental classroom, it seems that a crucial problem remains: If sameness is established temporarily through anthropomorphisms, ultimately, one will arrive at a point where understanding one's humanity and the establishment of an identity relies on the difference, the "contrast with animals." This means that the tension that animals are at the same time 'other' and 'like us' has to be resolved and that the human/animal dichotomy has to be perpetuated.

So, while both approaches have their merits, they share a blind spot. Matthewman at least partially attempts to develop a sense of animal identity when she stresses the sameness of human and other animals, if only at the margins of literary encounters between readers and fictional animals and only as some kind of halcyon interim. Welling and Kapel's proposal to focus on animal representation fully stresses the constructedness of animal alterity, too, which is quite in line with current arguments from the field of Critical Animal Studies, but it links being response-able with what I would call, cautiously following Derrida, an 'illusion of presence'. Critical Animal Studies refutes the claim that animal otherness creates an abyss between 'them' and ourselves, and it emphasizes that what we share with all animals can best be discussed negatively: finitude, for example, and embodiment, which for many means 'aging', 'pain', 'bodily desires', 'excretion'.[2] Under the headline of 'posthumanism', there is quite a discussion going on about these issues. But how to get posthumanism into the classroom? Welling and Kapel, for instance, are

---

2   It is of course possible to call this focus on negativity into question, as, for instance, Sue Donaldson and Will Kymlicka do in *Zoopolis: A Political Theory of Animal Rights* (2011). While this is not the objective of this paper, I do explore the potential of their ideas (beyond the liberal-rights context in which they emerged) in "Ghostly Presences: Tracing the Animal in Julia Leigh's *The Hunter*" (forthcoming).

rightly skeptical of "theoretical esoteric that our students are likely to find boring, if not downright useless" (Welling & Kapel 113-4). What comes to mind may be Cary Wolfe's formulation—grounded on work by Luhmann and Derrida —that "we are not we; we are not that 'auto-' of autobiography that humanism gives to itself" and that therefore, animal studies must engage with the complex same-but-different nature of finitude. In the context of the EFL classroom, however, the "estranging prostheticity and exteriority of communication" (Wolfe 2010: 119) seems less an avenue for wild thinking than a straight road to turning students away, probably bored, surely bewildered.

Is there no way out of this conflict, then? An increasingly complex and abstract field of Critical Animal Studies on the one hand and a form of teaching that is inevitably bound to teleologies of estrangement from animals on the other (you start with animal stories, then learn the symbolism of fables and finally understand that animals are little more than allegories)? I think there might be a way, but it is crucial to discard the notion that we could "think like an animal" (cf. Matthewman 73) if thinking like an animal implies an undifferentiated animal collective instead of pointing to the human animal we certainly are. In the classroom, thinking like an animal cannot rely on the appropriation of animal voices that Matthewman seems to suggest in her discussion of a poem by Les Murray, "Pigs" (1993). Here are some excerpts:

Us all on sore cement was we.
Not warmed then with glares. Not glutting mush
Under that pole the lightning's tied up [...]
Us all fuckers then. And Big, huh? Tusked
The ball-biting dog and gutsed him wet. [...]
Us back in cool god-shit. We ate crisp.
We nosed up good rank in the tunneled bush.
Us all fuckers then.

Now, if working with this poem within the sameness/difference-framework suggested by Matthewman is supposed to foster ecocentric or animal-oriented attitudes, ecocritical pedagogy will without a doubt benefit from postcolonial ecocriticism. While Matthewman seems genuinely happy with the fact that "[t]he narrative of the poem follows the pigs looking back to their 'natural' state before factory farming" (74), readers more critical of the rhetoric strategies and the intricacies of anthropomorphism would maybe point out that the use of Pidgin does not only refer to a form of animal hybridity—"almost as if these animals have taught themselves the English language," as she says (75)—but that it creates parallels between the human speakers of Pidgin and Creole languages and pigs. One does not even have to be a postcolonial ecocritic or a posthumanist to comprehend the disadvantageous and complex enmeshment of the histories of theriomorphic degradation in the colonial context, and detect here a strange form of (ig)noble-savage thinking that links the 'natural' state of pigs with Pidgin/Creole languages.

But literature certainly has other advantages than providing privileged access into other minds. In *Uses of Literature* (2008), Rita Felski tries to map the tricky question of the nature of literary fiction, proposing four categories that are crucial to the experience of literature: "reading," she says, "involves a logic of *recognition*; [...] aesthetic experience has analogies with *enchantment* in a supposedly disenchanted age; [...] literature creates distinctive configurations of social *knowledge*" and, last but not least, "we may value the experience of being *shocked* by what we read" (Felski 2008: 15, emphases original). It is Felski's focus on seemingly banal experiences such as "recognition" that I think might strike a chord in ecocritics – Felski argues convincingly against the almost pathological concentration on elegant-abstract maneuvers of academic exegesis while finding oneself in a fictional character, or being enthralled by a film "is associated with more homespun and vernacular forms of aesthetic response driven by the dream worlds of mass culture" (52). However, in the context of an ecopedagogical discussion, the arguments developed by Felski are most relevant as they can be used to put into perspective claims to 'eco-correctness' and an instrumentalizing stance towards literature, as suggested by Matthewman when she proposes to "evaluate environmental texts in terms of their usefulness as a response to environmental crisis" (2011: 30). In contrast, Felski maps the large territory of literary fiction, open to the question of what literary fiction is and does.

Of course, as Felski is well aware, she is not the first to grapple with the intricate question of literature's "uses," and certainly, as she points out, her ideas are not completely novel: readers of her book, she says, "will detect in [the four categories she presents] the shadowy presence of some venerable aesthetic categories"—"anagnorisis, beauty, mimesis, the sublime" (Felski 2008: 15). At least two of these concepts have been crucial to the ecocritical debate as well: anagnorisis and, most importantly, mimesis. One only has to think of Lawrence Buell's definition of the environmental text, his preference for realist writing in his earlier, seminal works, or the still notable ecocritical interest in nature writing—each points to the fact that mimesis was and sometimes is conceived as the general antidote to abstraction, theorization and the *malaise postmoderne* in general. Moreover, what Timothy Morton describes as 'ecomimetic writing'— rhetorical authenticating devices such as "As I am writing this, the wind is blowing through the trees outside..."—strongly depends on an assumed anagnorisis: nature is solid and not to be doubted, and once we recognize ourselves as part of it, we will begin to think about it in the 'correct' ways. Let us now see how animals might disturb and challenge such facile ways of recognition.

*****

At one point in their discussion of "animal teaching," Welling and Kapel remind their readers that the "unfamiliar conceptual terrain" of animal studies in the classroom could cause some disorientation. But they add: "*Dis*orientation [...] has its own virtues" (107, emphasis original). I wish to second this claim by arguing that, indeed, what Felski describes as "shock" and "awe" are the better choices if we want to teach animality rather than anthropomorphism, and finitude rather than furry triteness. I will therefore now outline ways of teaching animals from the notion of disorientation rather than knowledge, holding that it is this very disorientation that engenders a very productive and necessary tension: the experience of not-understanding the 'wholly other' that is the animal (see Derrida 2008) while at the same time, personal experience and empathetic ability suggest otherwise.

The tension between the idea of abysmal otherness and experienced companionship and closeness, and the shock that measuring the distance between both positions encompasses, can be found in some of the finest texts in the focus of ecocriticism: J.M. Coetzee's *The Lives of Animals*, for example, which is all about the actual lives and suffering of animals while it features no real, suffering animal—apart from the protagonist Elizabeth Costello. Understanding this comes as a shock indeed, but as a very enlightening one (see Diamond 2008; Bartosch 2013: 255-77). It was Coetzee, too, who in an interview with David Attwell discusses a "certain elegance of poetic closure" in realist narratives and claims that today, such forms of closure no longer work. Literary fiction today adheres to a "poetics of failure," which he understands as being "ambivalent through and through" because it only offers a "program for constructing artifacts out of an endlessly regressive, etiolated self-consciousness lost in the labyrinth of language and endlessly failing to erect itself into autonomy" (Coetzee 1992: 7; 87). It remains open, however, whether this failure is in fact a failure of narratives generally, or whether the emplotment of failures of closures maybe succeeds in staging the very means of disorientation, uncertainty and not-understanding to which I am trying to expose myself, and the classroom. I think this idea is highly interesting with regard to the issues discussed in this paper.

In the context of teaching picture books, it will arguably not be the crucial aim to convey a sense of an "endlessly regressive, etiolated self-consciousness lost in the labyrinth of language and endlessly failing to erect itself into autonomy," but it will be possible to teach the tension of identity and alterity, and thus to bring closer to one's pupils what animality and finitude mean— always with the claim in mind that disorientation "has its own virtues" (Welling & Kapel 2012: 107; see also Jaques 2013). Such disorientation circumvents the problems that Christine Gerhardt has summarized as "the crux of consciousness-raising" in the ecocritical classroom: not only the 'ideological indoctrination'[3] but also the very vagueness of the concept of consciousness-raising might hinder a fruitful engagement with the medium of literary texts in the context of environmental crises (cf. 224). A pedagogical approach to teaching literary fiction—and this includes picture books of course—cannot ignore the basic insight of pedagogical research that plurivalent "images that invite interpretation and that appeal both emotionally and cognitively have [...] proven to be fruitful impulses" in the English classroom (Decke-Cornill & Küster 2010: 254, my translation). As far as openness to interpretation, on the one hand, and a challenge to visual and cognitive understanding on the other are concerned, the picture books I will discuss now seem ideal media for the negotiation of alterities and the value of literary fiction that engages with them.

John Marsden and Shaun Tan's *The Rabbits* at first sight seems to be very bleak, but I think it is remarkable that from an aesthetic perspective, the bleakness of the story contrasts with the lush and detailed graphic rendering. In fact, the visual elements of the book underline how serious children readers are being taken (see figure 1).

Fig. 1: Illustration from *The Rabbits*. *The Rabbits* by John Marsden and Shaun Tan, Lothian Children's Books, an imprint of Hachette Australia, 1998. Reprinted with kind permission.

Such a stance is reminiscent of E.T.A. Hoffmann's literary fairy tale of the "Nutcracker": In the framing narrative, the fictional 'Brothers of Serapion'

---

3   See also Bartosch & Garrard 2013; Parham 2006 and Pamela Swanigan's contribution to this volume.

argue that "children [cannot understand] the numerous fine threads that are woven through the whole and thus hold together a set of almost completely heterogeneous elements. They will concentrate on particularities at most" (Hoffmann 1998: 246; my translation). Hoffmann instead argues that children can indeed understand complex literary truths—this is the "Serapiontic principle." Complex literary truths is what we are looking for if we want to engage with the question of the animal in teaching environments, and trusting in young readers' ability to understand them is what we have to cultivate, within ourselves and in the perception of our pupils.

If understood as an anthropomorphic tale, *The Rabbits* tells the story of the colonial conquest of Australia by the British; the rabbits being the British colonizers and the 'we', apparently a marsupial, represents the aboriginal population. While the arrival is still somewhat awe-inspiring—note that height of the ship, and the pointed geometry of the 'European' rabbits (see figure 2)— their dominion soon turns into a nightmare. The visual means of conveying a sense of the strangeness and intimidating quality of the colonizing regime are impressive, and they are wonderful examples of aesthetic means of defamiliarization. The depiction of cattle, for instance, subverts common Western iconographies of peacefully grazing livestock, and the rabbit's harsh and merciless colonization of the land destabilizes familiar ways of depiction leporids with quite an impact.

Fig. 2: Illustration from *The Rabbits*. *The Rabbits* by John Marsden and Shaun Tan, Lothian Children's Books, an imprint of Hachette Australia, 1998. Reprinted with kind permission.

But the story disturbs and challenges its readers not only on the anthropomorphic level. For instance, it is not only the animal that is defamiliarized—likewise, the machines are heavily anthropomorphized, leaving it to the reader whether this is understood as a way of rendering the character of mechanistic reduction graspable in the visual code of nightmarish monstrosity or whether it opens up avenues for thinking about the constructive nature of anthropomorphisms in general. In any case, the machine-monster is a wonderful image of greed that works particularly well because it ascribes 'face' to technology—and thus calls for a discussion of anthropo- or theriomorphization as a means of constructing certain concepts of alterity. What is more, the fleeing mammals in the same picture, hardly visible at first sight, do not have such a face but only eyes. Notably, we share their perspective as we too are at the edge of a giant, monstrous maw. And while, in one of the most impressive illustrations, the reference to the 'Stolen Generations' certainly and clearly points to human history (see figure 3), environmental aspects and the engagement with forms of species invasion never allow one to read the story in strictly anthropocentric terms. Rather, the story disrupts the traditional lines of 'us' and 'them' by making 'us' all *humanimals* who suffer under colonial rule, technological hubris and the devastating effects of modernity.

Fig. 3: Illustration from *The Rabbits*. *The Rabbits* by John Marsden and Shaun Tan, Lothian Children's Books, an imprint of Hachette Australia, 1998. Reprinted with kind permission.

I am not arguing that the rabbits are *not* stand-ins for humans. In fact, the book indeed lends itself to Matthewman's approach of using animal narratives in order to discuss different forms of anthropomorphization and thus arrive at questions of identity and alterity. Yet, the book successfully blurs many dividing lines on which such moments of anthropomorphism rely, and I think that laying full stress on its rich and multiform aesthetic by means of which these moments are fostered is a very important ecopedagogical goal. The impact such aesthetic disorientations will probably have on pupils in a (European) EFL classroom allows thinking differently about human-animal relations. The discussion that may follow such rethinking seems to me to be more relevant than learning to accept that animals are stand-ins for human beings.

My second example is a German book by Wolf Erlbruch: *Ente, Tod und Tulpe* (translated as *Duck, Death and the Tulip*). Quite a contrast to the splendor of Tan's illustration, the graphics of Erlbruch's book are minimalistic and elegant. Again, it does not explicitly comment on the human-animal question, for instance, but it engages with the shared animality of both the human animal and the other ones: finitude. The story recounts the death of a duck—the duck literally *meets* Death and talks to him for a while until its end; and in the last scene, we see how Death says goodbye to the dead duck. This is how the narrative begins: "For quite a while now, the duck had had a strange feeling. 'Who are you?'—'How nice of you to finally see me. I am death. [...] I have been close to you since you were born. Just in case'." In a very simple and lyrically sparse language, the book discusses the fact that death is not something that suddenly strikes you and therefore may reasonably be ignored as long as possible. Instead, since birth, it is close to... to whom? Who, again the question comes up, is "us?" This work, too, renders difficult a clear-cut dualist division as the duck is both presented as an actual animal that enjoys swimming and other poultry pastimes and as a metaphorical device. This becomes clear in some unobtrusive puns, for instance: discussing death with Death, the duck suddenly gets goose bumps—language conventions such as animal metaphors can be discussed in this context and shed light on our practice of calling chickens easily scared, foxes cunning and cows stupid and illustrate, *sensu* Welling and Kapel, the constructedness of animality.

The duck in the book is anything but 'chicken-hearted', however, and duck and Death become something like friends; playing a while, sleeping and talking about being dead in a way that is both gentle and, by virtue of its graphic and verbal rendering, oriented towards children's capacity to understand these issues: "Down below they could see the pond. How silent it was – and lonely. 'This is what it is like when I am dead, then', thought the duck. 'The pond – alone. Entirely without me'." Upon which Death replies, "'When you are dead, the pond will be gone, too'"—not bad, philosophically speaking, for a children's book. The inevitable happens, nevertheless: "During the next weeks, they visited the pond less and less often. Most of the time, they sat on the grass, talking little. When a cool breeze went through the duck's feathers, it felt coldness for the first time." The duck dies, Death lays a little tulip on it and places both on the little river. Death, we learn at the end, is even a little bit sad to have lost his friend – but, and these are the last lines, "such is life."

Reader responses to the ambivalences of text-image relations are crucial in both books. However, I assume that in the second example, those reactions are even more relevant for ecopedagogical means. It is most likely that grown-ups reading the book together with children will be deeply moved by both narrative and pictures. The children, on the other hand, may then soothe the grown-ups, possibly having learned an important lesson about finitude by learning that this lesson continues to be difficult—for grown-ups, teachers, ducks, and Death himself.

In any case, the dividing lines between humans and animals, challenged by Critical Animal Studies and in environmentally conscious curricula, are blurred. Not by claiming a total sameness but by destabilizing the frames of reference by virtue of which we normally think and talk about them. This destabilization is a very fruitful one. Since disorientation in a work of literary fiction always resolves its own conundrum by emplotting its condition of being true-but-not-real in meaningful narrative sequence, teaching animals by teaching disorientation, or the poetics of failure as described above, follows a crucial pedagogical objective: understanding something by not really understanding it, thus granting it some impregnable space of its own. By troubling the dividing line between humans and (other) animals and the role of metaphors (as in *The Rabbits*) and by approaching the complex and daunting implications of a shared finitude of human and animal beings via elegantly reduced words and images (as in *Ente, Tod und Tulpe*) children's literature can succeed in that task, too.

With a particular focus on the pedagogical challenges and the potential of ecocritical readings, Berbeli Wanning suggests that the relationship of culture and nature might be thought of not in terms of unity or sameness but with regard to its articulations of difference (cf. Wanning 2008: 116). She does not suggest a strict dichotomy, however, but follows systems theory scholar Niklas Luhmann, stating that differences must not be seen as means of division but of reflection. It is therefore important, she explains, to focus on the tension of the separation of nature and culture, which can be questioned and relied on at the same time in literary texts. This comes close to what I have been trying to suggest in this paper and shows how for any green pedagogy, ecocriticism and Critical Animal Studies provide perspectives that enable the "exploration, interpretation and practical engagement with the ways literary texts allow us to experience nature" (117, my translation). Even if these ways form a maze.

By teaching picture books, such mazes may be explored if we follow the various text-image relations, paying equal attention to the words on the page and the sights we encounter. Surely, this does not have to—and will not—result in factual knowledge. In ecocriticism, a lot has been said about the gaze and the power of fiction to stage human-animal relations that evolve around the gaze. If we think about what Critical Animal Studies and posthumanism describe as the "necessity of an ethics based not on ability [...] but on *compassion* that is rooted in our vulnerability and passivity" (Wolfe 2010: 141)—finitude, that is—then we might learn to understand that the gaze as well as the maze can and should inform our teaching of (picture) books. Engaging, via word and image, with the provocation that is a 'poetics of failure' is an avenue for thinking about aesthetic ways of engendering a sense of such literary ethics. Even—or maybe especially —in 'easy' texts such as children's picture books, the aesthetic play and the effect of negation that engenders literature's mostly non-propositional, non-discursive language can help to emplot the 'failure' of understanding the other in ways that leave space for its alterity, but also for an acceptance of ambiguity— of the peculiar and fragile dividing lines between human and animal in general but also, and more specifically, of the questionable clarity of anthropomorphisms in picture books. These books ask us to look at them closely, to question our gaze as it were, and possibly to be moved to tears.

This stance towards literary readings accepts and embraces the notion that animals are material and vulnerable creatures just as humans are but that they, at the same time, cannot be appropriated by the texts we read. The kind of exposure such a reading grounds on does not, as Anat Prick argues in *Creaturely Poetics*, primarily "yield a moral 'reading'"—it is "antiphilosophical; it does not produce arguments or truth claims about its object" (5). It takes shared vulnerability as the starting point for empathetic exposure as exemplified, for instance, by the famous anecdote of Friedrich Nietzsche, who in Turin held a horse's head and cried for compassion with it. This episode is recalled by Derrida in *Memoirs of the Blind*, where he writes: "The eye would be destined not to see but to weep. [...] [T]o have imploration rather than a vision in sight, to address prayer, love, joy, or sadness rather than a look or a gaze. [...] [T]he blindness that reveals the very truth of the eyes, would be the gaze veiled by tears" (1993: 126-7). While posthumanist ethics and the tenets and explorations of Critical Animal Studies may be too complex a challenge for young learners in the English or the EFL-classroom, such aesthetic engagements with 'blindness' are indeed possible, and they might be essential lessons for any ecopedagogical practice.

In an article on the connection between "Ecocriticism and Education for Sustainability" (2007), Greg Garrard concludes that "[g]iven limited curriculum space, ecocritics have to make an unenviable choice" between canonical literatures and critical interpretive engagements on the one hand and systemic, applied, ready-to-use environmentalist contents (378). He reports how his students, after a literature class on sustainability, did neither feel that their commitment was strengthened nor undermined, but felt that their relationship to the environment had been "complicated" (377). Garrard concludes that ecocritics apparently have to vacillate between their own ecocritical position, choice of texts and pedagogical objectives, and the one purported by 'traditional' literary studies. I would like to suggest this tension as a very productive one and maintain that traditional approaches of teaching and reading literary texts may offer fruitful counter-perspectives to the scientistic view of contemporary educational practice. It may well be that anthropomorphization, for instance, must be overcome because the human subject must learn to decenter itself in the way Decke-Cornill and Gebhard (2010) have discussed it. But it is also true that anthropomorphic narratives convey a sense of an animist and affective stance towards the world which cannot (and should not) be completely retrieved but which offers a relevant perspective of interconnectedness in times of detachment, crisis, and insecurity (cf. Decke-Cornill & Gebhard 2010: 21; see also Bartosch & Garrard 2012).

The tension between both notions is the productive force we seek, and this force can help us come to terms with, and not appropriate, the manifold otherness with which we are surrounded and engender response-ability. For pedagogy this means that, as Luce Irigaray reminds us, since we as yet "lack an education and cultivation with respect to meeting the other as other," such forms of education are not an "intellectual luxury" but "perhaps the most important step [...] towards our becoming human" (Irigaray 119) That 'the other' can be addressed and taken seriously in its alterity through various perspectives, most notably postcolonial ones, has been shown repeatedly in educational contexts (see, for instance, Burney 2012). The problem of taking seriously animal otherness is a persistent one, however. Probably, the insecurity and disorientation fostered by encounters with the "w/holy other" (Derrida) resists our common ways of the production of knowledge even more – while inter- or transcultural studies still produce fruitful results in the context of, for instance, globalized economies and forms of vocational education. I have tried to tackle this quandary by stressing the fruitfulness of an engagement with otherness that does not fall into forms of appropriation; rather, I have sought moments of aesthetic experience that have shown the disorientation that often frames human-animal encounters to be pivotal. In *The Rabbits*, the abyss between human and animal, deepened by the rhetorical force of anthropomorphism, could thus be questioned. In *Ente, Tod und Tulpe*, the complex entanglements of human-animal finitude was addressed. Notably, in both books, it is the interplay of aesthetic form and representation or content that provides these challenging moments of disorientation or, in the words of Coetzee's poetics, failures of closure. It is down to us whether this is seen as a disadvantage or whether cultivating a "gaze veiled by tears" can be understood as the prerogative for our becoming human(e). Which is, after all, what we try to foster by our pedagogical practice.

Works Cited

Bartosch, Roman. *EnvironMentality. Ecocriticism and the Event of Postcolonial Fiction.*
      Amsterdam and New York: Rodopi, 2013.
— . "Ghostly Presences: Tracing the Animal in Julia Leigh's *The Hunter*" (forthcoming).
— & Greg Garrard. "The Function of Criticism. A Response to William Major and Andrew
      McMurry's Editorial". *Journal of Ecocriticism* 5.1 (2013). 6 pp.
Burney, Shehla. *Pedagogy of the Other. Edward Said, Postcolonial Theory, and Strategies for
      Critique.* Frankfurt am Main et al.: Peter Lang, 2012.
Coetzee, John M. *Doubling the Point. Essays and Interviews.* Ed. David Atwell. Cambridge,
      MA: Harvard UP, 1992.
Daston, Lorraine & Gregg Mitman. "Introduction". *Thinking with Animals. New Perspectives
      on Anthropomorphism.* Eds. Lorraine Daston & Gregg Mitman. New York: Columbia UP,
      2005. 1-14.
Decke-Cornill, Helene & Lutz Küster. *Fremdsprachendidaktik.* Tübingen: Narr Verlag, 2010.
Derrida, Jacques. *Memoirs of the Blind. Self-Portraits and Other Ruins.* Eds. Michael B. Naas
      & Pascale-Anne Brault. Chicago: U of Chicago P, 1993.
— . *The Animal That Therefore I Am.* Ed. Marie-Louise Mallet. Trans. David Wills. New
      York: Fordham UP, 2008.
Diamond, Cora. "The Difficulty of Reality and the Difficulty of Philosophy". Stanley Cavell
      et al. *Philosophy and Animal Life.* New York: Columbia UP, 2008. 43-89.
Donaldson, Sue & Will Kymlicka. *Zoopolis. A Political Theory of Animal Rights.* Oxford:
      Oxford UP, 2011.
Erlbruch, Wolf. *Ente, Tod und Tulpe.* München: Verlag Antje Kunstmann, 2007 [translation:
      Duck, Death and the Tulip. Wellington: Gecko Press, 2011].
Felski, Rita. *Uses of Literature.* Malden/Oxford: Blackwell, 2008.
Garrard, Greg. "Introduction". *Teaching Ecocriticism and Green Cultural Studies.* Ed. Greg
      Garrard. New York: Palgrave Macmillan, 2012. 1-10.
— . "Ecocriticism and Education for Sustainability". *Pedagogy. Critical Approaches to
      Teaching Literature, Language, Composition, and Culture* 7.3 (2007). 359-83.
Gerhardt, Christine. "Literature, Nature, and the Crux of Consciousness-Raising".
      Ecodidactic Perspectives on English Language, Literatures and Cultures. Eds. Sylvia
      Mayer & Graham Wilson. Trier: Wissenschaftlicher Verlag, 2006. 223-33.
Hoffmann, E.T.A. "Die Serapionsbrüder" [1819-1821]. In: *Werke.* Augsburg: Weltbild
      Verlag, 1998. 5-967.
Ingensiep, Hans Werner & Heike Baranzke. *Das Tier.* Stuttgart: Reclam, 2008.
Irigaray, Luce. "How Can We Meet the Other?" *Otherness. A Multilateral Perspective.* Eds.
      Susan Yi Sencindiver, Maria Beville & Marie Lauritzen. Frankfurt am Main et al.: Peter
      Lang, 2011. 107-20.
Jaques, Zoe (ed.). *Children's Literature and the Posthuman. Animal, Environment, Cyborg.*
      London & New York: Routledge, 2013.
Marsden, John & Shaun Tan. *The Rabbits.* London: Hodder, 2010.
Matthewman, Sasha. *Teaching Secondary English as if the Planet Matters.* London & New
      York: Routledge, 2011.
Murray, Les. *Translations from the Natural World.* Manchester: Carcanet Press, 1993.
Parham, John. "The Deficiency of 'Environmental Capital': Why Environmentalism Needs a
      Reflexive Pedagogy". *Ecodidactic Perspectives on English Language, Literatures and
      Cultures.* Eds. Sylvia Mayer & Graham Wilson. Trier: Wissenschaftlicher Verlag, 2006. 7-
      22.

Pick, Anat. *Creaturely Poetics. Animality and Vulnerability in Literature and Film.* New York: Columbia UP, 2011.

UNESCO. *Shaping the Education of Tomorrow.* Paris: United Nations Educational, Scientific and Cultural Organization, 2012.

Wanning, Berbeli. "Kulturökologie in didaktischer Perspektive: Neue Tendenzen für den Literaturunterricht". *Standard: Bildung. Blinde Flecken der deutschen Bildungsdiskussion.* Eds. Paul Ingwer, Fritz Tangermann & Winfried Thielmann. Göttingen: Vandenhoeck & Ruprecht, 2008. 115-27.

Welling, Bart H. & Scottie Kapel. "The Return of the Animal: Presenting and Representing Non-Human Beings in the (Post-)Humanities Classroom". *Teaching Ecocriticism and Green Cultural Studies.* Ed. Greg Garrard. New York: Palgrave Macmillan, 2012. 104-6.

Wolfe, Cary. *What is Posthumanism?* Minneapolis & London: U of Minnesota P, 2010.

Ecocritical Sensitivity with Multimodal Texts in the EFL/ESL Literature Classroom

Janice Bland (Paderborn)

According to children's literature expert Peter Hunt, when discussing children's literature

> we are dealing with a parallel universe to the world of canonical literature, a universe of very large numbers of texts with a massive cultural influence [...] and in many ways more complex, more *difficult* to talk about than other literatures. (Hunt 2001: 2, emphasis in the original)

The "massive cultural influence" of children's books is mirrored by the enormous influence of textbooks employed in classrooms around the world, many of which are in English. Possibly the largest global market for school textbooks is English as a Foreign Language (EFL). However, EFL teaching now occurs in state education with ever-younger children, and very often in multicultural/multilingual classrooms, so the distinction between EFL and ESL/EAL is gradually becoming blurred.[1] For example in immersion contexts, where over 50 per cent of schooling takes place in English, and in Content and Language Integrated Learning classrooms (known as CLIL), reading authentic children's literature can be an essential component of EFL education. Therefore the cultural influence of children's literature in English is of great significance.

This chapter considers whether the use of children's literature in EFL education can support an eco-consciousness, as possibly the first step towards pragmatic environmentalism. EFL textbooks, as opposed to authentic literature, are frequently aimed at as wide a market as possible, and therefore tend to a

---

1   There is much confusion over the EFL/ESL/EAL acronyms. As many children worldwide are plurilingual even before starting school, ESL (English as a Second Language—the acronym used by applied linguists researching second language acquisition)—and EAL (English as an Additional Language—the acronym preferred in the UK context)—really mean the same in mainstream schooling. They mean the English language support needed by children from a non-English speaking background in an English-speaking context. EFL, on the other hand, refers specifically to the learning of English in non-English speaking countries.

conservative and middle-ground ideology believed to appeal to stakeholders in the majority of teaching situations:

> Foreign language education has been characterized up to now by the search for a 'middle landscape'. [...] By refusing to be ideological, this approach has in fact espoused a middle-ground conservative ideology, recognizable by its positivistic, pragmatic bent, intent on assimilating conflicts by minimizing them. (Kramsch 1993: 12)

The uncritical approach described by Kramsch is in stark contrast to the urgent need for an environmentally aware pedagogy. This is true for all school subjects, of course. However, I will argue that literary texts offer a medium that can be particularly influential and potentially beneficial in the EFL classroom with young learners and lower secondary school students. Drawing on the example of climate change, Richard Kerridge states:

> Many features of global warming defy political response and cultural representation. Its extent is global. Fifty years may pass, or more, before the effects become plain. It confronts us with possibilities so frightening as to demand urgent action, yet, even when few scientists deny it is happening, a degree of uncertainty remains that those who want to do nothing can seize upon. (Kerridge 2006: 533)

In literature, the storyworld, a term used in narratology to capture the "ecology of narrative interpretation" (Herman 2005: 570), allows readers to create a vivid mental model of what otherwise might be ignored. This is one of many arguments for using literature in education. However, in this chapter I would like to consider the opportunity of ecopedagogy with young learners and novice secondary students, who are not yet fluent readers of extended prose in English. Quite apart from motivational reasons for including work by masterful storytellers and illustrators in EFL, and language acquisition reasons for including children's literature in language teaching (Bland 2013), major children's literature often deals with themes that are invaluable for a critical, dialogic pedagogy. The urgency of the interdisciplinary topic of environmental conservation as a global issue and ethical debate is expressed succinctly by Andrew Goatly, who reminds us that neglecting the environment in favor of the classic global issues list of race, class and gender is "rather like addressing the problem of who is going to fetch the deck-chairs on the Titanic, and who has the right to sit on them" (Goatly 2000: 277). Although ethics have traditionally been anthropocentric whereas ecology refuses to see man as an utterly distinct species (particularly the philosophy known as deep ecology), both ethics and ecology "share the assumption of an interconnection between *local* and *global* issues and are, therefore, transcultural and transnational in orientation" (Zapf 2008: 847, emphasis in the original). According to Buell (2005: 136), "an increasing number of critics approach environmental issues from the standpoint of cultural studies, conceiving of nature, particularly under modernization, predominantly in terms of its manipulation or reinvention by human culture." Can ecocriticism join the established race, class and gender studies as an important ethical literary discourse in the classroom? If so, surely this must begin as early as possible, as young children are still very much involved in discovering the world and are relatively unfettered by cultural baggage. Children are as close to nature as they are to culture—or rather, not yet subject to "the dualistic separation of humans from nature promoted by Western philosophy and culture" (Garrard 2012: 24), which is seen by many as the origin of the environmental crisis.

Hunt writes (2001: 18), "children's literature (like all other literatures) reflects—must reflect—the culture that surrounds/permeates it." Due to the hidden ideology in all texts, critical literacy—by which is meant learning to read literature, textbooks, the internet *critically*—is a major competence to aim for in order to empower students. However, the literature of "downtrodden" groups, which would include postcolonial literature, literature reflecting gender diversity, as well as children's literature, is rather less likely to latently reflect the dominant ideology and status quo, and thus can already be implicitly empowering:

> One aspect of the (potential) subversiveness of children's literature may be that, as
> with the literature of other downtrodden groups, its subversiveness exists in passing
> its messages without the knowledge of the ruling elite. (Hunt 2001: 17)

Why is "subversive" literature desirable in the EFL classroom? One consequence of enculturation into the dominant Western culture is to teach children to believe in certain binary "opposites," including male/female, reason/emotion as well as culture/nature. Just as some ecofeminists argue that the identification of women with emotion and nature—originally meaning women are somehow less reasonable and less human—can now be welcomed and seen as hope for change from the destructive culture versus nature dichotomy, so children's connection to nature can be seen as a source of strength. I argue that this can be supported by choosing books for the EFL classroom in an ecocritical light. The texts we offer children should be evaluated for their environmental suggestiveness, as opposed to the crude anthropomorphism and Disneyfication—with the "saccharine, sexist, and illusionary stereotypes" (Zipes 2007: 25)—of many EFL textbooks for young learners (and of course also mediocre quality children's literature).

I therefore suggest a pedagogical concept for supporting eco-consciousness in the ESL/EFL-literature classroom. The approach of CLIL means that the educational content of an English lesson is as important as language acquisition opportunities. There are many examples of children's literature where the environment plays an active role; I will introduce briefly six picturebooks and graphic novels. If picturebooks communicate environmental sensitivity to young learners with as yet minimal English, this will normally take place as collateral learning:

> Collateral learning in the way of formation of enduring attitudes, of likes and dislikes, may be and often is much more important than the spelling lesson or lesson in geography or history that is learned. For these attitudes are fundamentally what count in the future (Dewey 1938: 48).

A more explicit ecopedagogy can be an aspect of learning with multimodal texts in the secondary school. I will examine literary texts suitable for a variety of levels: *The Stranger* (Van Allsburg 1986), *The Rough-Face Girl* (Martin and Shannon 1992), *Zoo* (Browne 1992), *Flotsam* (Wiesner 2006), *We're Going on a Bear Hunt* (Rosen and Oxenbury 1989) and *The Savage* (Almond and McKean 2008). Each of these books can promote important competences in the language classroom, such as communicative, literary and intercultural competences and visual literacy. In this chapter, however, I will examine in turn whether the books can also fulfill one of the four criteria proposed by Lawrence Buell, as a 'rough checklist' of ingredients that might be noticeable in a work that is environmentally oriented:

1. The nonhuman environment is present not merely as a framing device but as a presence that begins to suggest that human history is implicated in natural history.

2. The human interest is not understood to be the only legitimate interest.

3. Human accountability to the environment is part of the text's ethical orientation.

4. Some sense of the environment as a process rather than as a constant or a given is at least implicit in the text. (Buell 1995: 7-8)

1. The nonhuman environment as a presence

It is not at all unusual for picturebooks and children's literature in general to feature a detailed portrayal of the landscape, in pictures as well as in words. Of course childhood is not all innocence and ease in beautiful settings, and never has been. Yet a celebration of the natural environment for younger children honors the ideal of a harmonious balance, an upbringing with and through nature and her changing seasons. Chris Van Allsburg's *The Stranger*, a picturebook suitable for the primary or lower secondary school EFL classroom, goes further. The narrative describes in a matter of fact tone the strangely mysterious events of one golden autumn. The story encourages the reader to quite literally understand a natural phenomenon as one of the characters. Investing natural objects and phenomena with a life force is known as animism; it results in a dialogic communicative interplay, extending beyond the human characters. To McDowell, writing on ecocriticism,

> [d]ialogics helps first by placing an emphasis on contradictory voices, rather than focusing mainly upon the authoritative monologic voice of the narrator. We begin to hear characters and elements of the landscape that have been marginalised. [...] We can analyse the interplay of these different languages for an understanding of the values associated with the characters and elements and for a sense of how characters and elements of the landscape influence each other. (McDowell 1996: 374)

In some children's literature, nature is not a mere backdrop to more important human-centered concerns, nature herself becomes a character in the story. *The Stranger* appears to go even further, by personifying autumn in the figure of the stranger. It can be considered a magic realist text, as something magical and inexplicable enters a realistic setting. The stranger is a character who enters the life of a farming family when he is accidentally hit by Farmer Bailey's truck. He seems to have lost his memory in the accident, and joins in the farming at "the time of year Farmer Bailey liked best, when summer turned to fall" (Van Allsburg 1986: picturebooks are always unpaginated). The illustrations are rich with the golden colors of the harvest. Like the opening shot of a film, the opening panorama of this autumn scenery is seen from the bird's eye view, as if the reader/viewer is sitting in the branches of the trees. Van Allsburg subdues the cultural elements of the location and allows the autumnal landscape to draw us in:

> The trees frame the panorama as if they are in control of what is shown. The viewer's gaze is directed not towards the truck but into the distance, guided by the river and the bordering trees. The colours underline the clear border between culture and nature. The colours used for the natural environment are warm browns and greens, while a cold, metallic blue is used for the truck. In all, the truck and the house in the distance look insignificant and forlorn in this supreme natural landscape. (Bartels-Bland 2011: 11)

Already on the next page we leap downwards to the worm's eye view, a quite unusual and thought-provoking angle from which to contemplate the stranger lying in the road. This is the visual viewpoint of a small animal in the road near the stranger's head. Showing a scene from such a skewed angle has been called "very deliberate manipulations of the reader's viewpoint" (Lewis 2001: 161). With such examples of the literal or visual viewpoint in picturebooks we can very graphically demonstrate and bring about an understanding of the related concept of figurative point of view so vital to literary literacy. The angle from which we view the stranger in the road will "encourage thoughts on what it would be like to be in the stranger's position, having been hit by a truck. Which in turn might stimulate thoughts on the plight of animals being run over" (Bartels-Bland 2011: 12). Similarly, the figurative point of view in a purely verbal narrative refers to the angle or filter through which we perceive the storyworld, sharing the vision of the focalizer. After his accident, the stranger remains initially on the friendly Bailey farm, and the seasons appear disrupted. At last the stranger's memory returns, and he realizes he must go back to his natural environment. In this symbolic picturebook, the equilibrium in nature is restored and the seasons return to normal when the family sadly lets their new friend, the stranger, go.

Figure 1: Illustration from *The Stranger* by Chris Van Allsburg © (1986). Used by permission of Houghton Mifflin Harcourt Publishing Company. All rights reserved.

The portrayal of autumn takes place both in the personification of the stranger, and in the illustrations of farm life, dominated by warm yellow, red and brown tones. This attention to the setting allows the teacher to elicit a meaningful interaction on the seasons. In contrast, young learner EFL textbooks mostly simplify the pictures as well as language, and frequently offer trivialized representations of the environment. It was shown in a recent study that EFL textbooks for beginners had less environmental content than books for more advanced students: "The fact that environmental issues seemed to occur less often in coursebooks for lower proficiency students might be attributed to materials writers believing that, at this level, students lack the language tools needed to interact on this topic" (Goatly and Jacobs 2000: 261). Children's literature that fulfills Buell's criteria, on the other hand, and implicates human history in natural history, can offer EFL students a dignified representation of nature. This is the natural world taken seriously:

> Beginning with the idea that all entities in the great web of nature deserve recognition and a voice, an ecological literary criticism might explore how authors have represented the interaction of both the human and nonhuman voices in the landscape. (McDowell 1996: 372)

This provides a creative opportunity for the EFL classroom: writing thought bubbles and dialog for the various characters and natural phenomena. The Baileys have a daughter, who observes the mystery. But her words and thoughts are not reported in the narrative. The stranger communicates by body language and facial expressions, which are clearly represented in the illustrations. He never actually speaks:

> Katy, their daughter, peeked into the room. The man on the sofa was dressed in odd leather clothing. She heard her father whisper '... must be some kind of hermit ... sort of fellow who lives alone in the woods.' The stranger didn't seem to understand the questions Mr. Bailey asked him. 'I don't think,' whispered Mrs. Bailey, 'he knows how to talk.' (Van Allsburg 1986)

Asking students to write thought or speech bubbles for Katy will help them to clarify and verbalize their own ideas on this story. Asking them, in addition, to provide the stranger/the autumn with a voice, ensures that the environment plays a central role when young learners respond to this picturebook.

Rafe Martin's *The Rough-Face Girl*, illustrated by David Shannon, is an Algonquin Indian *Cinderella*. The many fairy-tale Cinderellas have, naturally, influenced and enriched each other across the centuries as well as across the continents. In this sense *The Rough-Face Girl* is also dialogic, it communicates with other fairy-tale versions of *Cinderella*, and encourages intertextual dialog in the classroom, as children retell to each other the versions they know. A comparison of different fairy-tale versions in the EFL-literature classroom offers abundant interaction potential. It should also be pointed out that there are no definitive versions of fairy tales, as "each teller brings to a tale something of his/her own cultural orientation" (Yolen 1982: 298), and that there are no absolute meanings in literary texts—an important lesson in literary literacy. Yet from a pedagogic and literary perspective there are, of course, differences. Disney has not only sugared the natural environment, but also heroines such as his Cinderella, and too much sugar without awe and respect is detrimental to health in many ways. In this sense, *The Rough-Face Girl* is closer to older European versions of *Cinderella*, for the important ingredient of *action* on the part of the heroine is central to the tale: "But in the fairy tales wishes have a habit of happening—wishes *accompanied by the proper action,* bad wishes as well as good. That is the beauty of the old stories and their wisdom as well" (Yolen 1982: 303, emphasis in the original).

The picturebook is vivaciously narrated; the author Rafe Martin is a professional storyteller and is able to tell a good tale of the downtrodden girl who is victimized by her sisters and protected neither by her father nor her community. The girl's chores include tending the fire:

> The two older daughters were cruel and hard-hearted, and they made their youngest sister sit by the fire and feed the flames. When the burning branches popped, the sparks fell on her. In time, her hands became burnt and scarred. Her arms too became rough and scarred. Even her face was marked by the fire, and her beautiful long black hair hung ragged and charred. (Martin and Shannon 1992)

The patterns in Martin's text help students notice the language. There is close parallelism: "became burnt and scarred" and "became rough and scarred," as well as the rhyme scarred/charred. Typical of authentic literature, *The Rough-Face Girl* is also rich in lexical chains; in the quotation above there is a "fire" chain: sit by the fire, feed the flames, burning branches, popped, sparks, burnt, scarred and charred. This patterning of language creates rhetorical energy, and helps build a rich mental lexicon (Bland 2013: 156-187).

The Rough-Face Girl's sisters receive elegant clothing from their father, and seek to marry the wealthiest man of the village, the Invisible Being. However, the sister of the Invisible Being tests whether the finely dressed girls can see him. They fail the test. The abused but indomitable Rough-Face Girl, on the other hand, is able to see a life force in the humble natural things surrounding her. Despite sneers and laughter, she fashions coarse clothing in order to leave home and seek her fortune:

> Then she found dried reeds and, taking the little broken shells, she strung a necklace. She stripped birch bark from the dead trees and made a cap, a dress, and leggings. Then, with a sharp piece of bone, she carved in the bark pictures of the sun, moon, stars, plants, trees, and animals. (Martin and Shannon 1992)

Figure 2: Front cover of *The Rough-Face Girl* by Rafe Martin © (1992), illustrated by David Shannon © (1992). Used by permission of Puffin Books, a division of Penguin Group (USA) Inc

Dressed in this way, she ignores the taunts of the villagers who come out of their wigwams, "They pointed and stared. 'Look at that ugly girl!' they laughed. 'Look at her strange clothes! Hey! Hey! Hey! Go home you ugly girl! You'll never marry the Invisible Being!'" However, the heroine has faith in herself, is active and resourceful. Shannon demonstrates in the double-page spreads, that as she walks beyond the village the courageous girl can divine the true nature of things. She sees in the "great beauty of the earth and skies spreading before her [...] the sweet yet awesome face of the Invisible Being," thus she is able to describe the Invisible Being to his sister. Brother and sister, in turn, can see what the villagers blindly missed, the Rough-Face Girl's inner beauty. They accept and cherish her already before her fairy-tale transformation scene, which takes place when she bathes in the lake, when her scars vanish and her beautiful hair becomes as "long and glossy as a raven's wing."

With the Algonquin Indian *Cinderella*, the EFL students may learn about intertextuality, about the oracy of fairy tales, and the value of different versions. These are literary and intercultural competences. The language of *The Rough-Face Girl* displays the lexical richness and idiom principle that characterizes well-written authentic literature (Bland 2013: 8), there is stylistic cohesion such as marked lexical repetition, lexical chains and the phonological patterns of rhythm and alliteration. In addition, the illustrations support communicative competence, as there is so much in the visual text that is not explicitly stated in the verbal text, and demands verbalization in the EFL classroom. An ecocritical competence might be supported by the appreciation of the environment as a presence in the picturebook. Although the "Ecological Indian is clearly a stereotype of European origin" (Garrard 2012: 135), it is evident from *The Rough-Face Girl* that dwelling with a deep sense of attachment to the land is considered praiseworthy and even heroic. "Dwelling" in the ecocritical sense means living and working responsibly, in harmony with nature. The central theme of *The Rough-Face Girl* therefore contrasts dramatically with recent European versions of Cinderella, where the heroine's heroic status derives from her sweet passivity and splendid magical outfit at the ball. Jane Yolan criticizes the Disneyfied heroine in the strongest terms:

> To make Cinderella less than she is, then, is a heresy of the worst kind. It cheapens our most cherished dreams, and it makes a mockery of the true magic inside us all – the ability to change our own lives, the ability to control our own destinies. (Yolen 1982: 299)

For our stories influence us, whether we hear them, watch them, play them, read them in EFL textbooks or in children's literature. And fairy tales are among the most influential of texts:

> The worlds portrayed by the best of our fairy tales are like magic spells of enchantment that actually free us. Instead of petrifying our minds, they arouse our imagination and compel us to realise how we can fight terror and cunningly insert ourselves into our daily struggles, turning the course of the world's events in our favour. (Zipes 2007: 31)

Although the terror we must fight is certainly less tangible than the dragons and witches of fairy tales, the point Yolen makes and Zipes echoes is crucial: the desirable goal of "taking control of our own destinies," as well as the recognition "that human history is implicated in natural history."

2. Humanocentrism – the only legitimate way?

Anthony Browne's *Zoo* (Kate Greenaway Medal winner) is a landmark picturebook. It was employed for a series of lessons delivered by a graduate student for her M.Ed. thesis focused on "Exploring the use of picturebooks in a foreign language class: *Zoo* (Anthony Browne) in the *Hauptschule*, 5th grade" (Möhle 2008). The children in this class (11—13-year-olds), typically for a German *Hauptschule*, which caters for low-achieving children, were entirely inexperienced with regard to reading (including reading picturebooks) for pleasure. We can assume most of these secondary students associate books with school learning—a domain where they have experienced failure as a rule.

Zoo combines outstanding pictures with a serious examination of the relationship between man and animals, and the concept of keeping animals in cages. The inexperienced 5th-grade readers were well able to grasp the messages to be found in the pictures, with support from the teacher, and thoroughly enjoyed the unfamiliar experience of shared and thoughtful reading. Some of the children were able, even in a sequence of just three lessons, to discover the contradictions between the dialog spoken by an initially thoughtless family visiting the zoo and the close-up images of the very beautiful but very beleaguered animals.

The cage as image is everywhere in the picturebook, beginning symbolically with a pet hamster in a cage on the title page. On the way to the zoo the family is caged in by the traffic. Zoomorphism begins as an irate lorry driver stuck in the traffic jam transforms into a roaring gorilla. Whereas the animals behind bars are subdued, the human visitors are shown as impatient or bored—gradually morphing into various animals. As we follow a family of four through the zoo, the elder of two boys narrates the day. The male members of the family appear almost as entrapped by tedium as the animals: "Me and my brother wanted to see the gorillas and monkeys, but we had to see all these boring animals first" (Browne 1992). Teachers know that when children are bored they will start monkeying around. The boys buy a "funny monkey hat" each in the gift shop, and their behavior becomes ever monkeyish. The non-human great apes suffer in their enclosures. The orang-utan—beautifully drawn as all the animals are—is called a "miserable thing" by the narrator because it will not show its face or move from its corner. Browne combines the hyperrealism of his animals with surrealism in portraying the (male) humans. Many of the human visitors observing the immobile orang-utan have animal features and thus appear less real, and "they are seen as alienated from the natural world" (Bradford, Mallan, Stephens and McCallum 2008: 82). Disturbingly, illustrations in young learners' EFL textbooks are usually bright, cartoon-like and unreal. One realistically drawn zoo visitor placed centrally in the background seems lost in thought. He is bearded and wears old-fashioned clothes, and suggests an allusion to Charles Darwin.

The animals communicate their anguish with their body language, which can be "read" by the sensitive mother, but not by the rest of her family visiting the zoo. None of the animals in *Zoo* represent a "demand" image,[2] they do not seem to seek eye contact with the reader, suggesting they have given up any expectations. The most moving image is the extreme close-up of the gorilla's face on one of the last recto pages, not looking into our eyes, but apparently establishing eye contact with the distressed mother in the opposite image on the verso. The emotional power of *Zoo* is due to the persuasive pictures, encouraging even the inexperienced reader to bond with the silent animals, and —given sufficient time—achieve a critical distance to the squabbling and unthinking human visitors at the zoo, some of whom are allegorically depicted as more "beastly" than the animals. In one of the final pictures the role reversal is complete when the young narrator is trapped behind bars in his dream and asks rhetorically "Do you think animals have dreams?" An EFL classroom may not necessarily go so far as to ponder the point some ecocritics make that "the startling conclusion must be that the species we most thoroughly anthropomorphise is our own" (Garrard 2012: 162). Nonetheless, the meaning of words like "brutal," "beastly," "feral," "bitch," "bearish," "swine," "bestial," "wolfish" and other terminology that sets humans way above animals might usefully be discussed in the EFL classroom. I would whole-heartedly concur with Ramke:

> it would be a waste of beautiful authentic literature to introduce a multilayered picturebook like 'Zoo' by Anthony Brown in the EFL classroom, just to employ new vocabulary or grammar rules. In contrast to many school-based textbooks [...], authentic English picturebooks can be much more than just a tool for foreign language learning. They can help pupils to become critical interpreters of texts. (Ramke 2011: 10)

---

2   The "demand" gaze (Kress and van Leeuwen 1996: 118) refers to when characters gaze directly into the viewer's eyes, establishing contact and demanding empathy.

Figure 3: From *Zoo* by Anthony Browne © (1992). Reprinted by permission of Farrar Straus and Giroux Books for Young Readers and The Random House Group UK Limited. All rights reserved

3. Accountability to the environment as an aspect of the storyworld

Michael Rosen and Helen Oxenbury's *We're Going on a Bear Hunt* is a picturebook rendering of the rhythmic camp-fire chant, with its sing-song pattern and beat. This book is more suitable for young learners in the primary school, as the language is very patterned and the story is like an adventure for little children. *We're Going on a Bear Hunt* recounts how a father and four children successfully cross the long wavy grass ("swishy swashy"), the deep cold river ("splash splosh"), wade through the thick oozy mud ("squelch squerch"), wander through the big dark forest ("stumble trip"), run through a swirling whirling snow storm ("hoooowoooo"), and at last enter a narrow gloomy cave ("tiptoe tiptoe"). The double-page spreads are alternatively in color and black and white. The black and white pictures carry the action forward with the rhythmical text, which changes very slightly at each obstacle (long wavy grass, deep cold river, thick oozy mud and so forth) and close-ups of the family preparing to negotiate the next landscape, for example by removing their shoes.

> We're going on a bear hunt.
> We're going to catch a big one.
> What a beautiful day!
> We're not scared.
> Uh-uh! A river! A deep cold river.
> We can't go over it.
> We can't go under it.
> Oh no! We've got to go through it! (Rosen and Oxenbury 1989)

The double-page spreads in color have very little text, merely the onomatopoeic expressions quoted above. The family is dominated and dwarfed by the natural landscape, which is luxuriously rendered by Oxenbury. We see in turn a silent, empty beach, a grassy hillside with wild flowers, a river with water so clear that it mirrors the trees, a gleaming marsh landscape where the colors, wildlife and movement are mostly to be seen in the dramatic and windy sky, a mysterious forest of gigantic trees, and a snowstorm that engulfs the now tiny and insignificant family. Each of these landscapes is so dominant and powerful that the process of the family is slow and hesitant—until they finally enter the dark, gloomy cave, where there is indeed a bear. The story now comically reverses as the family rushes back through the different weathers and landscapes, chased by the bear. On the return trip they dash through all six landscapes crowded one after another on a single double-page spread, the breathless rhythm of the pictures now underlining the hectic chase.

Some very successful picturebooks now exist both as book and DVD (which can be bought together), and a comparison of the two media can be productive. The film version of *We're going on a Bear Hunt* is an extremely faithful rendering of the book as it very simply animates Oxenbury's beautiful watercolor illustrations. In the filmed version of this picturebook, however, the story ends with the family back home, hiding under the pink covers of the enormous family bed, announcing: "We're not going on a bear hunt again." For preschool children, the excitement over, this is a fitting ending, a happy, safe homecoming. But in the picturebook version, the author and illustrator were perhaps thinking of the older brothers and sisters who may read the picturebook aloud to the preschoolers when they created this book, and, fortunately for school-aged EFL learners, added one final double-page spread. The bear wanders back alone along the silent beach, which is now darkening as night falls and the sun sets in the mist over a sparkling sea. There is no cheerful family. All at once the bear is the focalizer, and suggests loneliness and dejection. One double-page spread may seem a small gesture, but as there are only twelve full-color double-page spreads in the picturebook altogether, it is very significant. It creates a vacuum that wants filling, and can promote not only an interesting discussion, but even a completely new perspective, or schema refreshment (Cook 1994: 182). Why did the family want to hunt the bear? Do bears, other animals, other living creatures have rights? Is it possible to see human beings as anything other than the center of all life? The director of the film version decided to omit the final double-page spread; and so the chance of a first glimpse at the subject of anthropocentrism is lost if the EFL classroom only considers the film. It can, however, be highlighted by studying the gap between the film and the book.

Figure 4: From *We're going on a Bear Hunt* by Michael Rosen © (1989), illustrated by Helen Oxenbury © (1989). Reproduced by permission of Walker Books Ltd, London SE11 5HJ.

Contemporary picturebooks, such as David Wiesner's *Flotsam* can be highly complex and break the mold in several ways, beginning with length. In order to use *Flotsam*, which celebrates the wonder and magic of the natural environment, a secondary-school classroom first has to relearn some lessons, particularly that pictures are not "simple" to read and that narratives do not have to be linear. *Flotsam* begins realistically, a boy on the beach studies the sea life around him using a magnifying glass and microscope. He is always in close physical contact with the sand, water, plant and animal life, while his parents read in their deck chairs. A mighty wave washes an old Melville Underwater Camera onto the beach, and the boy has the film inside developed. As soon as the film is ready, the boy dashes back to the beach to study the images. The photos show underwater worlds with little cities created of shells, and tiny creatures that live among the sea horses and fish. Finally there is a photo of a child holding up a picture, and this embedded picture shows another child holding up a photo. Using his microscope, the boy is able to discover that the embedded picture shows more and more embedded pictures of children holding up a photo. No less than eleven children from around the world, stretching back at least a hundred years, have found the camera and the mystery it contains. The boy finally throws the camera back into the sea, having first taken a photo of himself holding the print with the embedded pictures, so that the secret of the parallel worlds can be carried by the waves and sea life to another child in another country, who is waiting to receive it. Vivienne Smith, referring to Kress and van Leeuwen's "demand image," identifies in *Flotsam* a double layer of demand:

> Characters, or eyes, look out to the reader towards or through, something else, and challenge us to notice not just what is depicted, but the very notion of seeing itself. A crustacean stares out, framed by a human eye. Later, a human eye, framed and magnified by a hand lens, looks at the crustacean. The demand here is clear: Reader! Slow down. Step aside from the daily action. Look! Looking is seminal to this text. (Smith 2009: 87)

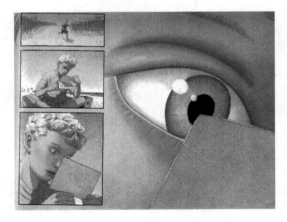

Figure 5: Excerpted from *Flotsam* by David Wiesner © (2006) Used by permission of Clarion Books, an imprint of Houghton Mifflin Harcourt Publishing Company. All rights reserved.

Wiesner creates all his images with great respect for detail and accuracy, from the past fashions and realistic beach settings of the children who had discovered the camera previously, to the natural world and the fantastic underwater parallel worlds. Valuing, illuminating and magnifying detail in this way highlights the wonder of the natural world, which flows seamlessly into the underwater magical worlds, and challenges the reader to look with far more care, as the boy does, at what is being destroyed.

Interestingly, *Flotsam* is a wordless picturebook. According to Jacques Lacan, the Symbolic, linear, logical and patriarchal human language supplants the thing itself, the Real. Possibly the images in multimodal texts bring us closer once again to the Real of our infancy, before we shared language. For when we experience the world only through language, we are "trapped in the alienating prison-house of language, so can never capture the real animal (any more than our real selves)" (Rudd 2009: 247). However, and this is of course highly relevant for the EFL classroom, it is also the Symbolic, that is language, which allows us "imaginatively, to animate any 'thing': animals, certainly, but also vegetables, flowers, dolls, clocks [...] where animism rules, where all things are democratically, anarchically even, given a voice" (Rudd 2009: 247-248). With multimodal texts we can offer our students images as well as language, and begin much earlier with environmentally relevant topics in the EFL classroom.

4. The environment as a (healing) process

David Almond and Dave McKean's *The Savage* is the last text I would like to consider in the light of Buell's criteria. The environment as a process, not a given, is of central relevance to education, as threats to this process are reciprocally threats to mankind: "The threats that preoccupy environmentalists are not only to wildlife and wilderness but also to human health, food, and shelter, and they are global as well as local" (Kerridge 2006: 533). I have inserted the word "healing" into the fourth criterion, which admittedly renders it rather more anthropocentric than the original wording: "Some sense of the environment as a process rather than as a constant or a given is at least implicit in the text" (Buell 1995: 8). *The Savage* is a brief multimodal text with a young implied readership. As such, it does not contain the extended, detailed prose of the texts Buell mentions when explaining his fourth criterion (works by James Fenimore Cooper and particularly by his daughter Susan Fenimore Cooper). However, I propose *The Savage* for a slightly revised fourth criterion, as it highlights man's connection to wilderness and the past as an aspect of healing.

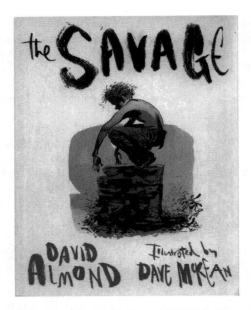

Figure 6: Front cover of *The Savage* by David Almond © (2008), illustrated by Dave McKean © (2008). Reproduced by permission of Walker Books Ltd, London SE11 5HJ.

The Savage is about the healing power of storytelling, narrated by a boy called Blue after the death of his father. Blue creates a prehistoric savage, who lives in a cave in the local woods and exists almost without any of the trappings of human culture. *The Savage* is a magic realist text that interrogates the culture/nature dualism and reason/emotion dualism, and, through an embedded story, re-embeds the protagonist in nature and a more organic understanding of his place in the world. *The Savage* is, both in Almond's verbal text and McKean's illustrations, a study of pain, loss, and the wretchedness of bullying. The ferocious wildness of the images combined with a dark, poetic text creates a short but very complex graphic novel suitable for the lower to mid-secondary school. Blue begins creating the story of the Savage in words and pictures after the death of his father:

> Once I started writing the story, it was like I couldn't stop, which was strange for me. I'd never been one for stories. I couldn't stand all the stuff about wizards and fairies and 'once upon a time' and 'they all lived happily ever after'. That's not what life's like. Me, I wanted blood and guts and adventures, so that's what I wrote. (Almond 2008: 13)

In order to read and enjoy contemporary postmodern fiction, students in the secondary EFL classroom should understand certain literary conventions, and a preparation for the literary studies of upper school years can certainly begin already in the lower secondary school with children's literature. A postmodern trope frequent in magic realism, and one that is central to *The Savage*, is narrative metalepsis, which the teacher can explain as "jumping between story levels." Metalepsis is "a breaking of the boundaries that separate distinct 'levels' of a narrative, usually between an embedded tale and its frame story" (Baldick 2001: 153). While the embedded story created by the narrator Blue moves forward, and the Savage acts out what Blue desires but is afraid of (living a wild life in Burgess Woods and furiously attacking the bully Hopper), the embedded and frame story levels begin to intertwine and interact. Blue writes of the Savage:

> He wore a dog skin round his waist and chicken feathers on his head. When I drew him and wrote about him, I could see him, I could hear him, I could smell him. Sometimes, it was nearly like I was him and he was me. (Almond 2008: 31)

The above passage clearly illustrates the patterned and multisensory nature of the language, and *The Savage* is an excellent model for students' own creative writing. In other ways too *The Savage* encourages creativity, the illustrations are fierce and menacing, and suggest a horror that is gently alleviated by Almond's text. The story within the story has a different font, one that resembles juvenile handwriting. Blue's nonstandard orthography intensifies the childlike nature of the embedded story, while illustrating that spelling is a gradual process—like language acquisition—for native speakers as well as for EFL learners: "But of cors the savage had no words, just jabbers and grunts and gasps, and he new nothing abowt words. How cud he? But he was starting to lurn" (Almond 2008: 39). This is an entirely normal developmental stage of the literacy of native speakers, a discovery that heartens EFL students, who might be encouraged to try to edit Blue's story for him in groups, with the aid of a dictionary.

The language of the embedding story contains no nonstandard orthography. It is beautifully written, lexically dense and moving:

> I stared into the moon. I felt sad, small, frightened, furious, bitter, lost, lonely … But like I said, there's no words that can say how I really felt. I stared into the moon and I stared into the moon. Then I switched the light on again, and I got my notebook and my pen and I started writing fast and hard. (Almond 2008: 50)

Blue's wild and gripping story and the wildness of the woods and the Savage hidden there in a cave appear to bridge the culture/ nature dualism when the distinct narrative levels begin to dissolve. Blue's Savage is arguably his answer to the "paradox of masculinity:" the expectation that the male "seem savage and yet domesticated at one and the same time" (Nodelman 2002: 7). The ending of *The Savage* can be equally read as a magic realist text of mystery and healing, or as the story of a young boy coming to terms with the savage within himself:

He led me further into the cave, further towards the fire, and by the low light of it I saw him face-to-face like a reflection, and he was just like me, only weirder and wilder and closer to some magic and darkness and some dreams. (Almond 2008: 73)

The savage seems to connect Blue's present life to a prehistoric past, and to ancient forms of storytelling, when he reveals cave paintings of Blue and his family: 'It was me, there on the cave wall. I was drawn in charcoal and colored with the dye from leaves and earth and berries' (Almond 2008: 74). As a magic realist text the meaning is left open, offering the potential for the negotiation of interpretation in an EFL classroom.

Literacy, in the sense of understanding texts, is one of the central competences of English language learning. It is now largely recognized that English language teaching should be multidisciplinary, with approaches such as Intercultural Learning, Task-Based Language Learning and Content and Language Integrated Learning, whereby the English language is the medium in content-based classrooms. In this chapter I have argued for including literary English teaching in a content-based classroom. Moreover I have argued for the choosing of texts in the primary and lower secondary-school classroom that— through the imaginative potential of literature—engage dialogically with nature as well as cultural phenomena. The eco-pedagogical significance of literature is outlined by Zapf: "The need to 'think globally' requires not only empirical information, but reflection and imagination, a capacity and readiness to think beyond oneself and one's own immediate interests and life-world" (Zapf 2008: 850). This, I have suggested, may be prepared with primary and lower secondary EFL students, through the use of literary microforms such as picture books and graphic novels.

Works Cited

Almond, David, illus. Dave McKean. *The Savage*. London: Walker Books, 2008.
Browne, Anthony. *Zoo*. London: Random House, 1992.
Martin, Rafe, illus. David Shannon. *The Rough-Face Girl*. New York: Penguin, 1992.
Rosen, Michael, illus. Helen Oxenbury. *We're Going on a Bear Hunt*. London: Walker
     Books, 1989.
Wiesner, David. *Flotsam*. New York: Houghton Mifflin Company, 2006.
Van Allsburg, Chris. *The Stranger*. Boston: Houghton Mifflin Company, 1986.

Baldick, Chris. *Oxford Concise Dictionary of Literary Terms*. Oxford: Oxford UP, [2]2001.
Bartels-Bland, Cara. "Picturebooks and Ecocriticism: Chris Van Allsburg's *The Stranger*."
     *Children and Teenagers, C&TS, The Publication of the Young Learners and Teenagers
     Special Interest Group, IATEFL* 11.2 (2011), 11-3.
Bland, Janice. *Children's Literature and Learner Empowerment. Children and Teenagers in
     English Language Education*. London: Bloomsbury Academic, 2013.
Bradford, Clare; Robyn McCallum; Kerry Mallan & John Stephens. *New World Orders in
     Contemporary Children's Literature: Utopian Transformations*. Basingstoke: Palgrave
     Macmillan, 2008.
Buell, Lawrence. *The Environmental Imagination*. Cambridge, Mass.: Harvard UP, 1995.
— . *The Future of Environmental Criticism. Environmental Crisis and Literary Imagination*.
     Malden, MA: Blackwell Publishing, 2005.
Cook, Guy. *Discourse and Literature: The Interplay of Form and Mind*. Oxford: Oxford UP,
     1994.
Dewey, John. *Experience and Education*. New York: Touchstone, 1938.
Garrard, Greg. *Ecocriticism*. London: Routledge, [2]2012.
Goatly, Andrew. *Critical Reading and Writing*. London: Routledge, 2000.
Goatly, Andrew & George Jacobs. "The Treatment of Ecological Issues in ELT
     Coursebooks." *ELT Journal* 54.3 (2000). 256-64.
Herman, David. "Storyworld." *Routledge Encyclopedia of Narrative Theory*. Eds. David
     Herman; Manfred Jahn & Marie-Laure Ryan. London: Routledge, 2005. 569-70.
Hunt, Peter. *Children's Literature*. Oxford: Blackwell, 2001.
Kerridge, Richard. "Environmentalism and Ecocriticism." *Literary Theory and Criticism*. Ed.
     Patricia Waugh. Oxford: Oxford UP, 2006. 530-43.
Kramsch, Claire. *Context and Culture in Language Teaching*. Oxford: Oxford UP, 1993.
Kress, Gunther & Theo van Leeuwen (2006), *Reading Images: the Grammar of Visual
     Design*. London: Routledge, [2]2006.
Lewis, David. *Reading Contemporary Picturebooks, Picturing Text*. London: Routledge,
     2001.
McDowell, Michael. "The Bakhtinian Road to Ecological Insight." *The Ecocriticism Reader.
     Landmarks in Literary Ecology*. Eds. Cheryll Glotfelty & Harold Fromm. Georgia: U of
     Georgia P, 1996. 371-91.
Möhle, Manuela. "Exploring the Use of Picturebooks in a Foreign Language Class: *Zoo*
     (Anthony Browne) in the Hauptschule, 5th grade." Hildesheim University: unpublished
     MEd thesis (2008).
Nodelman, Perry. "Making Boys Appear: The Masculinity of Children's Fiction." *Ways of
     Being Male: Representing Masculinities in Children's Literature and Film*. Ed. John
     Stephens. London: Routledge, 2002. 1-15.

Ramke, Katharina. "From Picturebooks to Graphic Novels: Why and How to Employ Multimodal Texts in the Lower Secondary EFL Classroom." Hildesheim University: unpublished MEd thesis (2011).

Rudd, David. "Animal and Object Stories." *The Cambridge Companion to Children's Literature*. Eds. Mathew Grenby & Andrea Immel. Cambridge: Cambridge UP, 2009. 242-57.

Smith, Vivienne. "Making and Breaking Frames." *Talking Beyond the Page. Reading and Responding to Picturebooks*. Ed. Janet Evans. London: Routledge, 2009. 81-96.

Yolen, Jane. "America's Cinderella." *Cinderella. A Casebook*. Ed. Alan Dundes. Wisconsin: U of Wisconsin P, 1982. 294-304.

Zapf, Hubert. "Literary Ecology and the Ethics of Texts." *New Literary History*. 39.4 (2008). 847-68.

Zipes, Jack. *When Dreams Came True. Classical Fairy Tales and Their Tradition*. New York: Routledge, [2]2007.

When Pigs Cry
Teaching the Gaze, Materialities and Environmental Ethics with the film *Babe*

Kylie Crane (Mainz/Germersheim)

In introducing the term 'companion species' in *Where Species Meet*, Donna Haraway observes the way the Latin roots of 'companion' point to the gustatory (*cum panis*, together with bread) and the roots of 'species' allude to the visual (*specere*, to look, behold) (cf. Haraway 2008: 17-18). I wish to take up both of these senses in this contribution. That an analysis of a film, *Babe* in this case, might dwell on senses of seeing will not be surprising, really, although there are particular configurations of seeing that I wish to foreground in order to stress moments of ethical entry into the text. Exploring the gustatory is more unusual, but—together with visual renderings of human-nonhuman[1] relations— is key to interpreting the film within the environmental framework stipulated by this volume. *Babe*, as I will argue in the following, can be included productively in ecocritical pedagogical contexts, but also in classes that address issues brought forward by Critical Animal Studies (in particular, through the ethical moments of the gaze) and by food-oriented cultural studies, corresponding to the two senses put forward by the 'companion species'.

Before looking Babe in the eye, and before considering how pigs might (or might not) end up on the table, I think it felicitous to have a look at the environment, as it were, of the film. This entails reflecting on the specific

---

1   I use the term nonhuman to encompass all beings, organic and non-organic, that are not human. The term animal and the phrase non-human animal are both tricky. They seem to be hinting at a 'mass' of potentially indistinguishable others rather than a differentiated plurality, a point I will reflect on in the course of this paper with reference to the name of the film's protagonist. The term animal also belies a differentiated plurality in another mode: Speciesism. Often, the term animal brings a specific referent, albeit obscured; frequently this referent is implicitly mammalian. Substitution might help: replacing the word 'animal' with an 'unlikely' species such as crab, cockroach or caterpillar rather than, say, cat will prove the extent to which assumptions regarding species are present. In the class I taught in the winter of 11/12 from which this contribution emerges, I asked my students to write down two animals on a piece of paper before the class started properly. As I suspected, the cats and dogs clearly outweighed the snakes and flies, even birds.

pedagogical framework from which this contribution has emerged, initially, and also a close examination of the materiality of the film itself. Environmental humanities suggests, to me, an opportunity to foster thinking of students and of teachers about the classroom as well as the subject matter: As a sheep-dog-pig might, Babe calls upon us to consider our categories, our ways of seeing, and, in the most friendly, possibly naïve, way, to be polite to those we find beside us.

Teaching Environments

As this contribution emerged from the context of a conference called "Teaching the Environment," I would like to reflect on the two terms 'teaching' and 'environment' and the manner in which they interact, proposing, instead, the phrase "Teaching Environments" as a more fitting context for my contribution. The plural, and the loss of the definite article 'the', point in two directions: Firstly, to the environments of teaching and how they might be taken into close consideration; secondly, to the multiple environments which might be taught, in a move that stresses the plurality of meanings attributed to—indeed the plurality of—environments that surround us.

To address the first point, the environments of teaching. Whilst preparing the paper that preceded this contribution, I had to realize that my imaginations of what might be understood under the title "Teaching the Environment" might differ from those of Roman and his colleagues in Cologne, and indeed what you, 'dear reader', might conceive of as being appropriate. My contribution threatened to fall apart before it began. For, to address the latter concern first, my teaching practices are based at a university, and I am in the strange position —in Germany at least—of teaching English at university but *not* teaching burgeoning teachers. Instead, I teach the next generation of translators and interpreters. My teaching practices are hence not currently primarily considered in the light of 'Didaktik' or pedagogy of the kind that explicitly might be passed on. My students, if it is at all possible to consider them as plural-and-singular, are not learning to become teachers. If anything, I hope that my students might leave my classes thinking about the world—and hence also the environment, that small-and-large process that emerges through worlding—in different ways, in a different light. The teaching they will do is of the conversational kind, and of quotidian practices. Which might, of course, be passed on. But, again, in a different way than what perhaps many of the other contributions in this volume might suggest.

To come to the plurality I wish to emphasize by adopting the plural 'teaching environments': Certainly in the light of postcolonial studies and, more generally, postmodern thought, it has become increasingly difficult to consider identity, or text, as singular. Perspectives—or to use the phrasing of Sara Ahmed which moves away from a visual metaphor: angles (cf. Ahmed 2010: 37)— suggest a plurality of meaning. In the translation classroom I find it of particular relevance, although it might sound commonplace: The context from which we approach something, be it poem, film, fellow beings or world, effects a particular response. By stressing the plural, I wish thus to be deliberate regarding the multiplicities of environments both in the world at large, but also in the space of a specific classroom.

A further point of clarity is perhaps necessary. The environment in this paper takes the nonhuman, in particular nonhuman animals, as its subject. Pigs, mostly, but also ducks, cows, sheep, cats and dogs; rather than trees and rocks, fields and mountains, deserts and oceans. Certainly, these creatures are of and in our environments. If not in messy, mucky, dirty, noisy forms, then, often, in packaged, cooked and served forms. They are not necessarily the first thing that comes to mind when we meditate on the repercussions of the term 'environment'. Yet, as Elspeth Probyn quite succinctly puts it: "There is perhaps no area where the global inserts itself into the intimate and emotional lives of people than in the realms of food production and consumption" (2011: 99).

A Pig Called Babe[2]

At the center of this contribution is the 1995 film *Babe*, directed by Chris Noonan. It was a popular success on its release (cf. Mizelle 2011: 183), and its classification, contents, packaging and marketing frames it as a children's movie.[3] It is a well-known film, indeed many of the students from my class were already familiar with it, but a short description will help to contextualize what follows: In the film, the story follows a pig, Babe, from birth in a factory farm through an arbitrary rescue to a guess-the-piglet's weight stand at a quaint country fair, to a quaint country farm populated with a myriad of talking animals. Here Babe must avoid the fate of becoming Christmas Dinner which leads, finally, back to the fairgrounds, where Babe succeeds in winning a perfect score as a sheep-dog-pig as well as winning the hearts of the viewers, both intra- and extradiegetic.

---

2   This is the German title of the film, translated back into English.
3   In Germany, it has the broadest rating, for viewing from the age of 0; it has a MPAA rating of G and a rating of G in Australia, too. Pallavi Gogoi, however, suggests that the film was banned in Malaysia.

It is a film that is easy to watch. It has pleasant aesthetics, perhaps kitschy, probably cute. It has a happy ending. It does not confront the viewer with explicit renderings of animal suffering, factory farm mass-production, slaughter, pain, blood—unlike other films one might choose to show in a Critical Animals Studies or Ecocriticism class. Following from the objections that Major and McMurry raised in response to the CfP for the conference from which this volume of papers has arisen, I want to stress that not all that is ecocritical is doomsday (Greg Garrard, for example, sees (the analysis of) apocalyptic rhetoric as one of many modes of doing ecocriticism in his book by the same name). A text does not need "catastrophic urgency" (Major and McMurray 2012: 3) to be environmental, although I suspect (hope?) this is not their point. A careful, gentle, nuanced approach is, in my humble opinion, more likely to engender long-term engagements, particularly given the shock and horror strategies of media outlets that tend to polarize, particularly on environmental issues. It seems, for instance, that global climate change has become something of a religion, something one can choose to believe in or not. Working against this, in the slow, perhaps sheltered, environment of a semester's time at university means, for me, fostering critical thinkers, people who are prepared to do the footwork as it were and carefully walk their way through the issues, rhetoric and forms. An English classroom can be a place to do this. It is not a biology classroom or a religious classroom, but a classroom that looks towards language, and the ways in which language works to reveal and critique our relations with the world. A cultural studies classroom further emphasizes this emplacement.

Given the heterogenous 'body of students' in my classroom—some vegetarians and an activist vegan as well as some students whose presence in the classroom was probably more a function of their timetable than anything else—this approach of watching a 'gentle' film at the outset of the semester worked well to engender a sense of trust rather than of disgust.[4] We later read Singer, Heise, Berger, some Coetzee, Martel. And thus *Babe* served as a platform for transfer to more quotidian contexts; enabling a questioning of structures behind the day-to-day, rather than alienation.

---

4   Students are quite able of watching more confronting films 'on their own time', like for example *Earthlings*, and many did, and some were referenced in later presentations on topics of the students' own choice.

Animals in the Classroom, Animals in the Film

Susan McHugh, in her article "Bringing up *Babe*," draws attention to the media employed in the film, focussing on "the role of visual media in constructing nonhumans as historical subjects" (McHugh 2002:150). She references cyborg theory, in particular how it "suspends the value of the human in relation to technology in order to trace a similar displacement enacted along the boundaries of technology and animals" (McHugh 2002:150), suggesting that the film might be used as an exploration site of the constructions of nonhuman others. The entanglements of the various means of presenting characters in the film can be thus foregrounded.

Approximately 55 animal handlers are listed in the credits of the film; Jim Henson's Creature FX Shop (of Muppets fame) is given credit, as well as Fleece Fabrication for sheep animatronics; human actors and voice actors are also listed. The credits thus draw viewers' attention to the varying materialities of the film. The human-nonhuman opposition is disturbed by the various roles performed in the film: by humans performing as humans, by humans 'giving voice' to animals, by animals performing as animals, by machines performing as animals, by puppets performing as animals. And, if you will, by animals performing as (if they were) humans, by communicating in a language we can understand. Thus surface-level appearances of the film as a meeting of human and non-human animals are revealed in the credits as simulation.[5]

Drawing attention to the materiality of the film is to work through ways of being in the world, an intermediate step between text and the world, and hence a cornerstone of work done in environmental humanities. Discussions of the various means used to perform various beings might lead towards other films. Steven Spielberg's film *Jurassic Park*, based on Michael Crichton's novel of the same title, serves as one example; the various incarnations of Jim Henson's muppets, also in *Sesame Street*, works as a further example that emerges from

---

5   Susan McHugh coins the term *animalacra* to meet the "collective of simulacral animals" (McHugh 2002:150) in the film, with reference to Jean Baudrilliard. Her conclusion is more Deleuzian, though: "animalacra emerge not as humans pretending to be animals, machines pretending to be animals (or humans), or animals pretending to be humans (or machines), but as animals pretending to be other animals in such a way that humans and machines are implicated" (McHugh 2002:150) placing the sheep-dog-pig *Babe* at the centre of her analysis. McHugh also notes some disruption in the visuals of the film, missing dark hairs from the puppet pig's head, for instance, working towards "[t]he destabilization of the animal subject, so common in film media" (McHugh 2002:154). Such visual disruption is common to film, the noting of which has become a hobby in its own right (various internet forums are dedicated to the spotting of continuity mistakes) and the performance of which is also a profession of its own accord (body doubles).

Henson's Creature FX Shop's involvement in the production of the film. Both examples enable students (and teachers!) to draw on previous knowledge to contextualize the challenges that the relations in *Babe* suggest. The unfamiliarity that cyborg theory, for example, might present is kept in check with the familiarity of the representational modes.

As those familiar with the film will be aware, the communicative structures in the film establish particular species boundaries that constitute hierarchies, although this hierarchy privileges the nonhuman animal with the ability of greater comprehension. As the case is in any number of 'children's films', animals are anthropomorphized into speaking, cognizant, intelligent creatures capable of human speech. Whilst the animals comprehend human speech, the focalization of the film suggests that humans cannot comprehend the semiotics of the myriad of species by which they are surrounded. A number of scenes further suggest the ways in which such boundaries are upheld: On Babe's first attempt at being a sheep-dog-pig, a role that of itself works to confound species boundaries through the catalog nature of its description, he does not bark as a dog, nor grunt as a pig, but yells 'Woof, woof, woof'. The arbitrariness of signs, the 'stupidity of humans', the tenuity of cross-species performance all work to provide further discussion of moments of constitution of subjects.

The animatronic-puppet-real animal, McHugh's *animalacra*, thus works to test the boundaries of a number of dualisms. Cyborg theory enables the viewer of *Babe* to not just consider the cyborg nature of the animals as depicted on the screen. Importantly, after this first step, it enables the viewer to reflect back upon him/herself, to consider the multiple ways in which our existences are also a confusion of the human and nonhuman (both nonhuman animal and machine), of bacteria, computer, mobile phone and virus. In her essay "From Extinction to Electronics," Ursula Heise has suggested that "robotic or electronic animals have been discussed very little in studies of cyborgs" (Heise 2003: 59), offering, among other examples, the Tamagotchi, that fad of the late 90s (so not long after the release of *Babe*) as well as a close analysis of *Jurassic Park* as potential sites for thinking through these issues. Looking for the merits of the texts she examines, Heise suggests that *Jurassic Park*, *Do Androids Dream of Electric Sheep?* and Thomas Ray's *Tierra Ray* all recognize that "the experience of nature is heavily mediated by technology" (Heise 2003: 75). Her assertion, with particular reference to Dick's novel, that "[a]nimals are envisioned and assessed in terms of benefit or drawbacks they bring to human knowledge, experience, and comfort, not as beings with independent rights to existence" (Heise 2003: 76) is one that holds in my interpretation of *Babe*, and is key to understanding the relationships in the film. That anthropocentricism is disrupted by *animalcra*, reading Heise and McHugh together, is an interesting and valuable environmental point: The issue of mediation might run aground with the assertion that mediated experiences of nature are often going to be mediated by technology—film, documentary, books (and e-readers), broadcast, all these media use technology. To press an environmental point here is to let go of the opportunity to engage with other aspects I find just as (if not more) pressing in the text, in particular that of food. Although I would like to take pause in order to examine the further aesthetics of the film.

Story Matters

The use of a voice-over in combination with the inclusion of stylized 'rustic' text and the mice figures suggests a fairy-tale structure. The phrase 'There was a time not so long ago' with which the film opens recollects the typical English fairy-tale beginning 'Once upon a time', but only almost: It is not a direct quote. We are invited into a quasi-fairy-tale world, a close approximation. This phrase, in its entirety, is "There was a time not so long ago when pigs were afforded no respect except by other pigs. They lived in a cruel and sunless world" (2:30- 2:44). This almost-fairy-tale opening moves in a number of directions. It works to reference a fairy-tale setting, without exactly creating it: Given that many pigs indeed continue to live in "cruel and sunless worlds," the typical fairy-tale ending which works to (re-)establish order is questioned. Moreover, a number of dualisms within the film can be foregrounded by referencing structuralist readings of fairy-tales, taking care, however, to avoid reducing the film to these structures. My reading of the past tense of "They lived," for example, sees the deictic reference point of the fairy tale in a possible future (or maybe long-gone past) but certainly not in the present moment. (A similar effect can be read into the opposition of genders, to which I return later.) The aesthetics which reinforce the opposition of factory farm vs. family farm are not successfully upheld if the temporal reference point of the film is destabilized.

On a different level, the fairy-tale structure is reiterated through an off-screen voice. The omniscient narrator is performed by Roscoe Lee Browne, an African American (voice) actor. Given the knowledge of Browne's ethnicity, the statements he utters might be read as implying a plurality of ethnic being (e.g. "our valley," the use of an inclusive first person plural) but they are displaced by the absence of any people of color in the scenes which display human presences.[6] The voice hence is 'disturbed' by its very non-presence. This narrative framework also employs 'they' to reference the pigs. This forms a deictic gesture which places distance between this unbodied voice-over presence

---

6   Extradiegetic observations such as this give rise to a critique informed by postcolonial thought, which might be explored in more detail in other contexts.

and the creatures we encounter on screen; or, alternatively, between the viewer and the events on screen.

A further disruption is figured by the mice. The mice usually quote phrases from the scenes yet to come, thus preempting particular events. Their incessant giggling and chuckling, as well as their smurf-like voices, troubles the serious tone provided by Browne, and provides a way into the film that, whilst seemingly innocent, is actually a lot more engaging. The use of voice modulation (Chipmunk-style, for want of the correct terminology) to exaggerate their voices, and their presence as a quasi-choir, work to destabilize the singular authority of the voice-over narration, on the one hand, and to foreground the issues of (gendered, racialized, aged) voices otherwise audible in the film. The mice, further, are visually present in the film, often appearing in a faux spot-light, usually embedded in the scenes from the farm-yard, although they are otherwise absent from the story. Further visual clues associated with the mice, specifically the blending in of intertitles, "a formal device reminiscent of the vaudeville stage and early cinema" (McHugh 2002:159), work differently in that they, much like Browne's disembodied racialized voice, disturb the 'placedness' of the film, suggesting a historical context that is belied by the presence of particular technologies (to which I will return below). In combination, the two narrative frameworks might work with each other, inviting interpretations that focus on how they work *against* each other. Close attention to the specific aesthetics of the film (in this case, informed by narratology, an approach most university-level English students are familiar with) will provide clues for 'unpacking' the other, in particular ethical and political, themes broached in the film.[7] Importantly, the tension between the two narrative strains emphasizes a number of other dualisms at work in the film.

Negotiations of Difference

The film-world postulates a number of oppositions, beyond the historical (story-world) and the human-nonhuman. Spatially, the contrast between factory farm versus family farm is one which is first and foremost aesthetically coded. The initial scene depicts agriculture at the factory farm. The cages, feeding-machines, and truck that dominate the visuals of the scene are combined with wet weather to depict a gloomy world. The only individuated presence is the

7   My use of the terms ethical and political would probably make most scholars from these fields break out in an allergic reaction. As a sort of antihistamine: I use these terms in a shorthand to point towards the extratextual interbeing relationships that surround us as social beings in a world imagined as more-than-just-human.

disembodied voice of the narrator; the pigs are meat, mass-noun (see also below); humans are rendered faceless, wearing uniform-like black rubber boots and dark clothes. Machines, coldness, metal dominates the screen. Here, Babe is one of many babes, and it is only at the quaint country fair – a moment constituted through the gaze as I will address below – that Babe is called into the role as the film's protagonist. I find it significant that the aesthetics of the film foreground the transition from factory to family farm, as it draws viewers' attention to the interrelatedness of many of the binaries the film explores. The country fair of Babe's 'rescue', the country fair of Babe's *tour de sheep-dog-pig*, and the Hoggett farm form a stark contrast to the opening scene in their visual mode: A 'warmer' color palette, predominantly sunny weather (with the exception of some flashbacks), a marked increase in organic materials (wooden fences, grassy hills, trees etc. rather than metal and bitumen). This contrast of aesthetics also draws attention to the employment of technology in these two 'farm worlds'.

Whereas the cold world of the factory farm is dominated by metal and machines, the roles of technology on the family farm are marginal, but no less important for analyzing the manner in which the film constitutes this agricultural binary. Arthur Hoggett struggles with the microwave to heat up the meals his wife has left for him in her absence, for instance. The gate to the homestead is controlled by a quirky contraption that speaks to homemade solutions rather than mass-production. The introduction of the fax machine, whilst at the time of writing this contribution a near obsolete technology, works as a placeholder for media technologies, and hence representative of 'buying in' to a comprehension of the world that equates technological advancement with progress. Note, also, the employment of the horse for plowing: This speaks, on the one hand, to the 'traditional' aesthetics of 'traditional' family farms—an imaginary one, replete with nostalgic connotations, hence the scare quotes—but also to the instrumentalization of nonhuman labor, the radical othering of nonhuman animals that finds the horse itself uttering "each animal its own place" and that resonates rather all too well with the cat's assertion that "animals that don't seem to have a purpose really do have a purpose [...] probably the most notable purpose of all when you come to think about it" (1:03:22-1:03:31).

As Lulu Lucia, writing under the guise of Anonymous in *Cineaste* observes,

> [a]lways associated with Farmer Hoggett's wife, the cat is shown to share in this woman's lack of vision and imagination, able to function only in the most petit-bourgeois of social structures, fearing to change the system that oppresses yet provides for her (19).

She also notes it is the cat that "pushes Babe to crisis, not through deception, but through revealing the cold truth of human cruelty" yet, unlike Ferdinand who appears eccentric, she is, as "teller of the truth," quite evil (ibid). Both figures,

the female and the feline, Lulu states, "with our obsessive interest in grooming
and the like, [...] expose the very fragility of those roles" (ibid). Gender roles in
Babe are rather conservative on the whole, but the rigorous work done to
maintain them does not remain unseen.

The Eyes Have It

Two central ethical moments in *Babe* are constituted through vision. In the one,
the viewer looks on as Farmer Hogget looks at Babe, in the other, we watch as
Babe cries. The eyes, it is said, are the windows to the soul. And the eyes have
received quite some attention, seem ubiquitous: John Berger asks "Why Look at
Animals?"; in the film *Earthlings* we hear "[w]e must learn to see into the eyes
of an animal and feel that their life has value because they are alive" (17:39-
17:48); and from *The Animal That Therefore I Am*: "I [Derrida] often ask
myself, just to see, *who I am* – and who I am (following) at the moment when,
caught naked, in silence, by the gaze of an animal" (3). Haraway makes much of
this moment between Derrida and his cat, suggesting that he might have looked
back and, in doing so, contemplated his nakedness not in terms of his shame, but
as an encounter between two beings (Haraway 2008: 19-27). The visuality of
encounters is only one dimension, but for the film (as genre, and also this
specific film), these meetings of the eyes are crucial.

"The pig and the farmer regarded each other" (5:03-5:06) the narrator
instructs us, and hence the viewer also sees both pig and farmer, looking at them
as they look at each other. Rather than Derrida's embarrassment in front of his
cat, here we have the farmer regarding the pig, and pay careful attention to the
agency, indeed the order of appearance, in the quote: The pig regards the farmer.
It is a reflexive phrase, and, I argue, invites reflection. Consider the pig, look at
the pig, watch the pig as it looks back, watch yourself as you watch the pig as it
looks back. A moment constituted by sight invites insight, as the various
quotations above seem to suggest.

*****

As well as being a (rather cheap) play on words ("when pigs fly"), the title of
this paper references a specific turning point scene in the film, when 'our' hero
the piglet cries at the death of a sheep, is accused of killing said sheep and only
narrowly, and through the cooperation of a number of other species, escapes

becoming bacon and ham in the farmer's cottage. The moment of Babe crying at the death of the sheep Maa, occasional surrogate mother and key to sheep-dog-pig success, is read here as a gateway into the text in order to query animal ethics. If we decide that it is not okay to eat Babe if he cries, are we not proposing an anthropocentric argument? Is the suggestion 'if a being feels, hurts, yes cries, like a human, then it is not okay to submit this being to pain' one that only works to reinforce an anthropocentric view of our environment? Although I have no answer for this quandary, the question nevertheless warrants articulation: Is there a way that we might be able to engage in ethical relations towards and with non-human animals that does not rely on anthropocentric models of being? Or do we decide to ask a different question, equally warranting articulation: What ways can we imagine being in the world that are *not* anthropocentric? These are difficult questions, I think, and open the door to work done by animal activists and ecocritics; at the same time, I think these questions also open doors to work done by artists and authors, as ways of imagining being in a world that is not centered on the human (/artist).[8]

Drawing attention to the roles of the eyes, it becomes difficult not to notice the absence of eyes, particularly human eyes, in the opening scene at the factory farm. The shots instead primarily depict human feet. Unlike Farmer Hoggett, these humans resist the gaze of their fellow species. The unseen scenes of the factory farm and indeed slaughterhouse can be supplemented through viewing the 'Food' section of *Earthlings*, and/or by reading various chapters of Jonathan Safran Foer's *Eating Animals* as well as Barbara Kingsolver's *Animal, Vegetable, Mineral* in addition to the opening chapters of Michael Pollan's *The Omnivore's Dilemma*, to highlight those sources included in the bibliography.

Steven D. Brown and Ian Tucker, in an amusingly titled essay "Eff the Ineffable" included in *The Affect Theory Reader*, draw on Deleuze and Bergson to put forward the following:

---

8   Open-ended questions to which I have no definitive answer such as these foster a forum for discussion that enables an engaged critique, a theoretically informed problematising, and, also important, a careful tracing of positions. In opposition to the proposals outlined in the contribution by Pamela Swanigan at the conference from which this volume emerges, I always seek to provide a narrative of my own investments in the topics at hand to students. My impetus is *not* to produce 'thought-clones'. Rather, I believe that students at universities are able to position themselves with respect to certain issues, are able to formulate critique of written and spoken texts (so engage in discussions of theoretical texts but also to point out gaps in my own contributions) and can read my narrative as what it is: A (possible) narrative. So, in the classroom, such open-ended questions might give rise to readings and critique of Singer, of Haraway, of John Berger, but also of Yann Martel and J.M. Coetzee (in particular *Lives of Animals*, or in its 'extended version', *Elizabeth Costello*). Different questions might provide for parallels to George Orwell's *Animal Farm*.

> [A]n attention to affect allows us to propose that persons differ from other creatures and things only quantitatively, by the number and complexity of the planes of experience that intersect, and intensively, through the particular connections and engagements that the human body is capable of supporting. (233)

I wonder if the imagination of Babe as talking, sentient being beyond normal experiences of pigs—regardless of whether this experience takes its basis in pig as farm animal or pig wrapped in plastic in the supermarket—multiplies and intensifies these connections. Babe's naiveté, for example the misreading of a motherly trip to the slaughterhouse as a trip to heaven, appeals to the viewer's own naiveté in childhood at the same time it appeals to the viewer's greater understanding of the events, alluding, in a sense, to the viewer's comprehension of deeply entrenched narratives of the *Bildungsroman* type. At the same time, the despair Babe feels for other animals—beyond self-interest—invites the viewer to consider what the narrator has to say: "and the pig promised himself that he would never think badly of any creature ever again" (13:55-14:01).[9]

Bringing home the bacon

Animals as food is an important topic of environmental critique. In the last few years, it has received much media attention. Foer's *Eating Animals* engendered much debate[10] as well as further texts on the issue (for example, Pollan's *The Omnivore's Dilemma*, Kingsolver's *Animal, Mineral, Vegetable*, as mentioned above, as well as Eric Schlosser's *Fast Food Nation*[11] and in Germany also texts such as Karen Duve's *Anständig Essen: Ein Selbstversuch*). In *Babe*, the issue of eating animals is present at a number of levels. Babe, for instance, is naively unaware of his fate as Christmas roast until the other animals explain it to him.

(Remember: It is this naiveté that endears us, that calls upon us to 'see things similarly'. The pig, the baritone narration declares when he is about to be shot,

---

9   The narrator thus does what I have been careful not to do: Gender the pig.

10   Of particular relevance here, the chapter "Influence/Speechlessness" (117-148). The repetition of the title of the chapter over the first few pages draws attention both to the slippage between the two terms, presented graphically through the '/', and to the issue of eating animals, as Foer announces "On average, Americans eat the equivalent of 21,000 entire animals in a lifetime – one animal for every letter on the last five pages" (121). Further, his arguments on the cognate term 'influenza' reverberate well with discussions of *Babe* through the colloquial name for the H1N1 virus: swine flu.

11   Chapter 10, "Global Realization" (225-252) works well in the German classroom, as it starts and ends in Plauen, a town in Saxony, bringing the global reach of the chapter 'closer to home'.

"had a vague memory that shiny tubes produced food and guessed that some quite unexpected surprise would come out of the tubes' small, round mouths" (54:08-54:18). It is this slippage between the experiential world of the naive pig and the worlds of the film's viewers that works, albeit counterintuitively, to foster engagement in the issues explored. The work of the viewer to 'fill in the gaps' or to 'join the dots'—here, to see the gun as a gun (and not as a feeding machine)—functions to encourage similar interpretative practices in the world *beyond* the film (i.e. the viewers' worlds.).

It is quasi-anarchistic Ferdinand who most explicitly articulates this concern in the film. His logic: Dinner means death. Death means carnage. "Christmas means carnage" (27:14-27:16). This anorexic duck crows in best rooster manner from the thatched rooftop of the barn, convinced that his efforts to confuse his avian classification will ensure avoidance of the most dreadful fate of the oven. Elsie Hoggett, meanwhile, is concerned with the menu—ham or duck l'orange. Arthur Hoggett might be able to postpone Babe's slaughter, but only, first, by suggesting that Babe will make a nice leg of ham for next year's fair, thus only delaying the carnage and, second, by deferring the carnage to Rosanna, who only Ferdinand is able to name.[12] Babe's place of birth at a factory farm comes close to referencing mass production of animals, and although the aesthetics of the farm are rendered dark, they belie the grim reality of factory farmed pigs: The film, after all, follows the fate of the pig that got away (and, if you follow the trajectory of the film to its sequel, all the way to the big city—and not to the market (This little piggy *didn't* go to market)).

But, some words on the name of the film's protagonist, as a bridge between the individual and the masses. Responding to the question of the piglet's name posed by Fly, the surrogate mother, the piglet notes they were given no names to tell them apart from each other: "Our mum called us all the same" (7:45-7:49). Note, in particular, the use of the plural here: Grammatically unnecessary ("My mum called us all the same" works just fine), the phrase draws attention to Babe's status as one-of-many-Babes. Taken further, the one-of-many-Babes draws attention to the conditions of the factory farm that gave rise to this situation. It also reinforces the de-individualization of the circumstances of mass production, not just for the pigs but also for the faceless, nameless human animals in the opening scenes of the film.

The pig, then, is called Babe, a term that is linguistically applicable to humans, and not piglet (cf. also Smith 2002: 54). As Carol J. Adams and Marjorie Proctor Smith note, meat is a mass term, linguistically masking the

---

12 I think of the scene in the 1999 film *Fight Club*, when the group starts chanting "His name is Robert Paulson" after the character dies, the naming of fallen soldiers, the introduction of the individualised and named sufferer into media reports (for instance, most recently, of Jyoti Singh Pandey, whose name was repressed according to some media outlets).

multiple sources and multiple individuals that come to land on plates. Val Plumwood phrases this point as follows:

> Animals so conceived [as meat] are subject to both radical exclusion (as having a radically different nature discontinuous from that of the human meat consumer) and homogenisation—they 'drown in the anonymous collectivity' of the commodity form meat [...] [that] denies kinship and generates a conceptual distance of boundary between humanity and its 'meat' which blocks sympathy, reduces the risk of identification with those so designated, and silences them as communicative beings. (Web)

Babe as one-of-many works to emphasize the plight of becoming-meat.

The film proved to make a lasting impression, as consumption of ham and bacon went down considerably in Australia following the film's release. Brett Mizelle suggests "the film seems to have led some consumers to forsake pork at the request of their children, as it was reported to have led to a 40 per cent drop in pork consumption in Australia" (Mizelle 2011: 154). Mick Smith contends "the subsequent fall of pork consumption showed [...] some children did make uncomfortable connections (especially when it became known that the various pigs that played 'Babe' all ended in the slaughterhouse" (Smith 2002: 54)).[13] Further paratexts reinforce such assumptions, for example interviews with James Cromwell, who plays Arthur Hoggett in the film, indicating that he turned vegan from vegetarian as a consequence of his role in the film. The film also finds an internet presence in the Animals Australia website *www.savebabe.com*. The question is not so much 'Why is this the case?' but rather the pre-question 'What aspects of the film might give rise to such behaviors?' The latter, in contrast, draws our attention to the specific devices or aesthetics/rhetoric of the film, challenging us to contextualize our queries in different frameworks as well as to engage in something of a close reading. The effect of—indeed affect that leads to—these politicized responses/behaviors is one that requires politicized queries. A close tracing of investments into the materials, both by student and by teacher. And part and parcel to this is also the engagement of the teacher with the materials, in my opinion, one that should not be withheld from an environment of critical thinking. Babe's politeness and readiness to be exposed

---

13   Smith continues as follows "Such breakdowns in the anthropic imag(e)ination are however rare and their effects usually transitory given the overwhelming weight of messages that make meat eating normal or even necessary. It is much more common to see cartoon animals happily espousing their own edibility on television or even taking a more active role, as in the case of those smiling plastic pigs that stand on two legs wearing a striped apron and wielding a cleaver outside so many butcher's doors" (Smith 2002: 54). My interest in the film is to use it to point to the exception, rather than the rule. Not to suggest an overtly positivistic account of meat consumption, but to ask, instead, what makes the film 'special'; also, as outlined elsewhere in this contribution, I have had good experiences teaching this 'soft' text.

to new experiences is key to the success (read: life) of the character; and perhaps also to the success of the film in my classroom. And now, repeat from beginning: a hermeneutic circle.

That'll Do, Pig: or What'll Pigs Do?

A smiling pig graces the cover of the Little Brown Book group and the Virago editions of Margaret Atwood's *Oryx and Crake*. Those familiar with the tale 'inside' the cover can only read this as insidious. These are smart pigs, enhanced by biotechnology. And then there's Snowball and Napoleon, as well as Squealer (and yes aren't those fantastic names?), of George Orwell's allegorical and broadly read *Animal Farm*. Wilbur, a pig, is saved from slaughter by a spider called Charlotte in E.B. White's *Charlotte's Web*. The novel, preceded four years by an essay "Death of a Pig," it is a tale that resonates well with *Babe* (cf. also Mizelle 2011: 149-153). Closer to home, pigs emerge again: In *Food and Cultural Studies*, Bob Ashley et.al. observe of the pig "the values of civilization are generally held to exist in opposition to that animal's uncultivated characteristics" (2). Drawing on the work of Peter Stallybrass and Allon White, they observe that

> the pig is an ambivalent creature, a threshold animal that transgresses major oppositions between human and animal (the pink pigmentation of the pig disturbingly resembling the flesh of European babies) and between outside and inside (pigs were usually kept in close proximity to—and sometimes within—the house). (Ashley et.al. 2004: 7)

This ambivalence and familiarity makes the pig an intriguing subject, but so, too, do the troubling behaviors in its presence (in the sty, in the factory farm, 'at home' on the table). "A peasant" writes John Berger, "becomes fond of his pig and is glad to salt away its pork" (2007: 253): This "and" comprises a linguistic stumbling block in the ESL classroom and an ethical stumbling block in the cultural studies class. Some matters we might like to see separated, aestheticized, anaesthetized, they become confused when they, like Babe, enter the kitchen. Of a meeting of academics, Haraway writes of meat. With a hunted feral pig 'on the table', she writes:

> The crisis the party faced was a cosmopolitical one, where neither human exceptionalism nor the oneness of all things could come to the rescue. *Reasons* were well developed on all sides; *commitments* to very different ways of living and dying were what needed to be examined together, without any god tricks and with consequences. (Haraway 2008: 298)

Addressing the various claims and issues surrounding the consumption of (feral)[14] meat, Haraway argues: "Dialectics"—the cornerstone of the various approaches to *Babe* I outline in this contribution—

> is a powerful tool for addressing contradictions, but Bekoff and Lease [the colleague/hunter] do not embody contradictions. Rather, they embody finite, demanding, affective, and cognitive claims on me and the world, both sets of which require action and respect without resolution. (Haraway 2008: 300)

This is *Babe* in the classroom. A mess of entanglements, refusing an answer, and refusing to stop asking questions.

So: How might we teach environments? For instance, by using theory to probe a text to think about ways of being in the world. A text such as *Babe* provides a non-threatening platform for discussing ideas such as the cyborg—understood as the myriad ways in which borders between the human and the non-human (both animal and machine) are transgressed in the world around us—and the pathways and meanings of meat and food. The radical ways in which the film tests these boundaries—through the materiality of the film, through its use of anthropomorphized talking animals, and through the moments of meeting the gaze—can be juxtaposed against the less radical moments of the film, in particular its adherence to ideas of hierarchy, its gender politics and its fairy-tale like happy ending. In this way, a classroom of critical thought can seek to comprehend the seemingly challenging and to question the seemingly complacent. Ideally, these paths of critique will lead to ways into quotidian practices, both of teacher and of student. For a text to be environmental, for an approach to be environmental, means thinking back to the world, means considering practices of worlding.[15]

---

14   Feral is an interesting term that alludes, but only alludes, to biological knowledge. It speaks much more loudly to comprehensions of local/global, and hence is left open to postcolonially informed critique.

15   I would like to thank the students from my Critical Animal Studies class for pushing my thoughts. And also for pointing out, when faced with my perplexity, that children buying masses of goldfish after watching *Finding Nemo* were not killing clownfish, that is, working 'against' the film, but instead trying to rescue them by flushing them down the toilet.

Works Cited

Adams, Carol. J. & Marjorie Procter-Smith. "Taking Life or 'Taking Life'?" *Ecofeminism and the Sacred*. Ed. Carol J. Adams. New York: Continuum, 1995 [1993]. 295-310.

Ahmed, Sara. "Happy Objects." *The Affect Theory Reader*. Eds. Melissa Gregg & Gregory J. Seigworth. Durham & London: Duke UP, 2010. 29-51.

Anonymous. "A couple of furry black and white pets sitting around talking ... about *Babe*." *Cineaste* 22:2 (1996). 17-9.

Ashley, Bob; Joanne Hollows; Steve Jones & Ben Taylor. *Food and Cultural Studies*. London: Routledge, 2004.

Atwood, Margaret. *Oryx and Crake*. New York: Nan A. Talese, 2003.

Berger, John. "Why Look at Animals." *Animals Reader: The Essential Classic and Contemporary Writings*. Eds. Linda Kalof & Amy Fitzgerald. Oxford: Berg Publishers, 2007. 251-61.

Brown, Steven D. and Ian Tucker. "Eff the Ineffable: Affect, Somatic Management, and Mental Health Service Users." *The Affect Theory Reader*. Eds. Melissa Gregg & Gregory J. Seigworth. Durham & London: Duke UP, 2010. 229-49.

Cardoni, Salvatore. "James Cromwell: You don't own another creature." http://www.takepart.com/article/2011/12/27/james-cromwell-you-dont-own-another-creature (5 Sept. 2012).

Coetzee, J.M. *The Lives of Animals*. Princeton, New Jersey: Princeton UP, 1999.

— . *Elizabeth Costello*. London: Secker & Warburg, 2003.

Derrida, Jacques. *The Animal That Therefore I Am*. Trans. David Wills. New York: Fordham UP, 2008.

Duve, Karen. *Anständig Essen: Ein Selbstversuch*. Munich: Wilhelm Goldmann Verlag, 2012.

Ellis, Samantha. "James Cromwell: You Don't Own Another Creature." *Global Animal*. http://www.globalanimal.org/2012/01/02/james-cromwell-you-dont-own-another-creature/62175/#sthash.nkx2UhFw.dpbs (21 Dec. 2012).

Foer, Jonathan Safran. *Eating Animals*. New York: Little, Brown and Company, 2009.

Garrard, Greg. *Ecocriticism*. London: Routledge, 2004.

Gogoi, Pallavi. "Banning Borat." http://www.businessweek.com/stories/2006-11-05/banning-boratbusinessweek-business-news-stock-market-and-financial-advice (5 Sept. 2012).

Haraway, Donna. *When Species Meet*. Minneapolis: U of Minnesota P, 2008.

Heise, Ursula. "From Extinction to Electronics: Dead Frogs, Live Dinosaurs, and Electric Sheep." *Zoontologies: The Question of the Animal*. Ed. Cary Wolfe. Minneapolis: U of Minnesota P, 2003.

Kingsolver, Barbara with Steven L. Hopp & Camille Kingsolver. *Animal, Vegetable, Mineral: Our Year of Seasonal Eating*. London: Faber and Faber, 2007.

Major, William and Andrew McMurray. "Introduction: The Function of Ecocriticism; or Ecocriticism, What is it Good For?" *Journal of Ecocriticism* 4.2 (2012). http://ojs.unbc.ca/index.php/joe/article/view/281/399 (21 Dec. 2012).

McHugh, Susan. "Bringing up *Babe*." *Camera Obscura* 49 17.1 (2002). 149-87.

Mizelle, Brett. *Pig*. London: Reaktion Books, 2011.

Orwell, George. *Animal Farm: A Fairy Story*. London: Penguin, 2008.

Plumwood, Val. "*Babe*: the Tale of the Speaking Meat: Part I." *Australian Humanities Review* 51 (2011). 205-07. http://epress.anu.edu.au/wp-content/uploads/2011/12/babe1.pdf (22 Dec. 2012).

Pollan, Michale. *The Omnivore's Dilemma: A Natural History of Four Meals*. London: Penguin, 2007.

Probyn, Elspeth. "Swimming with Tuna: Human-Ocean Entanglements." *Australian Humanities Review*. 51 (2011). 97-114. http://epress.anu.edu.au/wp-content/uploads/2011/12/swimming.pdf (22 Dec. 2012).

Schlosser, Eric. *Fast Food Nation: What the All-American Meal is Doing to the World*. London: Penguin, 2007.

Singer, Peter. "All Animals are Equal." *Social Creatures: A Human and Animal Studies Reader*. Ed. Clifton P. Flynn. New York: Lantern Books, 2008. 337-54.

Smith, Mick. "The 'Ethical' Space of the Abattoir". *Human Ecology Review* 9.2 (2002). 49-58.

Van Dooren, Thom & Deborah Bird Rose. "Storied-places in a multispecies city." *HUMaNIMALIA* 3.2 (2012). http://www.depauw.edu/humanimalia/issue%206/rose-van%20dooren.html (30 Jan. 2013).

White, E. B. *Charlotte's Web*. New York: HarperCollins, 2001.

Babe. Dir. Chris Noonan (1995)
Earthlings. Dir. Shaun Monson (2005)
Finding Nemo. Dir. Andrew Stanton (2003)
Jurassic Park. Dir. Steven Spielberg (1993)

www.savebabe.com Animals Australia (21 Dec. 2012).

Transdisciplinary Encounters I: Approaching the 'Two Cultures'

Pedagogy and the Power of the Ecoliterary Text

Adrian Rainbow (Zürich)

> Mainstream education can help correct the current imbalances, help learners gain a sense of interconnection, and educate the next generation for a sustainable life even in the midst of climate change. To teach competences, tools and skills with this in mind, new educational principles have to take the place of current practices. The Western educational system has become as rigid as the development, production and economic infrastructures that it has both shaped and been shaped by.
> - Karen Blincoe, "Re-educating the Person" (205-6)

In this paper I focus on ecocriticism, ecopedagogy, ecoliteracy, and the role of literary texts within the field of pedagogy. I argue that the role of fictional literature is pedagogically undervalued across the breadth of education in terms of teaching scientific and ecological principles, and that the author/artist as an ecopedagog, "change agent" (Blincoe), and "nature endorser" (Love), has been understated in relation to consilience and bridging the science and the humanities. I also argue that the role of the fictional text is multifaceted but that ultimately it functions to facilitate the Freirean notions of conscientization and praxis: to instill knowledge, transform consciousness, and create a dialog that then enables individuals to be in a position to see the world differently, and which empowers them to be an active change agent. Drawing on theories of ecopedagogy, I contend that the literary text can impact the consciousness in terms of affectivity, emotion, empathy, and ethics. Building on this notion, I maintain that the integration of aesthetic texts with the objectified, impersonal world of scientific fact leads to an effective aesthetic form to "read" nature, and understand humanity's current antagonistic relationship with it. This amalgamation, I argue, represents a new kind of nature literature which can ultimately contribute to a better understanding of scientific and ecological realities. Consequently, the knowledge that the reader gleans from this scientific understanding can lead to new ways of biocentric thinking which ultimately can provide them with a deeper appreciation of the ecosystem and humanity's relationship to it. At the risk of sounding idealistic, the overarching goal for this form of literature is that readers are *affected*, impelled to change their behavior and even, potentially, might engage in activity that will lead to progressive societal and environmental change. As I will outline below, this transpires because fictional literature represents a narrative medium in which readers are emotionally, cognitively, and ethically affected by the aesthetic text. Consequently, they are then more open to accepting and internalizing scientific discourse that they might not normally be exposed to. Furthermore, I maintain that the application of this type of multifaceted and "interdisciplinary" literary fiction needs to be at the core of educational curricula in the humanities to represent and emphasize new flexible principles of education that provide a challenge to our current rigid educational system, especially in terms of teaching ecological awareness and environmental sustainability.

Conscientization and Praxis

To understand the pedagogical context of my paper, and how I deem literature to function so effectively, I will often be alluding to the aforementioned Freirean notions of conscientization and praxis. Conscientization is an idea at the heart of Paulo Freire's (1921-97) pedagogical methodology, and pertains to the awakening of the consciousness and the process of the individual becoming a self-reflexive critical thinker; it represents the shift from ignorance to understanding. In his works *Education for Critical Consciousness* (1973), *Pedagogy of the Oppressed* (1993), *Pedagogy of the Heart* (1998), and *Pedagogy of Hope* (1998), Freire outlines conscientization as the process of "re-education" that places the emphasis on self-reflexivity. He defines conscientization as the method of exposing the cultural, hegemonic, and political contradictions of society; it is a process of awakening consciousness in individuals so that they become critically aware of the epistemological premises behind the structures of meaning in society, the historical processes that define society, and their sense of purpose within these structures. It is the process of the "illiterate" becoming critically educated so that they can see reality as well as their place in it more clearly. Most importantly, it entails the realization that they have the power to change it. Arlene Goldbard provides this useful definition:

> Conscientization is an ongoing process by which a learner moves toward critical consciousness. This process is the heart of liberatory education. It differs from "consciousness raising" in that the latter may involve transmission of preselected knowledge. Conscientization means breaking through prevailing mythologies to reach new levels of awareness—in particular, awareness of oppression, being an "object" of others' will rather than a self-determining "subject." The process of conscientization

involves identifying contradictions in experience through dialogue and becoming part of the process of changing the world. (Goldbard 2006: 242)

Empowered with this clarity, knowledge and empowerment, individuals can then actively attempt to liberate themselves and to politically transform their environment and society.

Furthermore, by praxis I mean the transformation from theory to action. Before any tangible societal change can take place, there needs to be a spark of inspiration, passion, and a theoretical, philosophical, or politically conceptual thrust. Critical pedagog Peter McLaren explains that "only the conversion of knowledge into action can transform life. This concretely defines the meaning of practice: the dialectic movement between the conversion of transformative action into knowledge and the conversion of knowledge into transformative action" (McLaren 2000: xxv). In *Pedagogy of the Oppressed* (1970), Freire claims that "[h]uman activity is theory and practice; it is reflection and action" (168). Thus by "critical pedagogy," I mean the combination of conscientization, critical thinking, and praxis. This represents an educational approach that emphasizes the need for critical consciousness to actively challenge and subvert existing hegemonic structures of thought.

Context: Science and Scientific Pedagogy

The context for my argument is grounded in the notion that the current environmental crisis is largely a result of mainstream epistemology, ontology and education: how we think about the earth, what meaning we ascribe to it, how we visualize our place as humans in relation to nature and how we pass this information on to students. The way we think about this problem is influenced by many factors, some of which are a result of the way our educational disciplines and practices have been chosen, favored, and evolved. Science, and the way we have been teaching, learning, and thinking about science, can be seen to be one of the problems. At the risk of being reductive and construed as scientifically naïve and illiterate, I would argue that science generally is based on mechanistic, reductionist, impersonal thinking, on objective reason, instrumental rationality, and the principles of the Enlightenment, even if scientific discourse and the ways we think about and teach science is rapidly evolving. The mechanistic way of thinking we have embraced in the Western World since the scientific revolution of the 1600s leading to the Enlightenment and the Industrial Revolution has created an intensely anthropocentric ontological perspective. In *The Science Delusion* (2012), Rupert Sheldrake explains that

[s]ince the late nineteenth century, science has dominated and transformed the earth. It has touched everyone's lives through technology and modern medicine. Its intellectual prestige is almost unchallenged. Its influence is greater than that of any other system of thought in all of human history (13).

As a result, human domination of the earth has become justified and accepted as the hegemonic position, as scientists have continuously engaged in a *Frankensteinian* quest for knowledge and progress. Consequently, the earth is regarded as dead, inert matter to be used for human purposes. However, many contemporary scientists acknowledge this predicament, see the perils of this in terms of our disenchantment from the earth, and want to open science to new methodologies that will connect us more to nature, or to use John Berger's term: to enable "new ways of seeing." For, as Sheldrake states, "[d]ogmatic ideology, fear-based conformity and institutional inertia are inhibiting scientific creativity" (4).

This is reflected in terms of education and how we teach the environment and sustainability. Even though more and more scientists, institutions, and schools are adopting interdisciplinary approaches to environmental education, ecological studies is still predominantly taught in terms of mechanistic, objective science. Ernst Schumacher explains how "[s]cience and engineering produce 'know-how'; but 'know-how' is nothing by itself; it is a means without an end, a mere potentiality, an unfinished sentence. 'Know-how' is no more a culture than a piano is music" (66). He claims that "[e]ven the greatest ideas of science are nothing more than working hypotheses, useful for purposes of special research but completely inapplicable to the conduct of our lives or the interpretation of the world" (71). Sheldrake echoes this and explains that the problem is that "most of our experience is not mathematical. We taste food, feel angry, enjoy the beauty of flowers, laugh at jokes" (31). The immense popularity of popular scientists such as Richard Dawkins, Jane Bennett, Edward Wilson, Fritjof Capra, James Lovelock, Stephen Jay Gould, and Rupert Sheldrake, to name a few, suggests that scientific thought is adapting, becoming far more accessible, and sympathetic to the notion that our understanding of science needs to change. Yet, despite the credibility and popularity of these scientists, there is still a lack of concrete suggestions about how to create a new scientific way of thinking that avoids the dogmatic ideology and reductionism inhibiting scientific creativity.

Gaia theorist Stephan Harding explains that students "are not enlightened by the dry language of conventional scientific discourse" (2011: 91). He explains that

our scientific understanding ignores the equally vital contributions that our sensory experience, our ethical sensibilities and our intuitive capacities can make to a more holistic understanding of the Earth and our place within it. The problem, more succinctly put, is that our current educational paradigm emphasises quantities at the expense of qualities, and prioritises *facts over values* (91, emphasis added).

Thus, we need to reconsider the hegemonic position of mechanistic, mathematical, reductionist science within our educational curricula and to develop a new form of scientific thinking with sensibilities outside of the current rigid scientific paradigm. Moreover, we need a new idea of education; one that comprises a holistic approach that attempts to see beyond objective facts and reductionism and incorporates other values that will give us a new understanding of ecology and sustainability.

Scientists are crucial to humanists; we need to know the ecological facts, and the ecological crisis can and *must* be understood scientifically. But these facts need to be morphed with ethics and value systems and connected to individuals on personal, spiritual, and moral levels. Greg Garrard explains: "we need better ideas, feelings and values even more urgently than scientific breakthroughs" (2011: 23). In due course, critics are realizing this ethical and emotional void within scientific discourse. However, the challenge is how to transform rigid ways of thinking about science, and this is where the humanities can play a crucial role. Critical pedagog and consilience theorist Edward Slingerland explains:

> As natural scientists begin poking their noses into areas traditionally studied by the humanities—the nature of ethics, literature, consciousness, emotions, or aesthetics—they are sorely in need of humanistic expertise if they are to effectively decide what sorts of questions to ask, how to frame these questions, and what sorts of stories to tell in interpreting their data. (9)

Not only is this where the humanities can play a significant role, but where fictional literature as an aesthetic form can lead science, and scientific education, out of its current malaise. Harding's solution for the problems he outlines above: "In my experience, *storytelling* works best" (91, emphasis added). Fictional literature, and especially its emphasis on narrative, is the perfect affective domain to challenge and bolster scientific discourse and the archetypal scientific paradigms. Indeed, affectivity is key here: "Doing rock and mineral identification may elicit little emotional response from most students. But when the subject matter seems to confront one's personal lifestyle, political leanings or economic situation, then the topic may be perceived in a very different light" ("Student Motivations and Attitudes"). Feelings, ethics, motivations, values are the affective domain of literature, and are, according to theorists studying cognitive poetics and neuroaesthetics, the gateway to how we actually learn. The "affective dimension is not just a simple catalyst, but a necessary condition for learning to occur" (Perrier & Nsengiyumva 2003: 1124, qtd. in "Science Learning" 76). What I am ultimately advocating here is a return to John Dewey's philosophy about scientific attitudes and the belief that "science instruction should foster such mental attitudes as intellectual integrity, interest in testing opinions and beliefs, and open-mindedness rather than communicate a fixed body of information" ("Science Learning" 77), and that fictional literature is the best medium to facilitate this. After I have outlined what literature on the whole contributes to this discourse, I will come back to the notion of ecoliteracy and consilience, or the merging of science and the humanities.

The Power of Literature—The Power of Story and Narrative

Fictional literature has always been effective in setting up or destroying taboos, conventions, and social prejudices, thus contributing to changes in thinking which in turn instigated social and political change. For example, Upton Sinclair's *The Jungle* (1906) was instrumental in changing laws regarding the way the meat industry in the Chicago stockyards of the early 20th century operated as it introduced, through fiction, horrible truths behind the industry and led to the passing of the Pure Food and Meat Inspection Act. Similarly, Mary Wollstonecraft's *Maria* (1798) is argued to have led the way for feminist theory and for the vindication of the rights of women; Harriet Beecher Stowe's *Uncle Tom's Cabin* (1852) played an effective function in furthering the antislavery cause and the abolishment of the slave trade in the United States; Helen Hunt Jackson's novel *Ramona* (1885) had a political effect on the way American society viewed Native Americans; and Arthur Morrison's *A Child of the Jago* (1896), and any of Charles Dickens' novels for that matter, impacted housing and child labor laws considerably. These examples may suffice in demonstrating how literature can represent a catalyst for consciousness change in their respective cultures, and most importantly, to Freirean praxis and tangible changes in society. The ideas in the texts represented conscientization, while the subsequent political action, taken by "awakened" individuals, represented the praxis.

That a literary text can represent a cerebral and creative mediator that can change culture is illuminated by Hubert Zapf's work. For Zapf, "[l]iterature draws its cognitive and creative potential from a threefold dynamic in its relationship to the larger cultural system—a cultural-critical metadiscourse, an imaginative counterdiscourse, and a reintegrative interdiscourse" (2010: 138). He explains that:

> Literature is thus, on the one hand, a sensorium for what goes wrong in a society, for the biophobic, life-paralyzing implications of one-sided forms of consciousness and civilizational uniformity, and it is, on the other hand, a medium of constant cultural self-

renewal, in which the neglected biophilic energies can find a symbolic space of expression and of (re-)integration into the larger ecology of cultural discourses (138).

For critical pedagogy and ecopedagogy, this is crucial. Henry Giroux explains this in a different way when he states that artistic texts "become important as public pedagogies because they play a powerful role in mobilizing meaning, pleasures, and identifications" ("Private"). This, then, provides the reader with epistemological and ontological understandings, considerations that were potentially hidden or invisible. Italo Calvino confirms: Literature "gives a voice to whatever is without a voice, when it gives a name to what as yet has no name, especially to what the language of politics excludes or attempts to exclude" (qtd. in Re 1990: 153). This significantly empowers the respective literary work, especially in terms of politics and agency, as well as the author as a radical educator or "change agent," to use Karen Blincoe's term.

That this is important for ecocritical discourse as well is also reflected in Frankfurt School scholar Herbert Marcuse's ideas about art outlined in *The Aesthetic Dimension* (1977), which focuses on the categorical imperative: "things must change" (13). Marcuse claims that art can challenge accepted truths in the existing reality by focusing on its capacity to represent reality *and* to estrange reality. He argues that "the truth of art lies in this: that the world really is as it appears in the work of art" (xii), but that is also lies "in its power to break the monopoly of established reality (i.e., of those who established it) to define what is real" (9). He then explains that "in this rupture, which is the achievement of the aesthetic form, the fictitious world of art appears as true reality" (9). This "true reality" established in the world of art, "is that of another Reality Principle, of estrangement—and only as estrangement does art fulfill a cognitive function: it communicates truths not communicable in any other language; it contradicts" (10). This, then, has positive implications for the power of literature in relation to epistemology and ontology. Terry Eagleton espouses this power:

> If literature matters today, it is chiefly because it seems to many conventional critics one of the few remaining places where, in a divided, fragmented world, a sense of universal value may still be incarnate, and where, in a sordidly material world, a rare glimpse of transcendence can still be attained (Eagleton 2000: 208).

This transcendence and depictions of alternative realities and truth is crucial, and so is the connection of art to ethics and values.

Moreover, John Carey, in *What Good are the Arts?* (2005) makes an interesting case for the power of literature and its transformative effects, boldly claiming: "Only literature can moralise" (181). This view echoes many literary critics who deem that literature is an optimal vehicle for the internalization of moral beliefs. For example John Gardner, in *On Moral Fiction* (1977), claims that "art is essentially and primarily moral—that is, life-giving—moral in its process of creation and moral in what it says" (15). Noël Carroll, in "Art, Narrative, and Moral Understanding," explains that we are "naturally inclined to speak of [literature] in moral terms." He states that "certain kinds of artworks are designed to engage us morally, and with those kinds of artworks, it makes sense for us to surround them with ethical discussion and to assess them morally," and, thus, that "it is natural for us to think about and to discuss narratives in terms of ethics, because narratives, due to the kinds of things they are, awaken, stir up, and engage our moral powers of recognition and judgment" (1999: 141).

Although we need to be critically wary of such bold and essentialist assumptions about the role and function of art, and suspicious about any discussion of art representing "truth," it is useful to keep these claims in mind when discussing and promoting ecopedagogical texts. It is worth noting that narratives can function in relation to ethics because to understand morality, readers engage in a social process through reading the text, consciously and unconsciously, asking questions and analyzing different perspectives, which engages their moral compass, as well as their powers of empathy and compassion. The narrative, in this way, forces individuals to think, but also to *feel*. Arnold Weinstein, in *A Scream Goes Through the House: What Literature Teaches Us About Life* (2004), concludes: "Without literature, we would be bereft and impoverished creatures, denizens of a flat and dimensionless world, a world with no more depth than a photograph, that has no more scope than a résumé or a medical report. Art and literature go *in*" (xxiii, emphasis added). This ability to go *in* is a result of literature being able to appeal to values: to emotion, to empathy, to what it means to be human, to recognize that which is around us, and to understand what ramifications result from our actions.

Thus, it is the medium of literature that can deliver in this regard: it represents a pedagogical, ideological, and political tool; it appeals to values, morality, emotion, and the imagination, and thus, has a significant impact on human cognition, consciousness and the conscience. As such, it plays an important role in critical pedagogy in terms of leading the reader, or student, to developing new critical thinking skills, and new understandings that can lead to praxis. Most importantly, all of these aspects transpire through form: through language, imagery, exposition, plot, setting, characterization, dialogue, free indirect speech, as well as other aspects studied by philology, hermeneutics, and semiotics. The reader is engaged through "the suspension of disbelief," the enchantment of the story, the narrative. However, for an ecoliterary text to be effective in synthesizing the sciences and humanities, it needs to fulfill some further, crucial functions.

Ecopedagogy, Ecoliteracy, and Effective Ecopedagogic Principles of Learning

To touch upon the issues discussed above in relation to science, David Orr claims that "this crisis cannot be solved by the same kind of education that helped create the problems" (1992: 83). The problem is, as Arran Stibbe and Heather Luna explain, that "educational policy tends, even now, to revolve around twentieth-century skills—skills for commercial innovation, further industrialization of society, economic growth, international competitiveness, and financial prosperity" (2011: 12). The question thus arises as to how we construct a pedagogy of ecology/science/sustainability that can facilitate epistemological as well as ontological change. Garrard advocates that we need "a progressive pedagogy in which the keynote of student-centered learning is *responsibility* rather than *entitlement*" (2012: 3). We need to devise a pedagogy that focuses on planting seeds in the student/reader's consciousness in order to awaken their conscience, and lead them to action. This leads me to the ecological principles needed in order to teach for environmental stability.

In order to teach new skills, especially those surrounding the discourse of sustainability, and in order for ecopedagogy to foster conscientization and praxis, terms of ecopedagogy and teaching for sustainability, I maintain that students need to engage in a multifaceted process. They need to: develop a more future-oriented perspective on their own lives and events in the wider world; identify and envision alternative futures that are more just and sustainable; exercise their critical thinking skills and creative imagination more effectively; participate in more thoughtful and informed decision-making in the present; and "engage in active and responsible citizenship in the local and global community, on behalf of present and future generations" (Hicks 1999: 141). Moreover, a progressive ecopedagogical methodology should:

- highlight holistic and interdisciplinary approaches that stress empathy for nature and that re-enchant and reinvigorate positive affirmations of life
- represent a counterhegemonic critical position with the aim to demystify the normalized ideology (anthropocentricism, consumer capitalism, and neoliberalism)
- develop the reader's ability to ask "what then?" (Orr 1999) or "what ought to be?" (Prinz, 2007; Clark, 2011)
- provide moral and ethical guidance (Prinz 2007; Clark 2011)
- advocate pro-social behavior (Hoffman 1983; Eisenberg 2000)
- enhance the ability to recognize interconnections (Strachan 2011)
- stress "aspects of dialogicity and recurring occasions of negotiation" (Bartosch 2010)
- affect readers at psychological and cognitive levels (Stibbe & Luna 2011)

- engage "learners in personal reflection, dialogue and collaborative action required to put futures thinking into practice." (Wayman 2011)
- be critical, ethical, creative, inclusive, and systemic (Sterling 2011)
- critique the foundations of happiness (Morris & Martin 2011)
- stress "intuition, imagining, wisdom, spirituality and holism" (Blincoe 2011)
- provide "political strategies for reinventing the world" (Kahn 2010).

However, to return to my thesis, I wonder to what extent these principles can be applied to a reading of literature, or rather, how literary texts can be seen to be the perfect vehicle to teach and learn these skills. Although I have outlined already how I think literature can be a powerful didactic and epistemic tool, for the purposes of ecoliteracy and ecological education it must be a *specific* type of literature, which brings me to my last section about ecoliterary texts. I am interested in texts that can play a leading role in consilience and in ecopedagogy, those similar to John Parham's notion of novels that might inform a "humanist ecocriticism." These are text that: are scientifically valid and credible; educate to create and "maintain some semblance of deep ecological affinity for other species and/or the landscape/environment as a whole" (2011: 26); investigate the human connection to ecology, especially in terms of the responsibilities humans have in providing solutions or "political remedies" to the existing scientific problems (26-7). These exhaustive criteria, as I will demonstrate, represent a better methodology by which to understand ecology and, more importantly for pedagogical purposes, to teach science to students.

Case Study: Ecoliterary Texts

In order to avoid the pitfalls of scientific thinking outlined at the beginning of this paper, it is important to remember that literature has a favored position because of its *form* in the sense that scientific content is being disseminated through story, through narrative, through the dialog of the characters, for example, and not through mechanistic or reductionist scientific fact. This way, the reader engages in the pleasurable act of reading fiction, but s/he is learning valuable scientific information at the same time that can lead to a better understanding of science and ecology as well as alternative biocentric ontologies. There are many examples of effective ecoliterary texts, but I would like to focus specifically on Barbara Kingsolver's *Prodigal Summer* (2000) and Margaret Atwood's *Oryx and Crake* (2003) as case studies.

Kingsolver and Atwood as authors and critical thinkers are both extremely interested in ecology and science and the environmental crisis; in terms of intention and motivation, they are both highly political and committed. They can be seen to symbolize the author as "change agent" and "nature endorser"; they represent the committed artist who wields their literature as an ideological, pedagogical and, as I contend, scientific weapon. *Prodigal Summer* and *Oryx and Crake* attempt to portray science realistically when depicting the environmental crisis, whether this is in terms of the danger of bioengineering, pesticide use, species extinction, climate change, pandemics, or overpopulation; but *they are also* narratives, stories that evoke emotion, compassion, morality, values, and ethics. In terms of form, the wealth of scientific issues, real facts, are discussed mostly through character dialog; indeed this is the central medium through which much of the ecological information in both novels is communicated to the reader and not, for example, through an omniscient narrator. Atwood and Kingsolver are particularly effective in terms of their characterization. Although they are essentially disseminating scientific fact, environmentalist philosophy, and ecocritical theory, they are doing so through the natural dialog of characters that the reader has, arguably, identified with. The result is that their ecocritical political agenda (and I think it would be difficult to argue both authors do not have one), is not too heavy-handed, and that this method ultimately renders the texts less overtly polemical whilst still pedagogically and politically effective.

Although there are many passages within these two novels that could be used to highlight the principles of ecoliteracy, a significant scene to outline my case here is a passage in *Prodigal Summer* where two of the protagonists, Garnett Walker and Nannie Rawley, discuss the use of pesticides on their farms and the scientific "Volterra Principle." Garnett Walker represents the anthropocentric, short-sighted, point of view and, in terms of critical pedagogy, he is "illiterate" due to the education about ecology and farming that he received, blindly accepting Western science as it has evolved to date, a symbol of the rigid mechanistic way of thinking about science. Nannie Rawley, on the other hand, represents a much more ecocentric and biophilic ontological position in her approach to farming, and to nature and ecology generally. They understandably have a different way of thinking about pesticide use.

Arguing for the use of pesticides on his farm, Walker explains that he would lose all of "this year's new crosses" if he did not spray the caterpillars that are on his "seedlings like the plague" (274). In her rebuttal, Rawley, who wants to farm organically, explains how his use of pesticides will affect her crops by killing all of her beneficials and pollinators and "songbirds that eat the bugs," calling Walker a "regular death angel" (274). Rawley continues to explain to Walker about bugs and plant eaters and bug eaters, predators and herbivores, and how predator bugs reproduce more slowly than herbivores, but that this is generally normal in nature, if their relationship is undisturbed, due to a predator bug eating "a world of pest bugs in its life"; as Rawley explains, "[t]hey're in balance with each other" (274). However, in reference to the Volterra Principle, she explains:

> When you spray a field with a broad-spectrum insecticide like Sevin, you kill the pest bugs *and* the predator bugs, bang. If the predators and prey are balanced out to start with, and they both get knocked back the same amount, then the pests that survive will *increase* after the spraying, fast, because most of their enemies have just disappeared. And the predators will *decrease* because they've lost most of their food supply. So in the lag between sprayings, you end up boosting the numbers of the bugs you don't want and wiping out the ones you need. And every time you spray, it gets worse (275).

Thus, by explaining the Volterra Principle, Rawley educates her neighbor as to how insecticide use ironically increases pest numbers, and how he had harbored misinformation about ecological science. Important to note in this passage in terms of critical pedagogy is that "Garnett nodded. He found himself listening more carefully than he'd expected" (275); Garnett here has been educated about the truth of pesticide use. More importantly, we need to consider whether the reader is also nodding, and listening more carefully than s/he expected. The reader here has also learned something about the Volterra Principle.

If we take this passage out of its fictional context, the discussion about the Volterra Principle and the detrimental use of pesticides can come across as "the dry language of scientific discourse," to use Sheldrake's terms. However, this is exactly where literature and the humanities can play such a significant role. By the time this passage occurs in the novel, the reader has long been exposed to the dynamic characters of Nannie Rawley and Garnett Walker; this scene comes late in the novel and you can feel the tension between them and their different ways of thinking about the world and science/ecology. The reader is probably curious about how their differences and diametrically opposed ideologies are going to culminate and climax. The reader can hear them speaking as the characters have become entrenched in the reader's consciousness and as their dialog comes across as a completely natural and fluid part of the narrative. Of note here, however, is that the scientific dialog, although perhaps dry outside of the text, is incredibly salient. Kingsolver, however, communicates this creatively and imaginatively via her characters. The result is that this leads to affectivity in that it resonates much more with the individual reader than if he or she were reading scientific discourse. The cold, hard facts of science are here, as well as throughout the novel, subtly communicated through humor, compassion, empathy, values, ethics, and most importantly, through *story*. This is the value of the ecoliterary text.

Margaret Atwood's *Oryx and Crake* is a further example of how fictional literature can play a leading role in disseminating scientific information and ecological knowledge. As mentioned earlier, Atwood has a robust interest in science: "I grew up among the scientists—'the boys at the lab' mentioned in the Acknowledgements [in *Oryx and Crake*] are the graduate students and post-docs who worked with my father in the late 1930s and early 1940s at his forest-insect research station in northern Quebec, where I spent my early childhood" ("Perfect Storm"). She explains that several of her close relatives, including her brother, are scientists, "and the main topic at the annual family Christmas dinner is likely to be intestinal parasites or sex hormones in mice, or, when that makes the non-scientists too queasy, the nature of the Universe" (ibid). She admits to reading Stephen Jay Gould and Edward Wilson for pleasure, and keeps a keen eye on the latest scientific inventions and trends in popular science, biology and ecology. Her oft cited *Oryx and Crake* explicates her scientific knowledge, especially in relation to the pertinent ecological questions pertaining to the state of the earth today.

Indeed, the novel is rife with scientific allusions, and Atwood is quick to point out that the science in *Oryx and Crake* is not "science fiction" *per se*:

> Like *The Handmaid's Tale*, *Oryx and Crake* is a speculative fiction, not a science fiction proper. It contains no intergalactic space travel, no teleportation, no Martians. As with *The Handmaid's Tale*, it invents nothing we haven't already invented or started to invent. Every novel begins with a *what if*, and then sets forth its axioms. The *what if* of Oryx and Crake is simply, *What if we continue down the road we're already on? How slippery is the slope? What are our saving graces? Who's got the will to stop us?* ("Perfect Storm," emphases original).

An example from *Oryx and Crake* that elucidates some complications that can come from science can be seen in the passage when Crake is taking Jimmy on a tour of Watson-Crick and they visit the "NeoAgriculturals" Department. Donning bio-suits, they are given a tutorial about cultured meat grown from stem cells from one of the biotechnicians: "What they were looking at was a large bulblike object that seemed to be covered with stippled whitish-yellow skin. Out of it came twenty thick fleshy tubes, and at the end of each tube another bulb was growing" (237). Explaining to Crake and a horrified Jimmy that what they were looking at were essentially "chicken parts," or chickens without any heads, the technician explains that there is

> No need for added growth hormones... the high growth rate's built in. You get chicken breasts in two weeks—that's a three-week improvement on the most efficient low-light, high-density chicken farming operation so far devised. And the animal-welfare freaks won't be able to say a word, because this thing feels no pain. (238)

Through its depiction of bioengineering, genetic transformations, and biotechnological advancements, especially in terms of the dangerous 'bobkittens' and 'wolvdogs' who begin to act out of control (192-3), the novel illuminates the dangers of scientific progress. Atwood delves into many different scientific issues such as depleting resources (138-9), extinction (261-2), and the overall problems with science: "The whole world is now one vast uncontrolled experiment —the way it always was, Crake would have said—and the doctrine of unintended consequences is in full spate" (267). However, important for my purposes here is that Atwood, like Kingsolver, is disseminating scientific knowledge to the reader in the form of fiction. Indeed, the artificially-engineered meat she depicts in this passage and throughout the novel is based on scientific reality,[1] but communicated to the reader through character dialog and imaginative fiction. This is the role of the ecoliterary text.

More importantly in terms of critical pedagogy, however, is that both novels end openly as the authors place the reader in a position of responsibility to participate, to take responsibility to end the story, to transform any Freirean conscientization that was sparked during the reading into praxis as the last lines are read. Through their reading of the text, the "student" has received much scientific information but this is only significant in terms of being the seed for critical thinking, and for thinking that can lead to some sort of action. This, too, is the role of the ecoliterary text. Having acquired a position of responsibility, the reader is induced to act; ultimately, this is its ecopedogical success, especially in terms of *practical* ecocriticism. A brief analysis of the endings of these two novels will underline how they are effective ecoliterary texts.

Firstly, at the end of *Oryx and Crake*, the protagonist Jimmy, or Snowman, is standing in the bushes deciding whether to shoot the humans he has stumbled across, or to join them; should he return to the Crakers and carry on Crake's project, or neglect his responsibilities for them and arguably the future of the world? He is torn:

> "What do you want me to do?" he whispers to the empty air.
> It's hard to know.
> > *Oh Jimmy, you were so funny.*
> > *Don't let me down.*
> From habit he lifts his watch; it shows him its blank face.
> Zero hour, Snowman thinks. Time to go. (Atwood 2003: 432-3)

Atwood here positions the reader to ask what next? What ought to be? Zero hour. Time to go. What will *you* do? How will *you* react with your newly gleaned knowledge? How have the words on the page affected you throughout this dystopian, yet very prescient, novel? You need to make the choice. Atwood does not prescribe solutions or a course of action; the reader must do this. In terms of Freirean critical pedagogy, this is key: the "student" must think

---

1   To see how meat is being engineered from test tubes, see for example:
     http://www.smh.com.au/world/science/tuck-into-some-soggy-pork-straight-out-of-the-test-tube-20091130-k177.html

critically and must be making choices that they have arrived at independently; it is only through this process that they have become critical.

The ending of Kingsolver's *Prodigal Summer* is also significant in terms of ecopedagogy. The final chapter is focalized by a coyote mother who has been a central ecological symbol throughout the novel. The last lines of the novel read:

> If someone in this forest had been watching her—a man with a gun, for instance, hiding inside a copse of leafy beech trees—he would have noticed how quickly she moved up the path, attending the ground ahead of her feet, so preoccupied with her solitary search that she appeared unaware of his presence. He might have watched her for a long time, until he believed himself and this other restless life in his sight to be the only two creatures left here in this forest of dripping leaves, breathing in some separate atmosphere that was somehow more rarefied and important than the world of air silently exhaled by the leaves all around them.
>
> But he would have been wrong. Solitude is a human presumption. Every quiet step is thunder to beetle life underfoot, a tug of impalpable thread on the web pulling mate and predator to prey, a beginning or an end. Every choice is a world made new for the chosen. (Kingsolver 2000: 443-4)

The reader does not know whether Eddie Bondo, the coyote and wolf hunter, is watching, and whether he will shoot the coyote, or whether Deanna's continual efforts to educate him in terms of the interconnectedness of the ecosystem will have changed his mind about killing animals for human profit. More importantly here, the significance of this ending is about the effect Deanna's ecological knowledge has had on the *reader* who is forced into deciding here whether *they* agree with Kingsolver's protagonist's biocentric position, or Bondo's anthropocentric position. The choice has to be made, and while the whole novel makes a convincing argument for accepting the former, the choice is still with the reader. Thus, it still very much encourages the reader to make an active decision. *Prodigal Summer*, like *Oryx and Crake*, does not end in a closed circle with a trite clichéd utopian solutions or dystopian visions. Both novels are open, ripe with potentiality, and empower the reader with critical choice, a crucial aspect of ecopedagogical praxis.

Conclusion

> Acts of the imagination—literature and the arts—can help guide a society through crisis
> lest it slump into cultural desolation and economic depression. [...] deride and ignore the
> power of the imagination to our peril.
> - Alex Hunt, "The Ecology of Narrative" (183)

Of course there is currently no data that can empirically verify how the
imagination operates, how Freirean conscientization or reader response
functions, and whether reading a novel can truly affect our cognition, feelings,
or behavior, and make us scientifically and ecologically aware. However, many
cognitive scientists, such as Keith Oatley (1999; 2011), Peter Stockwell (2002),
Norman Holland (2009), Gerald Edelman (2004), and Lisa Zunshine (2008;
2010; 2012), among many others, are providing a strong case to suggest that
fictional literature *does* impact our consciousness significantly in terms of
emotion, cognition, and the construction of "truisms." Texts rich in moments of
consilience and ecopedagogical principles educate readers in terms of ecological
discourse by inducing them to feel, as well as think, and it is this imbrication
that can fuse the dichotomy between nature and humanity, the human and non-
human, and educate us in terms of our responsibilities in protecting our fragile
earth. Fritjof Capra proclaims that 'in the coming decades, the survival of
humanity will depend on our ecological literacy—our ability to understand the
basic principles of ecology and to live accordingly' ("The New Facts"). Reading
texts like *Oryx and Crake*, or *Year of the Flood*, or Kingsolver's *Prodigal
Summer*, or *The Lorax* for that matter, in conjunction with other forms of
biocentric learning, whether it is in a science lab or by taking a walk through the
forest, will consolidate the issues in the consciousness and *conscience* of the
student. Accentuating the ecoliterary text in mainstream educational practices
not only increases students' awareness of environmental issues and an
interconnection with nature, but it can make them more inclined to act and take
responsibility for decisions that impact the future. I propose that the texts
discussed here, as well as many others, can be seen as media that evade Charles
Snow's notion of the clashing point of 'two subjects, two disciplines, two
cultures' outlook, and that they are representative of what John Brockman calls
"The Third Culture," a space overlapping the old demarcations of the sciences
and humanities. Taught in conjunction with other disciplines, including science,
ecoliterary texts can provide students with a deeper and more critical
understanding of the issues, and, more importantly, their place within the
discourse.

Paul Hart claims that environmental education is on the ascendancy in
Western cultures as we recognize the need for a better understanding of ecology
and the ecological crisis we are facing. He states:

Societies are searching for new narratives that give guidance and inspiration to people and purpose to schooling. Within these narratives, that range from teaching young people to accept the world as it is, to those that encourage critical thinking more distanced from conventional wisdom and intended to change what is wrong, is one that insists on our moral obligation to the planet. (2007: 689)

Kingsolver and Atwood, as well as many others, are providing these narratives, and it is our role as educators to take advantage of the medium of fictional literature and ecoliterary texts to educate our youth in terms of ecological science, to spark their critical thinking, and to empower them with skills that can make a tangible difference in terms of environmental discourse. Schumacher claims that the task of education is "the transmission of ideas of value, of what to do with our lives" (1973: 66). The ecoliterary text, and the incorporation of it into our teaching practice, facilitates this process.

134 Adrian Rainbow

Works Cited

Atwood, Margaret. *Oryx and Crake*. London: Virago, 2003.
— . (2003). "Perfect Storm." http://www.oryxandcrake.co.uk/perfectstorm.asp?p=5. (March 28 2006).
Bartosch, Roman. "Call of the Wild and the Ethics of Narrative Strategies." *Ecozon@* 1.2. (2010). (5 January 2012).
Blincoe, Karen. "Re-educating the Person." *The Handbook of Sustainability Literacy: Skills for a Changing World*. Ed. Arran Stibbe. Totnes: Green Books, 2011. 204-8.
Capra, Fritjof. "The New Facts of Life." http://www.ecoliteracy.org/essays/new-facts-life. (12 July 2011).
Carey, John. *What Good Are the Arts?* London: Faber and Faber, 2005.
Carroll, Noël. "Art, Narrative, and Moral Understanding." *Aesthetics and Ethics*: *Essays at the Intersection*. Ed. Jerrold Levinson. Cambridge: Cambridge UP, 1998. 126-60.
Eagleton, Terry. *Literary Theory: An Introduction*. Oxford: Blackwell, 2000.
Edelman, Gerald. *Wider Than the Sky: The Phenomenal Gift of Consciousness*. London: Yale University Press, 2004.
Freire, Paulo. *Pedagogy of the Oppressed*. London: Penguin, 1970.
Gardner, John. *On Moral Fiction*. New York: Basic Books, 1977.
Garrard, Greg (2011). "Ecocriticism: The Ability to Investigate Cultural Artefacts from an Ecological Perspective." *The Handbook of Sustainability Literacy: Skills for a Changing World*. Ed. Arran Stibbe Totnes: Green Books, 2011. 19-24.
— . *Teaching Ecocriticism and Green Cultural Studies*. London: Palgrave Macmillan, 2012.
Giroux, Henry A. "Private Satisfactions and Public Disorders: Fight Club, Patriarchy, and the Politics of Masculine Violence". http://www.henryagiroux.com/online_articles/fight_club.htm. (14 June 2005).
Goldbard, Arlene. *New Creative Community: The Art of Cultural Development*. Oakland: New Village Press, 2006.
Harding, Stephan. "Gaia Awareness: Awareness of the animate qualities of the Earth." *The Handbook of Sustainability Literacy: Skills for a Changing World*. Ed. Arran Stibbe Totnes: Green Books, 2011. 89-93.
Hart, Paul. "Environmental Education." *Handbook for Research in Science Education*. Eds. S. K. Abell & N. Lederman New Jersey: Erlbaum, 2007.
Hicks, David. "Education for the Future." *Pedagogy of the Earth: Education for a Sustainable Future*. Eds. Carlos Hernandez & Rashmi Mayur. *Pedagogy of the Earth: Education for a Sustainable Future*. Mumbai: International Institute for Sustainable Future, 1999. 140-50.
Holland, Norman N. *Literature and the Brain*. Psyart Foundation, 2009.
Hunt, Alex. "The Ecology of Narrative: Annie Proulx's *That Old Ace in the Hole* as Critical Regionalist Fiction." *The Geographical Imagination of Annie Proulx*. Ed. Alex Hunt. *The Geographical Imagination of Annie Proulx*. Plymouth: Rowman & Littlefield Publishers, 2009.
Kahn, Richard. *Critical Pedagogy, Ecoliteracy, and Planetary Crisis*. New York: Peter Lang, 2010.
Kingsolver, Barbara. *Prodigal Summer*. New York: Harper Collins, 2000.
Love, Glen A.. *Practical Ecocriticism*. London: University of Virginia Press, 2003.
Marcuse, Herbert. *The Aesthetic Dimension: Towards a Critique of Marxist Aesthetics*. Boston: Beacon Press, 1977.
McLaren, Peter. *Che Guevara, Paulo Freire, and the Pedagogy of Revolution*. Oxford: Rowman & Littlefield Publishers, Inc, 2000.

Morris, Dick and Stephen Martin. "Complexity, Systems Thinking and Practice: Skills and Techniques for Managing Complex Systems." *The Handbook of Sustainability Literacy: Skills for a Changing World*. Ed. Arran Stibbe. Totnes: Green Books, 2011. 156-64.

Oatley, Keith. "Why Fiction may be Twice as True as Fact: Fiction as Cognitive and Emotional Stimulation." *Review of General Psychology* 3.2 (1999). 101-7.

—. *Such Stuff as Dreams: The Psychology of Fiction*. Chichester: Wiley-Blackwell, 2011.

Orr, David W. *Ecological Literacy: Education and the Transition to a Postmodern World*. New York: State University of New York Press, 1992.

— . "Ecological Literacy." *Pedagogy of the Earth: Education for a Sustainable Future*. Eds. Carlos Hernandez & Rashmi Mayur. Mumbai: International Institute for Sustainable Future, 1999. 52-65.

Parham, John (2011). "'For you, pollution'. The Victorian Novel and Human Ecology: Benjamin Disraeli's Sibyl and Elizabeth Gaskell's Mary Barton." *Green Letters: Studies in Ecocriticism*. 14 (2011). 23-38.

Prinz, Jesse J. *The Emotional Construction of Morals*. Oxford: Oxford UP, 2007.

Re, Lucia. *Calvino and the Age of Neorealism: Fables of Estrangement*. Stanford: Stanford UP, 1990.

Schumacher, Ernst Friedrich. *Small is Beautiful: A Study of Economics as if People Mattered*. London: Abacus, 1973.

Sheldrake, Rupert. *The Science Delusion: Freeing the Spirit of Enquiry*. London: Hodder & Stoughton, 2012.

Slingerland, Edward. *What Science Offers the Humanities: Integrating Body and Culture*. New York: Cambridge UP, 2008.

Sterling, Stephen. "Ecological Intelligence: Viewing the World Relationally." *The Handbook of Sustainability Literacy: Skills for a Changing World*. Ed. Arran Stibbe. Totnes: Green Books, 2011.

Stibbe, Arran and Heather Luna. "Introduction." *The Handbook of Sustainability Literacy: Skills for a Changing World*. Ed. Arran Stibbe. Totnes: Green Books, 2011. 9-16.

Strachan, Glenn. "Systems Thinking: The Ability to Recognise and Analyse the Interconnections within and between Systems'. *The Handbook of Sustainability Literacy: Skills for a Changing World*. Ed. Arran Stibbe. Totnes: Green Books, 2011. 84-8.

"Student Motivations and Attitudes". http://serc.carleton.edu/NAGTWorkshops/affective/environment.html. (12 April 2009).

Wayman, Sue. "Futures Thinking: The Ability to Envision Scenarios of a More Desirable Future." *The Handbook of Sustainability Literacy: Skills for a Changing World*. Ed. Arran Stibbe. Totnes: Green Books, 2011. 94-8.

Weinstein, Arnold. *A Scream Goes Through the House: What Literature Teaches Us About Life*. New York: Random House, 2004.

Zapf, Hubert. "Ecocriticism, Cultural Ecology, and Literary Studies" in *Ecozon@* 1.1 (2010). 136-47. (5 January 2012).

Zunshine, L. (ed.) *Getting Inside Your Head: What Cognitive Science Can Tell Us About Popular Culture*. Baltimore: John Hopkins UP, 2012.

— . *Introduction to Cognitive Cultural Studies*. Baltimore: Johns Hopkins UP, 2010.

— . *Strange Concepts and the Stories They Make Possible: Cognition, Culture, Narrative*. Baltimore: Johns Hopkins UP, 2008.

Scientific Encounters in Literature
How the 'Two Cultures' Can Profit from Each Other In and Outside the Classroom

Celestine Caruso (Cologne)

Introduction

In a speech that would open a new interdisciplinary controversy known as the "two cultures debate," Charles Pierce Snow lamented that it was "bizarre how little of the twentieth-century science has been assimilated into twentieth-century art" (Snow 1959: 172). According to Snow, "the intellectual life of the whole of western society [is] increasingly being split into two polar groups," namely that of the literary intellectuals and that of the scientists. Moreover, since both groups share a pronounced "anti-feeling of the other" (171), their attitudes are so different that on an intellectual, moral and emotional level they cannot find any common ground (169). Snow's speech not only initiated a debate that would create a field of interdisciplinary studies in science and literature, it also led to numerous studies that researched the differences in critical thinking skills of students of the sciences and the humanities (Williamson 2011). Findings of these studies, which were mainly conducted from the 1960s to the 1980s, seem to go in line with those stereotypical distinctions frequently used in the past, namely that science aims at gaining a so called "objective truth" and explaining natural observation processes by means of experimental, inquiry-based methodology, whereas literary intellectuals, on the other hand "aim at interpreting the world through the expression of the artist" (O'Hear 1989: 228).

Rather than following discussions about how science and literature are different, it is much more important to focus on similarities: how do science and literature converge? How are they mutually shaped by culture and how do they shape culture in return? How are they part of the same discourse (cf. Levine

1987, Flohr 1999)? Literary fiction, and novels in particular, have always shown that science and literature are interconnected not only because they are both human activities that are produced within the same cultures but also because both deal with topics such as the quest for "origins," the relationship between culture and the individual, or the evolution of the human mind.

Whereas nineteenth century literature has been abundantly analyzed regarding the role of scientific aspects, such as Darwin's theory of evolution in the works of Gillian Beer, John Chapple, and George Levine, twentieth-century writing has attracted less consideration in this debate. A closer look at twentieth century literature reveals that, contrary to Snow's statement and his 'two cultures' claim, the first half of the twentieth century shows a great interaction of science and literature, manifesting itself in the evolution of 'new' genres such as science fiction.

Apart from outlining different ways in which science is vividly represented in literature from the nineteenth century to the present, this paper illustrates the potential that science (in) fiction contains when used in a pedagogical context. The interdisciplinary nature of scientific topics in literature contributes to the classroom of young learners as it contains a variety of different learning outcomes, which will be extrapolated in the following with the help of different literary examples. The paper neglects those aspects of ecopedagogical and environmental debate that address topics of global eco-crisis and focuses on opportunities that need to be grasped whenever the meeting of the 'two cultures' is a friendly one. I will argue that even if Snow's critique is slightly outdated, it has not only laid the foundation of the two cultures debate, but it can be further regarded as one of the basic motives for ecocriticism and therefore ecopedagogy as such.

What Do Scientific Encounters in Literature Include?

The literary examples discussed in this paper have a strong emphasis on scientific and technological aspects and may include gothic fiction, (hard) science fiction, utopias, dystopias but also social comedies, or contemporary popular cultural products. Yet, these sometimes fundamentally diverging literary representations of science have one thing in common: scientific landmark events as well as industrial and technological progress, from Galileo's first telescope (1616) or Darwin's theory of evolution (1859) to Rutherford's foundation of nuclear energy in the 1930s, are always reflected in literary engagements. Literature reacts on notions of scientific progress, for instance, by pointing out dangers that formerly unknown technoscientific forces could impose on our society. It plays with hopes and fears of irreversible change brought about by scientific progress. Not only does literature incorporate scientific discoveries on the level of content, but it addresses the needs of societies that are constantly challenged by scientific progress. Thus, it offers means to critically engage with those effects of technoscience that science does not dare to express. These needs could be expressed by providing a critical perspective on the consequences of scientific progress which would "indicate wrong answers, and why they're wrong, as well as suggesting right answers and possibilities!" (Westfahl 1998: 195).

Hard sciences and literary fiction are interconnected and influence each other. At least in part, scientific research is shaped by the needs of society, which find expression in art and literature. Thus, it becomes relevant "[h]ow the culture tells stories, that is, imagines its life, subtly informs the way science asks questions, arrives at the theories that reshape the culture that informed them" (Levine 1988: 4).

Even if at first sight one may think that science has more influence on literature than the other way round, there is more than enough evidence which proves otherwise. Not only are science and literature elements of the same discourse, draw from and are shaped by the same cultural context (Levine 1987, Beer 1983, Gould 1997). Scientists, moreover, are increasingly willing to welcome literary support when they wish to popularize their views, as can be seen with Francis Crick, Stephen Jay Gould or Stephen Hawking (Limon 1990: 3).

Evolutionary biologist Stephen J. Gould (1997) stated that because of the strict limitations placed on scientific writing, "fiction can often provide a truer and deeper account of empirical subjects than genres supposedly dedicated to factual accounting" (105). Absurdly enough, especially the mother of hard sciences, physics, provides most material for fictional, imaginative scenarios, as for example the Higgs bosons that apparently jump back and forth in time and space, disappear and reappear in different places. Time travel in H.G. Well's *The Time Machine* or the communicative gadgets in *Star Trek* seem to be almost prophetic: "Star Trek is theory, NASA the practice" (Penley 1997: 19).

If this is the case, if not only science influences literature but literature also influences science, why can we not apply these findings to a pedagogical context? Why not teach literature through science and science through literature? As Levine emphasized, literature needs to be regarded as the laboratory of science. From this point of view literature becomes just as much a source of knowledge as science (Levine 1988: vii). Scientific discoveries make their claims in the same way as great literature does and "to get to the heart of the culture one can travel the road of science, the road of literature, or—better—both" (Levine 1987: 25). Of course this does not mean that the imaginations presented in literature need to be accepted as truth, but it rather implies that we can profit from situations where the two cultures meet.

The Development of Scientific Encounters from the Nineteenth to the Twentieth Century

Novelists of the nineteenth century such as Elizabeth Gaskell, Thomas Hardy, George Eliot and Charles Dickens often included scientific aspects like evolution and technological progress in their narrations, abundantly and brilliantly analyzed by Beer, Chapple, Levine, Greenberg, Brody, Postlethwaite and many others. This abundance of scientific encounters in literature had several reasons:

The nineteenth century was so rich in 'scientific fiction' because scientists were inhabitants of common culture and not isolated in laboratories yet (Greenberg 2009), as it was apparently the case in the first half of the twentieth century, Snow's time, when the language of science was too technical to be understood by the 'common' reader. Scientific knowledge was widely available and accessible for the average reader, as main scientific works such as Darwin's *On the Origin of Species* (1859) "still shared a common language with educated readers and writers of their time" (Beer 1983: 6).

Scientific publications from the twentieth century to today on the other hand have shown a strong tendency of being extremely specific, making use of scientific terms that only experts on that particular field are capable of understanding. Darwin's *Origin*, by contrast, had a vast readership. Nineteenth century science differed from twentieth century science not only in aspects of language, but also on the nature of scientific discoveries.

The nineteenth century was full of scientific discoveries, which were "visibly reshaping the society in the form of new technology in such areas as transportation, lighting, communication, medical treatment and mass production" (Flohr 1999: 3). Furthermore, it was in the course of the nineteenth century that the speciation of sciences such as physics, chemistry, biology or geology evolved from the general term of 'natural philosophy'. The term science was not used until William Wherwell's *Philosophy of Inductive Science*, published in 1840. Darwin's principles of evolutionary theory and the origin of men, which, in Freudian terms, inflicted the 'second blow on human pride'[1], had a violent impact on the culture of his age. Scientific landmark events of the twentieth century were equally fundamental as Darwin's theory of evolution but were often concerned with the 'micro-levels' of biology, chemistry and physics.

---

1   The first blow to human pride or narcissism was inflicted by the Copernican Revolution and the third by Freud himself and his psychosexual theory (Freud 1916).

Einstein's theory of relativity or the two fundamental laws of thermodynamics are less part of 'common knowledge' as they require a more specific understanding of the respective matter.

The apparent isolation of science in the twentieth century probably inspired Snow's 'two cultures' thesis. However, a closer investigation of early twentieth century literature reveals that science left indeed a strong impact on literary productions, which seems to contradict Snow's claim that little of twentieth-century science has been adapted to art.

Most obviously and perhaps stereotypically, science in literature can be found in science fiction, dystopian and utopian narratives. Even if the definition and distinction between these three literary genres is a complicated and controversial task, as they sometimes overlap in themes and methods, there seems to be some consensus on the question of origin. Whereas utopian literature stretches back at least to Thomas More's *Utopia* (1516), the first science fiction novel can be generally traced back to the nineteenth century, namely to Mary Shelley's *Frankenstein* (1818), even if the term 'science fiction' was not coined until the 1930s, by Hugo Gernsback's launching of *Amazing Stories: The Magazine of Scientifiction* (cf. Sawyer and Wright 2011).

The imagined worlds of science fiction generally operate on the basis of physical laws but "they subordinate those principles to changes caused by rationally explicable developments, primarily scientific or technological" (Booker 2009: 252). Their (futuristic) speculations about a specific technological or scientific aspect are related to more general ruminations on the possible development of human nature, society and culture brought about by this specific aspect while remaining as plausible as possible concerning the speculative element (cf. Kramer 2003: 186). In Richard Matheson's *I am Legend* (1954), for example, the specific aspect is the intrusion of a parasitic bacterium that changes human nature and physiology and ultimately leads to the global extinction of *homo sapiens* due to our species' incapacity of adapting to the invasive parasite. The commentary on society that the text provides, its depiction of loss, trauma and the struggle for survival, however, are represented in a realist manner and thus exemplifies science fiction's and dystopia's strive for plausibility.

What science, science studies and science fiction have in common is that they all supply potential approaches of how the material world is perceived, how we perceive ourselves and how the process of 'constructing knowledge' works:

> If at its worst s[cience] f[iction] can be the literature of all the worst aspects of science — technocratism, singularity of vision, domination of nature, inserting a new gadget into the same world—then at its best it might be considered the literature of science studies— concerned with the social consequences of developments in science and technology, insisting on dialectic exchange between the novum and the larger social world, sensitive to

the contingency of knowledge, and open to new ways of seeing and being. (Vint 2009: 421)

Surprisingly science fiction as a 'genre in its own right' started developing during the first half of the twentieth century, a time where according to Snow the two cultures apparently had nothing in common, as scientific discoveries were too specialized to be accessible to a common reader. This neglect on Snow's part could be explained by the fact that science fiction, as it is often the case with a body of literature that is on its way of forming a 'labeled' genre, was connoted as pulp fiction:

> Like many 'popular' forms, [science fiction] suffered from its association with mass-market modes of production such as pulp magazines and cheap paperback, its use of stereotypical characters, melodramatic plots, and prose that often veered between the colourless and the hyperbolic. (Sawyer and Wright 2011: 1)

This implies that this 'new' genre was not yet considered by literary critics as material that deserved a second, closer look. With time, however, several factors brought about the acceptance of science fiction as literature 'worthy of' academic discussion and analysis, some of which derived from academia and others from literary production within the genre itself: during the 1930s and 1940s "the brash, commercial mode of writing" (Parrinder 1980: xiv) of American pulp literature with its "superscience and sensationalism" (Sawyer and Wright 2011: 2), crudeness in style and language, was replaced by observable refinement of style, plotting, characterization, psychological and scientific depth. Solemn speculations of possible futures showed more self-consciousness in the "formal, narrative, linguistic and thematic experimentation of the New Waves in Britain and the United States in the mid 1960s" (2). Gender roles and gender identities, the exploration of "post-human landscapes," "virtual realities" inspired by computer science were further included in the decades after (cf. 2).

Another reason for the recognition of science fiction as a potential field of interest for literary scholars originated from within academia. The British cultural studies movement of the 1950s and 1960s replaced the ideal of 'high culture' as the driving force behind cultural progress with a redefined concept of 'culture' includes popular cultural products, such as popular literature, vaudeville, TV-drama, musicals, pop music etc.

The slow recognition of science fiction in academia might explain why Snow was not aware of this indeed vivid interaction between the sciences and literature. The genre of science fiction had not yet been regarded as 'literary' and still needed to fight its way into the departments of literary studies. Due to its virtual non-existence in the eyes of scholars and literary critics, Snow too was not aware of the great potential that this interdisciplinary literary genre could yield.

It was only later that the general acceptance of popular culture and science fiction in particular eventually opened up school curricula to some extend and resulted in the inclusion of science fiction (-related) texts into the canon, e.g. Huxley's *Brave New World* (1931), Orwell's *Nineteen-Eighty-Four* (1949), Burgess' *A Clockwork Orange* (1962), and Bradbury's *Fahrenheit 451* (1953).

Science Fiction in the Classroom

The use of science fiction in a classroom context is by no means limited to these, well-known and ever-green literary examples. An important lesson that the history of science fiction from its struggle for recognition until its acceptance into the classroom could teach is that the choice of classroom material needs to be more experimental and innovative. The science in science fiction could be of manifold use in a classroom context.

Science fiction is particularly suitable for children and adolescents as topics in science fiction texts often revolve around the formation of identity and the struggle of finding a place in society while at the same time science fiction has a strong emphasis on science and technology: "Science fiction characters are very likely to be involved in difficult journeys of self-discovery and self-determination as they embark on quests for friendship, freedom, or survival" (Stutler 2011: 46). Stutler points out that science fiction stories are both emotionally involving and intellectually stimulating as they make use of speculations and imagination on the one hand and scientific aspects and methods that the students can engage with on the other. Studying science fiction could motivate the students to phrase inquiries, make speculations and explorations, solve problems, and engage in communicative interactions. Guided by student interests and inclinations, the learning that emerges may be in the form of creative writing, play-acting, future studies, problem-based learning (PBL), or student-developed simulations (cf. Stutler 2011: 47).

Students not only acquire skills how to overcome the aforementioned challenges in society and culture, especially those revealed by scientific research, but "great science fiction can be a springboard to studies of history, Earth and space science, physical science, technology, government, life science, and the environment" (48). Advantages of using science fiction literature in a classroom context moreover include debates about the cons and pros of highly advanced technology, cloning, personal freedom, and medical research. Stutler (2011) further states that "students who are fascinated with the recently announced 'invisibility technology' may avidly pursue knowledge of electromagnetic waves and nanotechnology and use the elements of science fiction to write their own 'What if?' stories" (48).

The use of science fiction is not necessary limited to the literary classroom. One remarkable example of how literature influenced science and science fiction was actually included into biology classes of high schools is shown in Bixler's paper, "Teaching evolution with the aid of science fiction," published in *The American Biology Teacher* (2007). Bixler specifies several ways of how to use the interdisciplinarity of science fiction in the classroom that so far had only been concerned with the mediation of scientific facts. In analyzing short stories, novels, cartoons or films that are based on scientific principles, students could test their scientific knowledge by verifying or falsifying evolutionary mechanisms such as natural selection or the process of speciation.

In the *Outer Limits* episode "The Sixth Finger" (1963), the frustrated miner, Gwyllm Griffiths, volunteers for an experiment that involves an increased exposure to atomic rays, the apparent agents in evolutionary development of organisms. The ray exposure speeds up the evolution of Griffiths' body and mind and results in the growth of a sixth finger on each hand (among other effects). In an analysis of *The Sixth Finger*, students could

> [identify] flaws of the author's evolutionary scenarios, [analyze] what aspects of environment could lead to the adaptations of the organisms, or even whether the species' characteristics are adaptations [as for example the question whether it would be a] necessary adaptation for modern humans to have six fingers on each hand as depicted in the *Outer Limits* episode *The Sixth Finger*. (337)

Similarly, in an analysis of H.G. Wells' *The Time Machine* students could elaborate on mechanisms of adaptation and habitat isolation that, in the novel, lead to speciation of *homo sapiens* into two distinct species, the peaceful but lazy and dependent Eloi and the savage, carnivorous ape-like Morlocks, as Bixler further proposes (338).

Besides, popular fiction such as *Jurassic Park* (Crichton 1990, Spielberg 1994) can be adopted into the biology classroom by examining and verifying or falsifying aspects of cloning that are presented in the novel or film. *Jurassic Park* had a deeper impact on science than Crichton and Spielberg probably intended as it revived the almost fossilized area of paleontological research on the Jurassic and Triassic period and included studies that would provide evidence against the possibility of extracting DNA from a prehistoric mosquito encased in amber. Furthermore, it resulted in a mass production of paleontological documentaries about the fauna and flora of primeval forests. As a consequence, paleontological topics, which before had been considered quite obsolete, were (re)introduced in German biology classes (cf. Dierkes and Scheersoi 2012). As these examples show, the inclusion of science fiction into the classroom can offer new possibilities of testing the students' knowledge and understanding of biological concepts and could be applied after a teaching unit of e.g. evolution or cloning.

Literary analyses would normally not include a testing of the text on its reliability and 'truth'. In this case, however, and in the context of an interdisciplinary approach to teaching science through fiction and fiction through science it is highly beneficial and it offers both a new way of reading to scholars and a new facet of literature to pupils. Moreover, bringing the two cultures together in a biology classroom has learning potentials for both the scientist and the 'literary intellectual'. Not only can students of biology learn how to critically analyze scientific concepts presented in fiction, but by being exposed to the literary fiction of novels, short stories or comics, they would also foster their skills in visual literacy and other literary competences. In an interdisciplinary, pedagogical context, students of literature would have comparable learning outcomes when confronted with scientific encounters in literature as science students do when dealing with literary topics. Of course, in order to be able to identify mistakes or correct aspects in the presented scientific concepts students' (prior) knowledge about, e.g. basic evolutionary concepts needs to be activated. To analyze literature in the context of history can only be successful when it involves the knowledge of history and literature; similarly, to examine biological influences on literature requires a basic understanding of both biological and literary texts. Dealing with scientific fiction in both the biology and the literary classroom includes the increase of scientific competences, the so-called scientific literacy.

In the current curriculum for secondary schools in North Rhine Westphalia (NRW Kernlehrplan: 8) scientific literacy is defined as the knowledge to apply scientific methods, recognize scientific inquiries, to draw conclusions from given evidence about natural phenomena and its modifications imposed by human interference. It is further the prerequisite for the developments of both the individual's and the society's potential (9) when it comes to technological and scientific progress. Basic principles of evolutionary terms such as adaptation, natural selection, mutation, variation etc. are part of the national curriculum as well.

The necessity and importance of having a basic knowledge of scientific concepts such as the evolutionary theory becomes obvious when we regard the repeated "abuse of concepts and terminology coming from mathematics and physics" (Sokal and Bricmont 1998: 4), not only by 'obvious' opponents of evolutionary theory such as creationists but, according to physicist Alan Sokal also by literary critics and postmodern thinkers. Most literary critics are not trained scientists and might therefore lack an informed and balanced understanding of science. While wrong usage of scientific concept is always problematic, Sokal and Bricmont therefore scathingly rail against postmodern

cultural studies in general and constructionism in particular, writing that
scholarship that tries to bring together the 'two cultures' is nothing but
'fashionable nonsense', as the book title (Sokal and Bricomont 1998) already
suggests.

Scientific literacy needs to be a component of general knowledge, deeply
embedded into society and culture in order to avoid abuses of scientific concepts
on the one hand, as previously performed in the field of social Darwinism and
presently propagated by creationists and to improve a mutual understanding of
the 'two cultures' on the other hand. The need of interdisciplinarity when
teaching forms of literature such as science fiction can be a useful tool to
improve the aforementioned scientific literacy that Sokal and Bricmont refer to
as lacking in 'postmodern thinkers' (6).

Similar to science fiction, which often reveals a positive, opportunity-driven
view on scientific research, other, similarly recent genres can be taken into
account in a pedagogical context: Comics and their more fully-fledged, book-
length relative, the graphic novel, evolved around the same time as science
fiction and often also contain elements of science fiction. Furthermore, these
genres that represent a cross between artistic and literary elements equally
struggled for their place in academia and, consequently, school curricula.
Whereas in the 1950s comics were blamed for being a cause of juvenile
delinquency, today the educational potential of both comics and graphic novels,
especially for young adults, has been recognized by numerous pedagogical
studies (e.g. Cary 2004, Carter 2007, Donnerstag and Volkmann 2008,
Eisenmann and Summer 2012, Tabachnick 2009).

Usually associated with a young readership, comics can have an advantageous
influence on the literary socialization of children and teenagers: as Leubner,
Saupe and Richter (2012) argue, most teenagers aged twelve to fifteen years are
generally confronted with a 'reading crisis' that starts towards the end of
primary school and results in a steady decrease of both the interest in and the
actual reading of fiction, and can even be accompanied by an aversion towards
any reading activity in general (78). This crisis could be compensated by
utilizing potentially motivating literature more closely linked to the students'
interests and preferences. Tabachnick (2009) justifies the use of graphic novels
in a pedagogical context, stating that

> [s]tudents enjoy them not only because of their largely—although by no means
> exclusively—contemporary content but also because graphic novels fit students'
> sensibilities at a deep cognitive level. In sequential art, the experience of reading text is
> combined with the experience, omnipresent today on the electronic screen, of viewing:
> and, in good sequential art, the lyricism of poetic word choice is combined with the
> lyricism of striking visual images to create a stunning, hypnotic form of poetry [...]. (4)

Hence, graphic novels not only offer the opportunity to overcome the literary crisis teenagers are confronted with by offering new, potentially motivational literary material. When applied systematically in a pedagogical context, graphic novels can also foster visual literacy—a skill that is crucial in our technology and media driven society. Comics and graphic novels, especially from the 'superhero' subgenre, also frequently deal with scientific topics. In containing science fiction elements, they often represent hopes, fears and scientific speculations of the culture they are produced in.

In a classroom situation comics and graphic novels offer material for a cultural studies based analysis of the American myth of 'the self-made man' and the American (technological) dream. Batman relies on extravagant technology as tool to fight evil as well. As his 'powers' are not the result of a scientific accident but achieved by disciplined and extensive physical training he represents a self-made vigilante who shields Gotham city from evils that arise mainly from within the city's underworld and corruptive powers.

How superhero stories in comics and film have the to potential to increase scientific literacy can be further explored in works such as *The Science of Superheroes* (2002) or *The Science of Supervillains* (2005) by Lois L. Gresh. These popular scientific readings of comics provide the physical, chemical, molecular or evolutionary background knowledge of the used scientific principles and they precisely dissect scientific feasibility that underlies many superhero and supervillain narratives. In *Physics of Superheroes* (2006), James Kakalios, professor of physics and mathematics, discovers that in many cases the comic writers got their science surprisingly right. He provides an engaging commentary while introducing the reader to both classic and cutting-edge concepts in physics, including the question what Superman's strength tells us about Newtonian physics of force, mass and acceleration and how Iceman's and Storm's weather-manipulative powers illustrate the principles of thermodynamics.

In a more concrete classroom context, and with regard to Bixler's aforementioned ideas of how to use science fiction stories in the classroom, the evolutionary concept of mutation presented in the comic *X-Men* could be examined in order to point out mistakes and to investigate the two opposing evolutionary concepts of the saltationists and gradualists. Whereas gradualists claim that evolution proceeds in 'small steps' by a gradual mutation and variation of single genes, saltationists regard mutation as involving 'bigger leaps' that result in visible changes from one generation to the next (cf. Gould, 2002, Gould 2007, Theißen 2009). The superpowers of the *X-Men* are the result of a mutation of the so called X-gene, which activates itself with the onset of the 'mutants' puberty. Thus, the concept of mutation in *X-Men*, leading to extreme change from one generation to the next, can be identified very simply by the pupils as belonging to the 'saltationists' theory of evolution. In a next step it would be possible to let the students creatively rewrite plots in *X-Men* where they correct biological mistakes (Bixler 2007: 337) or apply gradualist patterns of evolution on the mutation that takes place in characters of X-men. In this way their knowledge about particular scientific facts could be assessed while creative skills are fostered. When applied in the classroom, comics and graphic novels that have an emphasis on scientific aspects thus bear potentials of fostering different, interdisciplinary competences such as scientific, literary and visual literacies.

Moving away from Dystopias

Scientific encounters in literature often include dystopia, tragedy and apocalyptic narrative whereas positive depictions seem to be less frequent. Dystopian representations of evolutionary theory in particular are often the result of negative connotations and misunderstandings, e.g. when evolution is understood as regression and degeneration, or when people fear that "there was a savage beneath the skin of every civilized man" (Pykett 2006: 192). Degeneration in this view is the result and symptom of over-civilization and of the pressure of urban modernity (193). Instead of focusing on worst-case scenarios and doom-driven prophecies, some of the optimism that science, often very idealistically, emits needs to be regained.

How contemporary literature that provides a positive image of the scientist or science can foster intercultural competences can be wonderfully explored in Paul Torday's *Salmon Fishing in the Yemen* (2007). As in Ian McEwan's *Enduring Love* (1998), *Salmon Fishing in the Yemen* (2007) also engages in contemporary debates between not only two but three cultures, i.e. science, literature and religion. In McEwan's novel, the characters are exposed to a situation of crisis, which results in a clash of their different world views. *Salmon Fishing in the Yemen* likewise addresses conflicting temperaments and convictions in a situation of crisis that is caused by an apparently unfeasible scientific project: Overcoming his initially severe doubts, scientist and fish expert Dr. Alfred Jones agrees to put the scientifically impossible into practice and to populate the Yemen with salmon. The Yemen is a habitat where salmonids are usually lacking due to entirely unfavorable climate conditions. Salmon, as anadromous species, usually need both cool freshwater for breeding and reproduction and marine water as the smolt migrate to the ocean. However, the Yemen is far too dry and hot to qualify as natural habitat. The project, initially a vision of sheikh and fish(ing) enthusiast Muhammad ibn Zaidi bani Tihama, soon catches the eye of the British news media and government who are desperately searching some positive 'news' about Middle-east relations. To make the colonization of salmon possible, the dry landscape that normally does not possess any permanent rivers but numerous wadis, partially dried river beds, needs to be adapted to the species' needs by building a dam. This dam would create aquatic systems where the salmon could not only survive, but potentially also breed. The adaptation of landscape and environment to a particular species is, in itself, a process that cannot be found in nature, where usually conditions of climate and temperature are the foundations and 'selective mechanisms' of the habitat with its particular species. Science and technology make this 'unnatural' process possible and create an entirely new habitat in a dried-out river bed in the middle of the desert.

The impact on landscape and culture triggers aggression towards the sheik's project of bringing a piece of Western technology into the Yemen. In the end, however, the project succeeds. With his idealistic struggle for and faith in the success of the project which results in the creation of (fish) life in a formerly waterless environment, Dr. Jones manipulates nature, or, in other words, he 'plays God'. However, in contrast to his literary predecessors Frankenstein, Dr. Jekyll and many other 'dystopian' examples of scientists who get punished for interfering with the powers of nature and playing God by creating life, here, the creation of 'unnatural' life eventually leads to fruitful intercultural encounters. In a cultural studies context, *Salmon Fishing in the Yemen* can be a useful resource for exploring the process of overcoming the clash of the two, or rather three, cultures on different levels: the friendship between 'science' and 'religion', represented by Dr. Jones and sheik Muhammad ibn Zaidi bani Tihama on the one hand and the transcultural understanding between Britain and the Middle East on the other.

Conclusion

Snow's attack on the neglect of scientific education by large parts of the literary intelligentsia is somewhat outdated and, as I have shown in this essay, does not apply to the majority of science fiction narratives from the beginning of the twentieth century. This objection notwithstanding, I think that Snow has had a point by stressing the need for a dialog between literature and the sciences,. That ecocriticism now grapples with the implications of scientific findings for literary scholarship proves the point, and one could thus even call Snow one of the founders of current ecocritism. He was wrong in stating that "little of the twentieth-century science has been assimilated into twentieth-century art" (Snow 1959: 169) as my examples show—especially the ones where science and progress are positively connoted. Snow, however, was not aware of this interaction between the 'two cultures', as genres such as science fiction, or media like comics or graphic novels had not yet been granted the status of "literary fiction" and, connected to that, had not yet accessed school curricula. But he was right in challenging the very divide between literary and scientific cultures. The struggle of overcoming this divide in which the 'recent' genres of science fiction, sci-fi comics and graphic novels have participated will hopefully teach us to be more experimental as well—not in a Modernist sense of literary avant-garde, but in a scientific, yet also playful, sense. This perspective allows us to perceive ecocriticism less in terms of an activist, environmentalist reorientation within literary university departments but as an attempt to eventually supersede the notorious distinction between literary and scientific cultures, as early ecocritics as Glen A. Love have always demanded.

Including science-oriented literature that has (not yet) gained its place in the contemporary canon into the classroom has obvious advantages. Science in fiction and the fiction of science are constructs that need to be critically analyzed. However, it is exactly in their pedagogical application that one of the advantages of scientific encounters as they have been discussed in the paper can be found: If we critically deal with science in fiction and verify or falsify underlying scientific patterns, scientific literacy can be fostered.

By dealing with graphic novels and comics that show different ways of scientific engagement, the teenage reading crisis can be compensated in and outside the classroom; and the process of understanding sequential art also includes practicing literary and visual literacy. All of these literacies and competences are part of the national curricula on the one hand and essential survival skills in a modern world, on the other. Therefore, experimental, interdisciplinary approaches of teaching literature through science and science through literature need to be facilitated as early as possible.

Works Cited

Beer, Gillian. *Darwin's Plots. Evolutionary Narrative in Darwin, Eliot and Nineteenth-Century Fiction*. London: Routledge & Kegan Paul, 1983.

Bixler, Andrea. "Teaching Evolution with the Aid of Science Fiction." *The American Biology Teacher* 6 (2007). 337-40.

Booker, M. Keith. "The Other Side of History: Fantasy, Horror and Science Fiction". *The Cambridge Companion to the Twentieth-Century English Novel*. Ed. Robert L. Caserio. Cambridge: Cambridge UP, 2009. 251-6.

Bradbury, Ray. *Fahrenheit 451*. New York: Simon & Schuster, 2011 [1953].

Brody, Selma B. "Physics in Middlemarch: Gas Molecules and Etheral Atoms." *Modern Philology* 85 (1987). 42-53.

Burgess, Anthony. *A Clockwork Orange*, London: Heinemann, 1962

Carter, James Bucky (ed.), *Building Literary Connections with Graphic Novels, Page by Page, Panel by Panel*. Urbana: NCTE, 2007.

Cary, Stephen. *Going Graphic: Comics at Work in the Multilingual Classroom*. Portsmouth: Heinemann, 2004.

Chapple, John A.V. *Science and Literature in the Nineteenth Century*. London: Macmillan, 1986.

Cramer, Kathryn. "Hard Science Fiction." *The Cambridge Companion to Science Fiction*. Eds. Edward James & Farah Mendlesohn. Cambridge & New York: Cambridge UP, 2003. 186-96.

Dierkes, Paul & Annette Scheersoi. "Dinosaurier." *Unterricht Biologie* 374 (2012). 2-10.

Donnerstag, Jürgen & Laurenz Volkmann (eds.). *Media and American Studies in the EFL-Classroom*. Heidelberg: Winter, 2008.

Eisenmann, Maria & Thersa Summer (eds.). *Basic Issues in EFL Teaching and Learning*. Heidelberg: Winter, 2012.

Flohr, Birgitt. "The Relationship Between Literature and Science in the Nineteenth Century. A Discussion of an Interdisciplinary Approach." *Essay for King's College*. London: King's College, 1999. http://www.itp.uni-hannover.de/~flohr/papers/m-res-meth1.pdf (12 Jan. 2013).

Freud, Siegmund. *Studienausgabe. Vorlesungen zur Einführung in die Psychoanalyse*. http://gutenberg.spiegel.de/buch/926/18 (18 Jan. 2013).

Gernsback, Hugo & T. O'Conor Sloane. (eds.). *Amazing Stories: The Magazine of Scientifiction* 1 (1926).

Gould, Stephen J. "Afterword: The Truth of Fiction." *The Dechronization of Sam Magruder*. George G. Simpson. New York: St. Martin Griffin, 1997.

— . *The Structure of Evolutionary Theory*. Cambridge (MA): The Belknap Press of Harvard UP, 2002.

— . *Punctuated Equilibrium*. Cambridge (MA): Harvard UP, 2007.

Greenberg, Jonathan. "Darwin and Literary Studies." *Twentieth Century Literature* 55.4 (2009). 432-44.

Gresh, Lois H. & Robert Weinberg. *The Science of Superheroes*. New Jersey: Wiley & Sons, 2002.

— . *The Science of Supervillains*. New Jersey: Wiley & Sons, 2005.

Huxley, Aldous. *Brave New World*. London: Vintage, 2004 [1931].

Kakalios, James. *The Physics of Superheroes*. New York: Gotham Books, 2006.

Leubner, Martin; Anja Saupe & Matthias Richter. *Literaturdidaktik*. Berlin: Akademie Verlag, 2012.

Levine, George. *Darwin and the Novelists: Patterns of Science in Victorian Fiction.* Cambridge (MA): Harvard UP, 1988.

— . "Introduction." *One Culture: Essays in Science and Literature.* Ed. George Levine. Wisconsin: U of Wisconsin P, 1987. 3-32.

Limon, John. *The Place of Fiction in the Time of Science. A Disciplinary History of American Writing.* Cambridge & New York: Cambridge UP, 1990.

Matheson, Richard. *I am Legend.* London: Gollancz, 1954.

McEwan, Ian. *Enduring Love.* New York: Anchor, 1998.

More, Thomas. *Utopia,* London: Penguin Classics, 2009 [1516].

O'Hear, Anthony. *An Introduction to the Philosophy of Science.* Oxford: UP, 1989.

Orwell, George. *Nineteen-Eighty-Four.* London: Secker and Warburg, 1949.

Parrinder, Patrick. *Science Fiction: Its Criticism and Teaching.* London: Methuen, 1980.

Penley, Constance. *NASA/Trek: Popular Science and Sex in America.* New York: Verso, 1997.

Postlethwaite, Diana. "George Eliot and Science." *The Cambridge Companion to George Eliot.* Ed. George Levine. Cambridge & New York: Cambridge UP, 2001. 98-118.

Pykett, Lyn. "Sensation and the Fantastic in the Victorian Novel." *The Cambridge Companion to the Victorian Novel.* Ed. David Deirdre. Cambridge & New York: Cambridge UP, 2006. 192-211.

Sawyer, Andy & Peter Wright (eds.). *Teaching Science Fiction.* London: Palgrave Macmillan, 2011.

Shelley, Mary. *Frankenstein.* London: Penguin Classics, 2002 [1831].

Snow, Charles P. "The Two Cultures and The Scientific Revolution" [1959]. Reprinted in: *Leonardo* 23.233 (1990). 169-73.

Sokal, Alan & Jean Bricmont. *Intellectual Impostures: Postmodern Philosophers' Abuse of Science.* London: Profile Books, 1998.

Stutler, Susan L. "From the Twilight Zone to Avatar: Science Fiction Engages the Intellect, Touches the Emotions and Fuels the Imagination of Gifted Learners." *Gifted Child Today* 34.2 (2011). 46-9.

Tabachnick, Stephen E. (ed.). *Teaching the Graphic Novel.* New York: The Modern Language Association of America, 2009.

Theißen, Günter. "Saltational evolution: hopeful monsters are here to stay." *Theory in Bioscience* 128 (2009). 43-51.

Torday, Paul. *Salmon Fishing in the Yemen.* London: Weidenfeld & Nicolson, 2007.

Vint, Sherryl. "Science Studies." *The Routledge Companion to Science Fiction.* Eds. Mark Bould; Andrew M. Butler; Adam Robert & Sherryl Vint. Oxon (NY): Routledge, 2009. 413-23.

Westfahl, Gary. *The Mechanics of Wonder: The Creation of the Idea in Science Fiction.* Liverpool: Liverpool UP, 1998.

Wherwell, William. "On the Inductive Sciences." *On the Philosophy of Discovery* [1860]. Ed. William Wherwell. London: General Books, 2009.

Williamson, Peter K. "The Creative Problem Solving Skills of Arts and Science Students—— The Two Cultures Debate Revisited." *Thinking Skills and Creativity* 6 (2011). 31-43.

Transdisciplinary Encounters II: Historizing Environmental Discourse

The Fall of Man and the Corruption of Nature:
A Medieval Perspective

Haiko Wandhoff (Berlin)

It seems quite obvious that ecological thinking and, more specifically, 'ecocriticism' is a modern or even postmodern notion. However, the historical roots of our ecological crisis might be deeper than it appears at first glance (White 1996). Ecological thinking—according to the relevant handbooks—has developed as a reaction to the ongoing damage done to the natural environment by Western industrialization throughout the past 200 years (see the survey provided by Glotfelty and Fromm 1996; Cronon 1995). In the pre-modern era, man's consumption of nature and destruction of the environment in most cases was not considered problematic, although, for instance, in the high and late Middle Ages major parts of Southern Spain were deforested to build up a maritime fleet. In northern Europe, too, there was a threatening increase of alluviation and soil erosion caused by a significant population growth and the conversion of woodland to arable land as well as mining territory. In the year 1285, for instance, "London had a smog problem arising from the burning of soft coal" (White 1996: 5). It was only in the 18th century, however, that the destruction of the natural environment became a topic of philosophical and scientific discourse. Exactly 300 years ago, the term *Nachhaltigkeit* ("sustainability") made its first appearance in a German treatise on wood farming. In 1713, Carl Carlowitz, a mining industry official, published a book in which he demands a new and sustainable way of wood farming in order to save the natural resources for future generations ("daß es eine continuierliche beständige und nachhaltige Nutzung gebe, weil es eine unentbehrliche Sache ist / ohne welche das Land in seinem Esse nicht bleiben mag"; Carlowitz 2013, qtd. in Fuhr 2013).

From then on, as many scholars have shown, the idea of a human destruction of nature has had its proper place in Western European and North American thinking (cf. Glotfelty and Fromm 1996). Ursula K. Heise recently underlined the discursiveness of this story and pointed out that at least for the past 200 years there seems to have been and still is a kind of narrative pattern or genre about man causing the decline and, moreover, the 'end of nature': "die

Geschichte des vom Menschen ausgelösten Verfalls und Untergangs der Natur, die sich von der Romantik bis zu den grünen Bewegungen der Gegenwart in immer wieder etwas anderer Form manifestiert hat" (Heise 2010: 10). Global climate change and the extinction of species, according to Heise, are only two of the most important dimensions of this narrative genre at the beginning of the 21st century.

In my article, I want to call to mind the fact that long before the above mentioned historical landmarks of ecological thinking, that is, long before Romanticism and even Carlowitz's idea of sustainable wood farming, there had already existed a discourse about the corruption of nature caused by man: the narrative of the fall of man causing damage to nature and the natural environment, as told throughout the Western (Christian) Middle Ages. It constitutes an important part of the Christian dogma of creation—a part, however, which is often overlooked or neglected. This can be seen, for instance, in Lynn White's essay on the "Historical Roots of Our Ecologic Crisis," which is said to have evoked a heated debate among Christians (cf. Glotfelty 1996: xxvii). White suggests that Judeo-Christian anthropology carries "a huge burden of guilt" for this crisis (White 1996: 12) because man "shares, in great measure, God's transcendence of nature" (White 1996: 10). The ecological and, therefore, ethical consequences of man's fall, however, are not mentioned in this article.

Alluded to already in the Bible and elaborated on by the church fathers, Latin as well as vernacular texts of the high and late Middle Ages point out time and again that the fall of man and the subsequent expulsion from paradise did not only affect *human* nature but *nature as such*, in other words: man's natural environment. Man's original sin not only turned humankind into faint mortal beings but also caused substantial "collateral damage" to nature. An example of this medieval version of 'ecological' thinking is Thomasin von Zerclære's didactic poem "Der Welsche Gast" (1215/1216), in which he even offers a remarkable theory of climate change caused by man. While the nature created by God and in its prelapsarian state had been in perfect harmony with itself *and* with mankind (seen as a part of nature, too), as the Book of Genesis tells us, almost everything in the natural environment changed with the fall (at least in the *sublunar* world).

Is it conceivable that this early version of a narrative concerning a damage done to nature by man might function as a kind of pre-text for the modern narrative genre of the 'end of nature', as pointed out by Heise?

Teaching the Environment:
Thomasin von Zerclære's Didactic Poem "Der Welsche Gast"

Thomasin von Zerclære was born in the 13th century in Friaul, a borderland between Germany and Italy. He is witnessed as a canon in the vicinity of patriarch Wolfger of Aquileja (also known as Wolfger of Erla and Wolger of Passau, a famous patron of Middle High German poetry). Around 1215/1216, Thomasin wrote his "Welsche Gast" ("The Italian Guest"), the first comprehensive German language treatise of court manners. As an illustrated handbook of courtly virtues and behavior, it is especially dedicated to young nobles, but also to be read, as Thomasin suggests, by *rîtern, vrouwen* as well as *phaffen* ("knights, ladies and priests"; 14695-6). The Middle High German quotations from "Der Welsche Gast" used in my article are taken from the edition by Rückert (1852); translations follow Gibbs and McConnell (2009). For the most up-to-date scholarship see Starkey (2013).

Containing roughly 15,000 verses divided into ten chapters, "Der Welsche Gast" closes the gap between Latin cleric culture and vernacular lay culture in high medieval Germany. A fundamental topic of Thomasin's book is the virtue of *staete*, an ideal of aristocratic behavior which is often mentioned in courtly romances, too. (The Latin equivalent for *staete* is *constantia*; I will translate it here as "constancy".) Dealt with especially in chapters II-IV, *staete* for Thomasin is the very foundation of other prominent court virtues such as *güete* ("goodness"), *êre* ("honor") or *mâze* ("temperance"), and thus the essential principle of true lordship and courtly behavior. To strengthen his argument and place it in a broader frame, he displays the cosmological implications of *staete*, achieving, as Christoph Huber puts it, "eine naturphilosophische Grundlegung seiner Morallehre" (Huber 1988: 25). Thomasin diagnoses and criticizes widespread unfaithfulness and inconstancy (that is: *unstaete*) in his times, especially among lords and nobles of the lay elite, and he reasons this to be a part of a greater, cosmological instability and inconstancy caused by *unser missetaete* ("our iniquity"; 2150), and this is the fall of man:

> alsô ist diu werlt gar
> nâch unserm willen manicvar
> worden, untriu und unstaete:
> daz ist durch unser missetaete. (2047-50)

> [Thus the world has become very unstable because of us, disloyal and inconstant. That comes as a result of our misdeeds. (81)]

According to Thomasin, nature as originally created by God was in perfect harmony (for the following cf. Huber 1988: 23-78). But then the fall of the first

humans from a state of innocent obedience to God to a state of guilty
disobedience introduced confusion, instability and infidelity in the natural
world. As a result, man's natural environment became an awkward and even
hostile force which, at least in parts, turned against the human race. Those who
are willing to open their eyes can observe this day by day in their own
surroundings as, for example, in the unsettled phenomena of the weather:

> die werlt wart gar staetic gemacht,
> nu hât si niht an staete kraft,
> daz mac sehen swer der wil.
> der werlde unstaete ist harte vil:
> sumers ist uns vor schûwer wê;
> winters vor îse und vor schnê;
> hiute ist regen und morgen wint,
> die uns oft beidiu schade sint;
> der donerslac nâch liehtem blicke
> der bringet vinster tôde dicke;
> ich sihe daz ez vil ofte snît
> hingegen des sumers zît,
> vil ofte ouch vil heiz ist,
> und komt der vrost in kurzer vrist.
> uns koment wolken dick ze lône,
> swenn uns daz weter dunket schône.
> diu werlt hât unstaete site,
> unser unstaete si volget mite. (2051-68)

[The world was created absolutely stable, but now it has no stability left, as anyone can see
if he wants to. There are many examples of inconstancy in the world: in the summer we
complain of showers, in the winter of ice and snow. There's rain today and wind
tomorrow, and both of them often cause us injury. A thunderclap after a lightning strike
often brings the blackness of death. I see that it often snows when summer is approaching,
and it is also often very hot, and soon afterwards the frost comes along. We often get
rewarded with clouds just when we thought the weather was fine. The world has fickle
ways, and our own inconstancy matches it. (81-2)]

For Thomasin, the vagaries of the weather serve as illustrations of a profound,
let us say, *climate change* caused by man. Indeed, the argument might remind us
of our current debates concerning weather changes as effects of global warming.
The fall of man seen as his initial act of *unstaete* ("inconstancy"), according to
Thomasin, deeply influenced his natural environment and as a result, nature lost
its inherent innocence and constancy, too. Without Adam's fall, we would still
live in perfect harmony with all the other creatures around us:

> Ich getar sîn wol gejehen,
> jâne möht nimmer geschehen,
> waere unser unstaete niht,
> unstaet diu an der werlde geschiht.

nu zwiu waere regen od wint?
waer Âdâm und sîniu kint
gewesen staet, zwiu solt der snê
uns würde nimer von kelte wê. (2069-76)

[I venture to declare that if we were not inconstant it would not come about that there was inconstancy in the world. Now why would there be rain and wind? If Adam and his children had been constant, why would there be snow? We would never suffer from the cold. (82)]

Crucial to Thomasin's argumentation is the notion that nature damaged by man in the end turns against humankind. The harm we did to nature in the beginning by our own malpractice came back at us later as a painful experience of travail and suffering. The human inconstancy, which initially infected the natural world, plants and animals, as it were re-infected us, finally making us weak, ill and mortal,

wan ir unstaet diu schât ir niht,
der schade uns vil gar geschiht.
si gît uns siechtuom vür gesunt,
swenn si sich wandelt zaller stunt. (2189-92)

[for its [nature's] inconstancy does not harm it: all the damage falls on us. It brings us disease in place of good health, by changing all the time. (82)]

According to Thomasin, the prelapsarian effect of overall *staete*, however, has not completely vanished. There still is a lot of constancy to be found in the natural environment if we observe it thoroughly. There is, for instance, the reliable succession of day and night, summer and fall, winter and spring, indicating that at least a part of primordial constancy is still left in the world. These consistent, stable and unchanging phenomena of nature can (and shall!) give us an impression of the very idea of the world's constancy:

Diu werlt behaltet noch ein teil
der staete, daz kumt uns ze heil:
wan wir behalten nihtes niht,
daz ist ein wunderlîch geschiht.
an der werlde staete lît
daz ieglîch dinc hât sîne zît.
bluomen unde loup, obez und gras
ie nâch sînen zîten was.
der obeze einz vürz ander gât:
einz kumt vruo, daz ander spât.
nâch sîner zît vellt loup und gras
und dörret daz ê grüene was.
sumers ist lanc der tac,
das winters niht gesîn mac. (2193-206)

[However, the world remains part of its constancy and that serves us well, for we retain
nothing at all, that's the remarkable thing. It is in the nature of the world's constancy that
every thing has its time. Flowers and foliage, fruit and grass, everything has its time. One
fruit comes before the other: one ripens early, the other late. Leaves and grass drop to
according to their time, and that which was green withers away. In summer the day is long,
which it cannot be in winter. (82)]

While nature has kept a good part of its *staete*, man alone has lost his constancy
almost entirely. His behavior, his manners and his tempers are unpredictable like
the weather; he follows his desires without restraint and his attitude swerves
between good and evil. Thus a sharp contrast between man and nature can be
observed after the fall, because nature even in its state of corruption and disorder
still shows a fragment of its original constancy. This could and should, as
Thomasin points out, remind us of our own moral degeneration. At the same
time it can give us a glimpse of nature's (and our own) ideal prelapsarian state
of harmony. Natures's remaining *staete*, in other words, can provide a model for
man's behavior in the postlapsarian world: how the planets in their circles
steadily revolve around the earth's globe; how the sun reliably rises and sets
every day—these relics of the ideal prelapsarian world, according to Thomasin,
can serve as shining examples of constancy for us, as uplifting models that we
are to adopt.

This is the didactic impetus of Thomasin's argument. It indicates that the fall
of man is, at least in parts, reversible, if man takes nature's remaining constancy
as a model for his own orientation. His particular blend of ethical and
cosmological arguments has (neo-)platonic origins. It was a crucial belief of
(Neo-)Platonists that the only true being is founded upon the forms—the eternal,
unchangeable, perfect types—located in the macrocosm, of which the particular
material objects down on earth are imperfect and corrupt copies. We perceive
these objects with our senses day by day but they are subject to perpetual change
and, thus, deprived of all genuine existence. But man on earth can do something
about his poor ontological state of being. Using his erect stance, he can look up
to the stars in the sky, where the true forms and ideas can be found, and take
them as celestial models for his own terrestrial being.

Thomasin blends this platonic theory of degeneration, whereupon the true, the
good and the beautiful constantly decreases from the (celestial) macrocosm
down to the (earthly) microcosm, with the notion of a fundamental distinction
between the sublunar and the superlunar spheres of the cosmos. According to
Aristotle, the sublunar world is made up of the four elements, a notion that dates
back to pre-socratic times. These elements are earth, water, air and fire; and they
are subject to an ongoing process of mixture and composition which constitutes
every living (and non-living) thing on earth. The constant mixture of elements
can also be described as a process of interplay and antagonism. The superlunar

cosmos, in contrast (and still according to Aristotle), is made of a particular fifth element, the so-called *quinta essentia*. In these spheres there is no antagonism at all: not a shifting mixture of elements but the pure celestial constancy of the fifth element, which for Thomasin, therefore, is the mother of all *staete*:

> Swaz oberhalbe ist des mân,
> daz hât ein vümft natûre besunder.
> dâ von sol iuch nehmen wunder,
> swaz zwischen mân und himel ist,
> daz hât staete zaller vrist.
> da ist niemêr natûr denn eine,
> dâ von muoz sîn ir site gemeine.
> gelîche der mit dem andern gât
> der sîn natûre ganzlîch hât. (2390-8)

[I have said, that which is above the moon has a separate, fifth 'nature'. For that reason you should not be surprised that whatever exists between the moon and the sky is always constant. Here there is only one nature, and they are obliged to share this trait. It is just like someone who goes along with another who completely shares his nature. (84)]

Constancy in "Der Welsche Gast," as I have shown, is not only a crucial court virtue but also a basic element if not a unifying power of the cosmos. The assumption of a unifying cosmic force is a widespread notion in medieval Neo-Platonism: Alan of Lille in the 12th century, for instance, chose *concordia* as the basic cosmic power; Boethius, in late Antiquity, had favored *amor* (see Huber 1988: 25-46). But this cosmic substance cannot be found in the same intensity everywhere: Underneath the moon, the force of *staete* is corrupted, meaning that it is weakened by the fall of man, though not completely perished and still clearly visible. Above the moon, in the never changing macrocosm of the *quinta essentia*, the cosmic force of constancy can be observed in its ideal form. And as long as the cosmic principle of *staete* can be perceived and dealt with in the natural environment, man should observe it and adopt it as an inspirational example for his own behavior. In the realm of morale, therefore, a step-by-step approach to the cosmic idea of constancy seems to be possible.

In his cosmological excursus, Thomasin blends three different theories of nature known in his time. First, the platonic degeneration theory with its natural descent of true forms from macrocosm to microcosm. According to Plato, this is the original state of the cosmos and not caused by man. Second, Aristotle's belief on a basic distinction between the sublunar world of the changeable four elements and the superlunar world of the eternally unchanged *quinta essentia*, or, as Thomasin puts it, "ob dem man ist staetekeit / da ist niht widerwertikeit" (2421-2; "above the moon is constancy and there no conflict is to be found"; 84). Third, the essential Christian notion suggested in the Bible and elaborated by the church fathers that only the fall of man caused the ontological and cosmological differences pointed at by Plato and Aristotle. This is why, according to Romans 8: 18-23, all living creatures have been waiting together with man for his revelation (see Böhme 1997: 108):

> I am of the opinion that there is no comparison between the pain of this present time and the glory which we will see in the future. For the strong desire of *every living thing is waiting for the revelation of the sons of God*. For *every living thing was put under the power of change*, not by its desire, but by him who made it so, in hope that *all living things will be made free from the power of death* and will have a part with the free children of God in glory. For we are conscious that *all living things are weeping and sorrowing in pain together till now.* (emphasis added)

The Fall of Man and the Degeneration of Nature

In his "Buch der Natur" ("Book of Nature"), a 14th century adaptation of Thomas Cantimprensis's "De natura rerum," Konrad of Megenberg writes: "Ain ieglich creatur ist belaidigt mit der sünd des ersten menschen" (Megenberg 1994: 472, 19-20). According to the Book of Genesis, in the beginning, God created an ideal community of man, flora and fauna. But everything changed when Adam and Eve tasted the forbidden fruit and man not only alienated himself from his own nature, his body, his emotions and his knowledge, but also from nature in general, that is: from the natural environment surrounding him (cf. Finckh 1999: 292). From now on, he had to suffer disease and death in his painful attempts to find means of reciprocation with his natural environment.

The fall of man is the beginning of the world as we know it. Without the *peccatum primi hominis*, there would be no masters and servants, no private property, no labor pains, no disease, no torturous dying (see Schreiner 1992: 41-2). Even the four elements of the sublunar world were contaminated by the fall, as Thomasin reflects in his book, too (see Huber 1988: 32-46). The same holds true for the four bodily liquids of humoral pathology: blood, phlegm, yellow bile and black bile have all lost their natural balance. Man's entire body, as we know it, is only a faint image of his angel-like prelapsarian archetype, as Hildegard of Bingen, Alexander Neckham and others pointed out (see Schipperges 1962: 133; Crombie 1959: 158). The fall distorted the harmonious partnership of man and woman and turned it into a harsh relationship of power and submissiveness. Sinful lust was initiated by the taste of the forbidden fruit, too, and dramatically reduced both man's mental and intellectual abilities. What is more, without the fall there would be no sense of shame.

But most important for our purpose is the fall's impact on nature: without the fall there would be no plagues of insects, no spots on the moon, no poisonous plants and animals. Without the fall there would be no eating meat, which indicates a hostile relationship of man toward beast, as Udo Friedrich points out: "Die Turbulenzen der Körperfunktionen, der Humores und Affekte, lassen den friedlichen Vegetarismus des Paradieses in einen artbezogenen Kannibalismus umschlagen, der von den Klerikern als Zeichen einer neuen Gewaltkultur gedeutet wird" (Friedrich 2008: 45). According to Konrad of Megenberg, the planets now have harmful effects on man where their effects before the fall, in contrast, were sanative: "ich gelaub, hiet der erst mensch niht gesünt, so het der stern kreft und ander creatur kain gewalt gehabt über den menschen" (Megenberg 1994: 489; cf. Schipperges, 1962: 133; Blank 1984). The fall of man left behind a damaged and deformed nature that had lost its sense of purpose. Thistles and thorns grow, trees wither and animals eat each other.

But this does not mean that man merely adopts animalistic features: "On the outside you are a beast akin the image of the world, on the inside you are a human being akin the image of God," Isaac of Stella writes (*foris pecus es, ad imaginem mundi* [...] *intus hom ad imaginem Dei*; qtd. in Friedrich 2008: 45). Without the fall, there would be no 'animalistic affects' such as anger and rage, neither would there be melancholy and grief or any destructive passions. Without the fall, there would be no menstruation, no unpleasant sweat and no labor pains. Without the fall, mankind would live in a world without violence and fear, where a bond of friendship would constitute a perfect commonwealth.

According to some medieval philosophers, this man-made corruption of the creational world is not static but considered as an ongoing process of decomposing. Like man, nature can be seen as a living organism that is exposed to an irresistible process of aging and, at last, dying. In his treatise "De miseria humanae conditionis," Pope Innocent III declares: "The world is constantly aging, macrocosm as well as microcosm; and the older they both get, the more their nature is being deformed" ("*Senuit iam mundus uterque, macrocosmos et microcosmos, et quanto prolixius utriusque senectus producitur, tanto deterius utriusque natura turbatur*"; qtd. in Friedrich 2008: 43-4).

In his book "Menschentier—Tiermensch," Udo Friedrich points at the overall meaning (*Sinnbildungsprozess*) of the medieval narrative of nature damaged by the fall of man:

Die Konfrontation mit den zufälligen Widrigkeiten der Natur, d.h. mit der Gefahr der Wildnis, mit Zonen geographischer Lebensfeindlichkeit, mit der miseria hominis – Alter, Krankheit, Tod – insgesamt, wird mit Hilfe des Sündenfallmodells in ein homogenes sinnhaftes Kausalgefüge transformiert: Raum, Zeit und Substanz, d.h. Natur, Geschichte und Körper unterliegen sichtbar der Hinfälligkeit, für die dem Menschen letztlich die Verantwortung übertragen wird. (Friedrich 2008: 49; see also Schreiner 1992: 43-4)

The narration of the fall causing damage to the natural environment consigns to man a great responsibility not only for himself but for nature, too. Still, what can he do to recompense or even repair the damage done? What can he do at least to relieve the distress? As Hildegard of Bingen or Konrad of Megenberg point out, man is quite capable of providing healing forces for himself and for nature as well. At least in small steps, through baptism and penance, he can bring relief to his own soul. The healing power of gems and herbage, for instance, which has been corrupted by Adam's deed and lessens day by day due to the existence of sinful people can, according to Konrad of Megenberg, be restored through prayer (Megenberg 1994: 472-3). This might be called the spiritual way of pious devotion. In his "Der Welsche Gast," Thomasin suggests another way—a way which is more based on the rational, 'scientific' thinking derived from ancient Greek philosophers. Fallen man, in this perspective, can regain his sense of orientation in the world if he uncovers and brings into focus those aspects of nature that still do show *staete* (constancy and stability) and thus remind him of a perfect world not corrupted by sin. If he takes the constant and unchanging features of his natural environment as a model for his own behavior, then he can —at least in small steps—restore the world before the fall. Both ways, the pious devotion on the one hand and the scientific as well rational surveillance of nature on the other hand, are no strict opposites but actually represent different discourses in medieval philosophy.

According to Christian medieval philosophy, is not man's inescapable destiny that nature should be irrevocably damaged by the fall. The opposite is true: the question how to deal with nature in its corrupted and deeply damaged condition, man's inner nature as well as nature surrounding him, becomes a question of ethics—a question of the right or wrong behavior, as Thomasin points out in his juxtaposition of *staete* versus *unstaete*. Thanks to his free will, every Christian soul is capable of restoring the lost paradise within and around him at least a little bit—be it through moral behavior or pious devotion (cf. Schreiner 1992: 69). If God's grace, then, is a given, too, man can free himself as well as nature from their common degeneration:

> Enthaltsamkeit ebnete den Weg zurück ins Paradies. Gelungene Gemeinsamkeit in der Sphäre des Öffentlichen und Privaten bedeutete Wiedergewinn von unbeschädigtem, paradiesischem Leben. Krankheit zu lindern, Leben zu verlängern und Beziehungen zwischen Menschen gerecht zu gestalten, kam dem Versuch gleich, Folgelasten des Sündenfalls einzudämmen und erträglich zu machen. (Schreiner 1992: 68-9)

But this is only possible because of the passion of Christ. The Christian salvation of mankind is understood not only as the introduction of a generation of a 'new man', a *homo novus,* in relation to Adam, the 'old man', but also as a re-creation of the world in relation to God-Father's first creation of the world. "Die Inkarnation des Wortes führt zu einer Restitution der Naturordnung im verklärten Kosmos, wo die gereinigten Elemente mit dem erlösten Menschen in der Hochzeit von Schöpfer und Schöpfung den neuen Himmel und die neue Erde konsolidieren" (Schipperges, 1962: 135; cf. Bronder 1972)

Conclusion

Confronted with a tremendous consumption of natural resources over the last 200 years, ecologist Eugene Stoermer and Nobel Prize-winning atmospheric chemist Paul Crutzen recently proposed the term "anthropocene" in order to do justice to the influence of human behavior on the Earth's atmosphere in recent centuries, which is, as they claim, so significant as to constitute a new geological epoch for the planetary lithosphere (Stoermer and Crutzen 2000; cf. Heise 2010: 14-20; McKibben 1989) The Judeo-Christian cultural tradition of the Middle Ages suggests that this time span would have to be broadened remarkably, however: the era of a considerable impact of mankind on nature, including severe climate change, begins as early as the fall of man—that is the transition of the first humans from a state of innocence to a state of guilt and sin. With his own expulsion from paradise, man has turned nature, too, into a hostile and even self-destructive force.

The analogy between the medieval narration of an initial man-made corruption of nature on the one hand and contemporary discourses about environmental changes caused by man, like global warming or the extinction of species on the other hand, is striking—at least at first sight. Although both narratives about an ongoing degeneration or even 'end' of nature caused by human interference have a different rationale, their main arguments seem very similar: man is considered responsible for the ongoing degeneration of nature; he is the one who, without need, left his place in the original unity of man and nature and, through his endeavor to transcendent nature, transformed the creational world into a place of hostility, terror, and death. Moreover, the decline of nature inevitably leads to negotiations about a new distinction of man and beast, and how the "the two communities—the human, the natural—can coexist, cooperate, and flourish in the biosphere" (Rueckert 1996: 107) or cosmos, as the Middle Ages would have called it (for actual tendencies of our 'posthuman' era of global species extension see the chapter "Das posthumane Menschentier" in Heise 2010: 115-49). Man's original 'sin', which results in a constant damaging of the natural environment, eventually threatens to destroy his own natural resources. This is what environmentalists tend to call the suicidal or self-destructive aspect in our "paradoxical attitude toward nature" (Rueckert 1996: 107).

But then and now, the 'end of nature' is not the end of the story; in a certain way it is rather the beginning (of a new morale)—for man is able to do something against this overall decline. He can reject his original sin and act (more) responsibly in the future: today, for instance, he can buy local organic produce or fair-trade items. In the Middle Ages, he could pray to God as well as, according to Thomasin, adopt appropriate cosmic principles as seen in his natural environment as models for ethically correct human behavior. These are possible ways to reduce our original sin step by step in order to eventually restore nature's (and our own) innocence.

But it would probably be a short circuit to derive from these similarities an actual effect of the medieval narrative of the fall of man as a corruption of nature on the modern, ecological version of story concerning the 'end of nature'. At the end of the Middle Ages, especially in humanist anthropology, man's imperfection and infirmity, caused by the fall, was transformed into a necessary requirement for outstanding cultural as well as technological and scientific achievements. Paracelsus, for instance, considered the expulsion from paradise an indispensable condition for man's invention of *kunst* (art, craft, and science), and he even claimed that this exactly would have been God's plan,

> das wir das werk nit als ein werk lassen bleiben, sonner erforschen und erlernen, warumb es daher gestelt sei. Dan können wir erforschen und ergründen, warzu die wolle an den schafen gut sei und die börsten auf dem rucken der seuen, und können ein ietliches ding dahin bringen dahin es gehöret und dazu die rohe speis kochen, wie sie dem munt wohl schmecket, und uns stuben für den winter bauen und techer für den regend (qtd. in Schreiner 1992: 43)

Paracelsus calls to mind notions of medieval philosophers such as Augustine, Hugh of St. Viktor, or Vincent of Beauvais, who already in the early and high Middle Ages considered the mechanical arts (*artes mechanicae*) a desirable compensation for man's deficiencies (cf. Schreiner 1992: 71n10). Man's imperfection, his ontological 'crippling', as Peter Sloterdijk (2009: 69-99) puts it, thus is transformed into a necessary condition for his supreme performances in culture, technology, and the sciences. This turn can be considered a very successful reinterpretation of a strong cultural story of decline ("*Abstiegsgeschichte*" according to Heise 2010: 13 & *passim*) into an even stronger *success story*. It makes perfectly clear that in the field of ecological thinking, too, we are dealing not only with *facts* but with *stories* and their inherent *narrative organization* (cf. Heise 2010: 17, 18, 43, 44, 76 & *passim*).

Be that as it may, it is stunning to see how deeply rooted the narrative of a damaged nature caused by man actually is in Western cultural thinking. Only in Judeo-Christian anthropology, as it seems, does man have such an outstanding position that he is even able to damage God's own creation. The harm he does to God's creatures is effectively the downside of man's God-given mandate to rule over his natural environment. Lynn White, Jr., has pointed at the radical anthropocentric implications of this conception:

> Man named all the animals thus establishing his dominance over them. God planned all of this explicitly for man's benefit and rule: no item in the physical creation had any purpose save to serve man's purposes. And, although man's body is made of clay, he is not simply part of nature: he is made in God's image. Especially in its Western form, Christianity is the most anthropocentric religion the world has seen. (White 1996: 9)

In ancient Greek cosmology, which incorporates a cyclical notion of time and the return of the ever same, for instance, such a thing as a damage to the 'huge' natural world done by 'small' man would barely have been possible. The same is true for animistic cultures, which assign to every living thing on earth an own and independent state of being. In contrast, the "anthropocentric arrogance" (Glotfelty 1996: xxvii) seems to be a certain feature of Judeo-Christian religion.

In order to find appropriate ways for "teaching the environment," that is, for an educational and even didactic implementation of ecological thinking and, more specific, "ecocriticism" (Rueckert 1996, Glotfelty and Fromm 1996), it might help to compare the different narratives, medieval and modern, of the damage done to nature by man, as pointed out above. The question, then, could be if it can really be ruled out completely that the old Christian narrative dealing with sin and guilt still—through 'subcutaneous' channels—affects our present, 'post-Christian' thinking about the relationship of man and nature. "Human ecology," according to Lynn White, Jr. (White 1996: 9), "is deeply conditioned by beliefs about our nature and destiny, that is, by religion." Is it possible, then, that at least some aspects of green ideology today might be influenced by old discourses and narratives about man's original sin, as provided by Christian salvation history? It is not easy to find a straight answer to this question but the idea itself proves quite inspiring.

According to historian Donald Worster, the actual crisis of our ecosystems implies a crisis of our ethical systems, too. Overcoming this crisis requires not only "understanding our impact on nature as precisely as possible"; it also "requires understanding those ethical systems and using that understanding to reform them. Historians, along with literary scholars, anthropologists, and philosophers cannot do the reforming, of course, but they can help with the understanding" (Worster 1993: 27).

My paper intended to show that in this context it might widen the focus on ecology and the environment if you bring the old, ancient, and medieval cultural narratives into play, too. Ecocriticism, roughly understood as "the study of the relationship between literature and the physical environment" (Glotfelty 1996: xviii) and performed as a certain kind of discourse analysis, thus can remind us of the fact that talking about nature and ecology is never just about 'how things are'. It is always and foremost a question of storytelling, deeply depending upon narrative patterns and narrative organization.

Works Cited

Blank, Walter. "Mikro- und Makrokosmos bei Konrad von Megenberg." *Geistliche Denkformen im Mittelalter*. Eds. Klaus Grubmüller et al. Munich: Fink, 1984. 83-100.

Böhme, Gernot. "Natur." *Vom Menschen. Handbuch Historische Anthropologie*. Ed Christoph Wulf. Weinheim & Basel: Beltz, 1997. 92-116.

Bronder, Barbara. "Das Bild der Schöpfung und Neuschöpfung der Welt als *orbis quadratus*." *Frühmittelalterliche Studien* 6 (1972). 188-210.

von Carlowitz, Hans Carl. *Sylvicultura oeconomica oder Haußwirthliche Nachricht und Naturmäßige Anweisung zur Wilden Baumzucht* [1713]. Ed. J. Hamberger. Munich: Oekom, 2013.

Crombie, A. C. *Von Augustinus bis Galilei. Die Emanzipation der Naturwissenschaft*. Cologne & Berlin: Kiepenheuer & Witsch, 1959.

Cronon, William (ed.). *Uncommon Ground. Rethinking the Human Place in Nature*. London & New York: Norton & Co., 1995.

Crutzen, Paul J. & Eugene F. Stoermer. "The anthropocene." *Global Change Newsletter* 41 (2000). 41.

Finckh, Ruth. *Minor Mundus Homo. Studien zur Mikrokosmos-Idee in der mittelalterlichen Literatur*. Göttingen: Vandenhoek & Ruprecht, 1999.

Friedrich, Udo. *Menschentier und Tiermensch. Diskurse der Grenzziehung und Grenzüberschreitung im Mittelalter*. Göttingen: Vandenhoeck & Ruprecht, 2008.

Fuhr, Eckhard. "Wider den Raubbau an der Natur." *WELT AM SONNTAG* 11, 17.03.2013, 22.

Glotfelty, Cheryll & Harold Fromm (eds.). *The Ecocriticism Reader. Landmarks in Literary Ecology*. Athens, Georgia: U of Georgia P, 1996.

Glotfelty, Cheryll. "Introduction: Literary Studies in an Age of Environmental Crisis." *The Ecocriticism Reader*. Eds. Cheryll Glotfelty & Harold Fromm. Athens, Georgia: U of Georgia P, 1996. xv-xxxvii.

Heise, Ursula K. *Nach der Natur. Das Artensterben und die moderne Kultur*. Berlin: Suhrkamp, 2010.

Huber, Christoph: *Die Aufnahme und Verarbeitung des Alanus ab Insulis in mittel-hochdeutschen Dichtungen. Untersuchungen zu Thomasin von Zerklaere, Gottfried von Straßburg, Frauenlob, Heinrich von Neustadt, Heinrich von St. Gallen, Heinrich von Mügeln und Johannes von Tepl*. Munich & Zurich: Artemis, 1988.

McKibben, *The End of Nature*. New York: Anchor, 1989.

Megenberg, Konrad of. *Das Buch der Natur. Die erste Naturgeschichte in deutscher Sprache*. Ed. F. Pfeiffer. Reprint Hildesheim et al..: Olms, 1994.

Rocher, Daniel. "La leçon des éléments à l'homme dans le Wälscher Gast." *Les quatre elements dans la culture medievale*. Eds. Danielle Buschinger et al. Göppingen: Kümmerle, 1983, 149-52.

Rueckert, William. "Literature and Ecology: An Experiment in Ecocriticism." *The Ecocriticism Reader*. Eds. Cheryll Glotfelty & Harold Fromm. Athens, Georgia: U of Georgia P, 1996, 105-123.

Schipperges, Heinrich. "Einflüsse arabischer Medizin auf die Mikrokosmosliteratur des 12. Jahrhunderts." *Antike und Orient im Mittelalter. Vorträge der Kölner Mediaevistentagungen 1956-1959*. Ed. Paul Wilpert. Berlin: de Gruyter, 1962, 130-53.

Schreiner, Klaus. "Si homo non pecasset... Der Sündenfall Adams und Evas in seiner Bedeutung für die soziale, seelische und körperliche Verfaßtheit des Menschen." *Gepeinigt, begehrt vergessen. Symbolik und Sozialbezug des Körpers im späten Mittelalter und in der frühen Neuzeit*. Eds. Klaus Schreiner & Norbert Schnitzler. Munich: Fink, 1992, 41-84.

Sloterdijk, Peter. *Du mußt dein Leben ändern. Über Anthropotechnik*. Frankfurt: Suhrkamp, 2009.

Starkey, Kathryn. *A Courtier's Mirror: Cultivating Elite Identity in Thomasin von Zerclaere's "Welscher Gast."* Notre Dame: U of Notre Dame P, 2013.

Thomasin von Zirklaria. *Der Wälsche Gast*. Ed. Heinrich Rückert. Quedlinburg & Leipzig, 1852. Reprint: Berlin: de Gruyter, 1965.

Thomasin von Zirclaria. *Der Welsche Gast (The Italian Guest)*. Trans. Marion Gibbs & Winder McConnell. Kalamazoo: Medieval Institute Publications, 2009.

White, Lynn, Jr. "Historical Roots of our Ecologic Crisis." *The Ecocriticism Reader. Landmarks in Literary Ecology*. Eds. Cheryll Glotfelty & Harold Fromm. Athens, Georgia: U of Georgia P, 1996, 3-14.

Worster, Donald. *The Wealth of Nature: Environmental History and the Ecological Imagination*. New York: Oxford University Press, 1993.

"A Deathless Love for the Natural and the Free":
Nature, Masculinity and Whiteness in 19th-Century America

Dominik Ohrem (Cologne)

"The history of spatial changes," as the ecofeminist philosopher and environmental historian Carolyn Merchant notes, "is a history of power changes" (Merchant 2010: 50). Few histories support this statement more evidently than those of the Americas and particularly the former settler colonies which are today the United States of America, where shifting power relations have worked to reshape continental space and replace indigenous socio-ecological systems from the very inception of colonial settlement. In American history, notions of nature and nation, environmental transformation and nation-building have been entangled in complex and often contradictory ways, thus rendering space and power inextricable cognates. In the course of the 19th century, as white America struggled to define the quintessence of "Americanness" and to fulfill its "destiny" of continental expansion, ideological entanglements between nature and nation not only came to the forefront in a more distinct and insistent manner, they were also bound up with prevailing ideas about race and gender, the meaning of whiteness, and the bounds of national identity.[1]

While an already considerable amount of scholarship has examined the interplay and entanglements of race, class and other axes of difference in the construction of American masculinities, I propose that nature plays a similarly important role for processes of gender construction. This essay seeks to explore 19th-century intersections of nature, nation, race, and gender from the specific

---

1   I use the term "whiteness" rather loosely for the purpose of this paper in order to refer to the hegemonic group in a system of racialized power relations. It is important to note, however, that the meaning of whiteness was somewhat fluid and subject to change throughout the 19th century. See, for instance, Jacobson 1998.

perspective of masculinity studies. It argues that white notions of Americanness, which developed and solidified in the course of the century, have to be understood as a product of these discursive entanglements and that Americanness, while never an uncontested concept, came to manifest itself most dominantly in a racialized masculine ideal I term "natural manhood."

The interconnectedness and intermingling of various discursive strands reminds us that, in a sense, Barry Commoner's ecological dictum that "everything is connected to everything else" (Commoner 1971: 33) also holds true on the level of power/knowledge (cf. Foucault 1977: 27-8), which is itself inseparable from the various worldly materialities—both human and non-human —to which it is connected in networks of mutual (re)production. While a taking into account of this complexity often appears to be, quite frustratingly, beyond the grasp—let alone the possibilities of presentation—of historiographical narrative, it is important that we modify the way we address, interpret, and teach the complexity of the past as well as its various discursive and material entanglements with the present. Teaching environments can, and should, mean a lot of things and should take into account different and even disparate disciplinary perspectives, positionalities, and politico-ethical agendas while attempting to foster possible alliances. From a historical perspective, as I intend to argue with this essay, teaching environments is bound to take into account the complex historical entanglements of nature with other factors such as race or gender in the production of sociocultural as well as environmental realities, which, in any case, are closely intertwined. This essay rests on the premise that human-nature relationships, both in their ideological and material manifestations, cannot be addressed in any adequate manner without situating them in broader and historically specific systems of power relations while, at the same time, nature has to be understood as an integral force in the shaping of these relations.

As Adam Rome has argued, in order "[t]o understand the course of environmentalism throughout the twentieth century, historians need to consider changes in ideas about gender, not simply changes in attitudes toward the environment" (Rome 2006: 443). Extending Rome's argument, I suggest we understand "attitudes" toward the environment as formed and negotiated in a complex discursive space that is itself bound up with and informed by contemporary discourses of, among others, race, gender and nationhood. An understanding of the history of human-nature relationships is thus tied to an understanding of the histories of inter- and intragroup relations as well as, and more specifically, with historical formations of human subjectivity, which are the product of, but may also produce shifts and ruptures in, systems of power relations. At the same time, the discussion of "attitudes" should not divert our attention from the materiality of these attitudes, that is, the way they became embodied by historical subjects and materialized themselves in both minor and large-scale transformations of the natural environment. While this essay is mainly focused on "nature" and "the natural" as ideological categories or "tools of power" (Sturgeon 2009: 19) embedded in and constitutive of a broader historical discursive space, it is not my intention to deny the independent material agency of non-human nature. Indeed, what may be termed a "material-discursive" or "naturalcultural" (cf. Haraway 2003) approach to history and historiography, which integrates into its framework an analysis of the mechanisms of power/knowledge and the material powers of nature, might be useful and necessary.[2]

Against the background of current attempts to promote and foster an Education for Sustainability and consequential "changes in mind-sets, values and lifestyles, and the strengthening of people's capacities to bring about change" (UNESCO 2012: 5), environmental education, whatever its precise criteria, definition, scope, and politics,[3] needs to incorporate a historical perspective regarding the role, meaning and efficacy of nature in varying ideological and material contexts. With an eye fixed on changes in the present and future, environmental education and pedagogy need to consider the uses and misuses as well as the powers of nature in the shaping of historical realities which themselves extend into the present as, for instance, in the form of lasting or even irreversible transformations of the natural world or in realities of environmental (in)justice. With the analysis of 19th-century discursive intersections of nature, nation, race, and gender, this essay intends to serve as an example of the manifold ways in which hegemonic and marginalized groups as well as those "in-between" have employed, modified, and/or been affected by nature. This also means that the history component of environmental education cannot be reduced to environmental history in a narrow sense, but needs to address how different human and non-human histories—of natural environments, nations, racialized and gendered groups and so on—overlap, conjoin, and intertwine. A historically informed perspective on nature and constructions of "the natural," I argue, should, as a critical corrective, accompany all reflections on environmental education as well as environmental agendas more generally.

---

2   With regard to the study of gender and the natural environment, the promising field of new material(ist) feminisms attempts to integrate both language/discourse and human (bodily) as well as non-human materialities into its approaches. See, for instance, Alaimo/Hekman 2008; van der Tuin 2011.

3   Recent books dealing with this are, for instance, Garrard 2012; Jones/Selby/Sterling 2010.

Nature/Nation, Nature's Nation: 19th-Century Ambiguities

It is received academic wisdom that, in the process of colonizing the place they perceived as the New World, Euro-Americans placed themselves outside of and above nature and defined the "civilization" they erected against either a savage, dangerous, and morally as well as physically corrupting wilderness or against a "virgin forest" that could be transformed into a fertile and productive garden by means of manly exertion (Carroll 1969; Nash 2001: 23–43). Euro-American discourses of wilderness were centered on the dichotomy of civilization and savagery, and often went hand in hand with a form of cultural racism directed against Native Americans and African Americans, slave or free, who were discursively located on the far side of civilization, closer to the brute forces of nature, which they seemed unable to transcend (Pearce 1988; Vaughan 1995).

While most of the early colonists, Puritan or otherwise, had thus brought with them an essentially antagonistic conception of the relationship between humans and nature, by the early 1800s many Americans developed a more ambivalent attitude. To be sure, even in colonial and early national times some had articulated their anxiety about the unrestrained conquest and transformation of wilderness. Such voices, however, had been drowned out by a cultural majority for which wilderness was, at best, a potentially reclaimable wasteland. By the 1850s, most white Americans took pride in the fact that, as one contemporary put it, "while yet scarce 'hardened into manhood'," they had already "swept across the 'impassable' mountains, overspread the great valleys, and penetrated in immense numbers through the wildernesses [...] to the very shores of the Pacific Ocean" (qtd. in Greenberg 2005: 22). From this perspective, the transformation of a "howling wilderness" into productive farmland, towns, and cities was proof of the ingenuity and superiority of white America over both wild nature and "inferior races" of Indians or Mexicans.

Narratives of territorial expansion and wilderness conquest were centered on heroic male protagonists that wrested lands from the hands of hostile tribes of savages or, supported by technological innovations, settled and improved "virgin lands" in the name of Manifest Destiny (Smith 1950). The latter type of narrative often involved what David Nye (2003: 1) has described as "technological creation stories," which placed technologies like the mill, the plow, or the irrigation dam at their center. They offered an alternative to narratives of violent conquest and white-Indian race war, analyzed so elaborately in Richard Slotkin's work on the myth of the frontier (see, for instance, Slotkin 1973). At times, however, both types of narrative seemed to intersect—and then, as the editor of *The United States Magazine and Democratic Review* John L. O'Sullivan put it in 1845, the American was "armed with the plough *and* the rifle" (qtd. in Horsman 1981: 219, my emphasis).

And yet, the nineteenth century also brought an appreciation of wilderness in its own right and not merely as raw material to be claimed for agricultural or other uses. Increasingly, what George Bancroft in his *History of the United States of America* described as "the useless magnificence of nature" (Bancroft 1837: 266) came into view and would prove to be not that useless after all. In the first half of the century, as white Americans coped with the question of the identity of a young republic apparently lacking the cultural sophistication of the Old World, some increasingly turned to the natural abundance and the natural history of their continent. While nineteenth-century nation-building and white nationalist discourse were often tied to industrialization, technological innovation, and the conquest of the Trans-Mississippi West, American nationalism also manifested itself in the increasingly influential notion of the United States as "Nature's Nation," an exceptionalist narrative that understood American "character" as inherent in its natural environment and shaped by the "physical impositions of geography" (Miller 1956: 210, 1967). Beginning in the early decades of the century, white Americans developed what scholars have termed a "scenic" or "romantic nationalism" (Hyde 1990: 21; Miller 1996: 7) that was expressed, for instance, in the increasingly popular genre of landscape painting. Notions of the sublime were associated with the landscapes of the American West, which had been disdained as a desolate wasteland only a few decades before. Here, too, places like Yellowstone and Yosemite Valley were set apart as the first national parks. Transcendentalists like Henry David Thoreau and naturalists like George Perkins Marsh or John Muir offered powerful counter-narratives to the unrestrained subjugation of the natural world and thus helped to forge the beginnings of the conservation movement at the end of the century (Nash 2001: 84–95, 122–40).

Since the mid-twentieth century, historians have addressed nineteenth-century Americans' contradictory attitudes towards nature. The fascination with the "pristine" sublimity of wilderness was often opposed by an antagonistic pioneer mentality towards nature; this persisted into the twentieth century through a competing veneration of what Perry Miller has termed the "technological sublime" (Miller 1961; Kasson 1976; Marx 1964). These contradictions are not easily resolved, nor can they be explained by means of a simple trajectory "from conquest to conservation." Rather, the meaning and relevance which nineteenth-century Americans attached to wilderness were negotiated in a complex discursive space that was itself bound up with contemporary discourses of race, gender and nationhood. In particular, both the drive towards wilderness conquest and what may be termed an early proto-environmental ethic, the latter of which manifested itself in elegiac narratives of a vanishing wild America (cf. Mitchell 1981), were influenced by the increasingly powerful American nationalism. In many ways, the early 1800s laid the groundwork for the expansionism dominating the "Age of Manifest Destiny" between the War of 1812 and the beginning of the Civil War in 1861.[4] Thomas Jefferson's purchase of the vast Louisiana territory from France in 1803 doubled the nation's territory with the stroke of a pen and, along with the early expeditions of Lewis and Clark, Zebulon Pike and others, supported the idea of a continental destiny that demanded the expansion of the republic "from sea to shining sea" (Kastor 2004; Kukla 2003). As O'Sullivan proclaims in an 1839 article, the "national birth" of the United States marked "the beginning of a new history" which "separates us from the past and connects us with the future only" (O'Sullivan 1839: 426).This imagined American future lay not primarily in a development over time, but in an expansion through space. History, as Myra Jehlen has shown, was replaced by geography, as white Americans "described their national origin and growth as an impulse of the land itself" (Jehlen 1986: 6). Benedict Anderson's well known dictum that nations "loom out of the immemorial past and [...] glide into a limitless future" (Anderson 2006: 11–2) is thus only partially true for the American context: for nineteenth-century nationalists it was not so much an "immemorial past" that defined the nation's origins, but the essence of a national destiny inherent within the continental body itself and—for the time being—defined by its physical boundaries.

What interests me in what follows is the way in which, throughout the nineteenth century, the discursive entanglements of nature, nation, and race became an integral part of both American exceptionalist narratives of nation-building and a gendered and racialized ideal of Americanness, both of which were in full bloom at the turn of the twentieth century. From the early 1800s onward, as I will argue, the intermingling of these discourses both materialized itself in, and was mediated by, a specific ideal of masculinity.

The Rise of "Natural Manhood" and American Nationalism

In his 1893 address "The Significance of the Frontier in American History," the historian Frederick Jackson Turner proposed a concept of American identity that was defined by an unremitting struggle against the continental wilderness, where "man" and "nature" clashed over and over again as American civilization advanced farther westward:

> Facing each generation of pioneers was the unmastered continent. Vast forests blocked the way; mountainous ramparts interposed; desolate, grass-clad prairies, barren oceans of rolling plains, arid deserts, and a fierce race of savages, all had to be

---

4   For the War of 1812 and the rise of American nationalism see, for instance, Rossignol 2004.

met and defeated. The rifle and the ax are the symbols of the backwoods pioneer. They meant a training in aggressive courage, in domination, in directness of action, in destructiveness.(Turner 1920: 269)

Turner's "Frontier Thesis"—far from original in his times and rather a scholarly reiteration of a common and widespread popular ideology—located the origins of Americanness in the spaces of the western frontier. As the "meeting point between savagery and civilization," the frontier effected the "perennial rebirth" of both American society and a specific type of American masculinity: strong and rugged, fiercely independent, and with a "masterful grasp of material things, lacking in the artistic but powerful to effect great ends" (Turner 1961c: 61). The colonists that had disembarked from the *Mayflower* had been Europeans, but soon enough their contact with the vast American forest had turned them into wilderness-taming men of the frontier. In the process, civilized Europeans temporarily regressed into a more primitive condition, at times dangerously close to savagery, only to finally re-emerge as fully fledged Americans. "The men of the 'Western World' turned their backs upon the Atlantic Ocean," as Turner has it, "and with a grim energy and self-reliance began to build up a society free from the dominance of ancient forms" (Turner 1961a: 85). In Turner's version of America, for *fin-de-siècle* scientific racists only the latest manifestation of the triumphant "Anglo-Saxon" march through history, Americans' relationship with nature was best represented by the figure of the assertive and tenacious frontiersman. Wilderness, according to this narrative, was far from a Thoreauvian enclave of spiritual regeneration and it was not humble immersion but aggressive intrusion which defined the mythic frontiersman's relationship with nature. "In American mythogenesis," as Richard Slotkin puts it, "the founding fathers were not those eighteenth-century gentlemen who composed a nation at Philadelphia. Rather, they were those who [...] tore violently a nation from implacable and opulent wilderness" (Slotkin 1973: 5).

Around the turn of the twentieth century, the works of Turner, along with those of other frontier ideologues like Theodore Roosevelt and Frederic Remington, reproduced and bolstered narratives of nationhood centered on figurations of "natural manhood." With this term I intend to address a specific and increasingly powerful category of identity based on an intersection of whiteness, masculinity, and American nationality that was able to transcend other axes of difference such as class, region, and, in a more limited way, ethnicity, and that was primarily characterized by an intensive and extensive, though by no means necessarily harmonious, relationship with the natural world. The rise to hegemony of natural manhood was tied to a nineteenth-century re-evaluation of nature—either as a relentless adversary in a process of nation-building or a sublime emblem of national identity, but more often in an uneasy blend of both—as a source and object of American nationalism. However, natural manhood was also both involved in and the result of a continuing struggle over the bounds of national identity, concerns over the future of white supremacy—particularly with regard to black emancipation and resultant demands of social, political, and economic equality—and the unhinging of earlier ideals of white middle-class manhood in the context of a developing market capitalism (Griffen 1990).The term natural manhood thus not merely refers to figurations of American masculinity in close contact with nature, but also to a typology of masculine identities that embodied a notion of original Americanness. Natural manhood walked the mythical line between "savagery" and "civilization," and it was precisely this ability which, in contemporary discourse, constituted its difference from and superiority over both racially "inferior" forms of, for instance, Native American, African American, and Mexican masculinity, but also over the apparent decadence and effeminacy of the Old World.

While natural manhood is already emergent in the antebellum era, the late nineteenth-century ideological milieu of what Roderick Nash has termed the "wilderness cult" (Nash 2001: 141) and a burgeoning white supremacist and masculinist nationalism offered a particularly fruitful environment for the hegemony of natural manhood. At the same time, and somewhat paradoxically, natural manhood increasingly stood at the center of concerns over the virility and future of white American manhood and accompanying ideas of masculine renewal, discussed in more detail in the final part of this essay.

Natural manhood did not remain unchallenged, nor do I want to imply that all white Americans acted according to this ideal. What is argued in this essay, however, is that, as the century progressed, natural manhood became an increasingly powerful masculine identity in the sense of Raewyn Connell's concept of hegemonic masculinity, by which she refers to a historically specific normative ideal based on the marginalization and subordination of other forms of masculinity and femininity (Connell 2005: 76–81). How and to what effect natural manhood advanced from a marginalized and even abject type of masculinity to a hegemonic ideal might tell us something about nineteenth-century endeavors of white American self-definition, the discursive entanglements of nature, nation, race, and gender by which they were accompanied and influenced, but also, to borrow a term by Sarah Carter (1993), about the "categories and terrains of exclusion" carved out or reshaped in the process.

The rise of natural manhood to an American ideal of masculinity in many ways paralleled the growing fascination with nature in general and wilderness in particular, and its discursive association with issues of American nationhood. As favorable notions of wilderness became more acceptable throughout the antebellum era, so did figurations of masculinity that were associated with it.

During the colonial and early national period and well into the nineteenth century, the fear of violent death in the wilderness was paralleled by a similarly powerful fear of degeneration into a "savage" state associated with Native Americans. From Puritan times onward, liminal characters, already present in medieval English literature in the form of hunters, outcasts, or herdsmen, populated the American imagination as well as the actual frontiers of settlement (Calloway 1986; Yamamoto 2000). Wandering the fringes of civilization, fur traders, trappers, and other "natural men" were always in danger of being permanently absorbed into the wilderness; indeed, the specter of a degenerated white manhood loomed large in American discourses of savagery and civilization. "White savages" or "half-breeds" ominously hinted at the dangers inherent in the expansion of American civilization over the continent. Even in the late eighteenth century, backwoods- or frontiersmen were commonly mentioned with contempt and, if anything, were *un*-American and barely recognizable as viable citizens of the young republic. Due to the "wildness of their neighborhood," as John Hector de Crèvecoeur lamented, these men were "a mongrel breed, half civilized, half savage, except nature stamps on them some constitutional propensities." More often, however, they were "no better than carnivorous animals of a superior rank" (Crèvecoeur 1912: 52, 46).

Like vagrants, paupers, and other "disorderly" persons, frontiersmen belonged to a despised class of rootless, unsettled men, who threatened the republican order and the ideal of republican manhood based on "manly virtue, sociability, and civic-mindedness" (Kann 1998: 13). Rooted in individual landownership and economic independence, republican manhood was closely tied to the discourse of Jeffersonian agrarianism. In his *Notes on the State of Virginia* (1782), Jefferson celebrates the rural "middle ground" as an idyllic and economically productive landscape in contrast to both savage wilderness and an urban populace already being corrupted by commerce and industry. At the center of the *agrarian* ideal stood the *masculine* ideal of the self-reliant yeoman farmer who, as patriarch of the family farm, wrested a living for himself and his family from nature in the name of what Jefferson envisioned as the "empire of liberty" (cf. Onuf 2000).

Gradually, however, the persistence of the yeoman farmer as an ideal of American manhood was paralleled by the transformation of the frontiersman from degenerate outlaw to heroic conqueror of the wilderness, vanguard of civilization, and archetype of natural manhood. While Jeffersonian agrarianism was centered on independent farmers peacefully securing their claims to the soil by mixing their labor with it, an emerging nineteenth-century frontier discourse posited heroes of civilization violently wresting lands from the hands of hostile and cruel savages. The potency of this masculine ideal is already evident in the literary construction of the first and most widely celebrated wilderness hero of American history, Daniel Boone. A reluctant and unsuccessful farmer, as his biographers tell us, Boone was permanently drawn to the forests, went on extensive hunting trips and, in the 1770s, blazed a trail through the Appalachian Mountains into Kentucky. He was captured by Shawnee Indians, adopted into their tribe, and after four months eventually returned to white civilization when he heard of an impending Indian attack on Boonesborough, a town he had founded along the Kentucky river (cf. Faragher 1992). Significantly, Boone, a liminal and ambiguous figure inhabiting the contested space of the frontier with its shifting alliances and unstable belongings, is discursively transformed into a white hero of civilization for whom racial divides are clear and fixed. John Filson's Boone "autobiography," published as an appendix to his 1784 book *The Discovery, Settlement and Present State of Kentucke*, may count as one of the founding documents of the national mythology of the frontier. In Filson's narrative, which set the tone and topic for countless other stories of frontier and wilderness conquest, a white man enters a landscape of both threatening otherness and natural magnificence. Despite the menace of prowling wolves and murderous savages, Filson's Kentucky is a "second paradise" and its abundant nature "a series of wonders, and a fund of delight" (Filson 1784: 44, 41).

Filson's narrative was firmly embedded in an emergent discourse of frontier expansion, but it also offered material for the construction of natural manhood as a distinct masculine type, a task that would fall to subsequent antebellum writers. Throughout the nineteenth century, well over a hundred books about Boone were written, among them Timothy Flint's *Biographical Memoir of Daniel Boone*, first published in 1833 and the most widely read American biography of the century (Faragher 1992: 323). Flint's Boone no longer belonged to the group of social renegades condemned by the likes of Crèvecoeur, nor was he merely celebrated as an exceptional individual. Instead, Boone represented a new form of masculinity, the "new man" and American envisioned by Crèvecoeur. This original American masculinity, however, was not that of the yeoman farmer, but of the hunter and the backwoods pioneer, "a remarkable class of people, almost new in the history of the species, trained by circumstances to a singular and unique character" (Flint 1833: 50). To Crèvecoeur and most of his contemporaries, the loyalty of this "remarkable class of people" to the progress of a white agrarian civilization was questionable at best. Quite unlike the notion of frontier Americanization proposed by Turner a century later, Crevecoeur's backwoods settlers seem wholly and irretrievably overwhelmed by the "proximity of the woods" and while the *Letters* at times betray a certain ambivalence regarding both the value of wilderness and the benefits of civilization, his protagonist Farmer James, as the name suggests, presents himself as an advocate not of wild nature but of the cultivated garden.

However, for Flint and other antebellum writers it was Boone and those who followed after him in this imagined fraternity of white frontiersmen—myth-historical figures like Davy Crockett, the "King of the Wild Frontier," as Disney would later have it—that embodied an Americanness now increasingly defined by an aggressive version of Manifest Destiny. For Flint, Boone's loyalty was unquestioned: his alliances with Native Americans, whom he was able to control and overcome due to his intimate knowledge of their "savage modes" (Flint 1845: 58), were strategic and temporary. Just as wilderness had to be infused with the language of the sublime in order for it to become American, natural manhood had to be "cleansed" of the stain of the non-white and the taint of savagery. As Flint clarifies in the *Biographical Memoir*,

> [w]e suspect that the general impressions of the readers [...] is, that the first hunters and settlers of Kentucky [...] were a sort of demi-savages. Imagination depicts them with long beard, and a costume of skins, rude, fierce, and repulsive. Nothing can be wider from the fact. These progenitors of the west were generally men of noble, square, erect forms, broad chests, clear, bright, truth-telling eyes, and of vigorous intellects. All this is not only matter of historical record, but in the natural order of things. The first settlers of America were originally a noble stock. These, their descendants, had been reared under circumstances every way calculated to give them manly beauty and noble forms. They had breathed a free and a salubrious air. (Flint 1845: 107-8)

Boone, in the words of the journalist Charles Wilkins Webber, was a "Romulus of Saxon blood" and thus safely located within the bounds of an Anglo-Saxonist ideology of whiteness on the rise by the middle of the century. The very "traits" that defined a man like Boone, his "invincible self-reliance" and the "deathless love for the natural and the free," were increasingly celebrated as core elements of white masculine Americanness (Webber 1854: 171, 163).[5]

Somewhat unsurprisingly, the idea of America as a "natural civilization" (Jehlen 1986: 5) strongly intersected with other ideological currents of white antebellum America and sat particularly well with its expansionist endeavors. As Susan Schrepfer and Donald Sackman explain,

> Nature's Nation is a close cousin to Manifest Destiny. Both terms sublimate the facts of conquest and cast national expansion as the unfolding of a script written by a deity or nature rather than resulting from political acts of domination. (Schrepfer/Sackman 2010: 118)

The veneration of the wilderness heroes of the colonial and early national periods in antebellum discourse was thus much more than a nationalist reinterpretation of the American past, but also powerfully involved in the construction of normative models of white masculinity for a nation in the midst of a process of unprecedented territorial expansion (Greenberg 2005; May 1991).The 19th century is replete with examples of white Americans, among

---

5   For the rise of "Racial Anglo-Saxonism" in the antebellum era see Horsman 1981.

them presidents like William Henry Harrison and Abraham Lincoln, who rose to fame and power in part because they themselves were perceived or presented as natural Americans. Already during the antebellum era, the benefits of the "masculine dividend" were greatly increased by the (sometimes rather tenuous or even entirely imagined) association with the western frontier. Andrew Jackson, for instance, became president because of his popular image as a rugged frontiersman, Indian fighter, and son of the wilderness born in a log cabin in the midst of the American forest. As George Bancroft described him, he was the personification of American natural manhood:

> A pupil of the wilderness, his heart was with the pioneers of American life towards the setting sun. [...] Under the beneficent influence of his opinions, the sons of misfortune, the children of adventure, find their way to the uncultivated West [...] and teach the virgin soil to yield itself to the plowshare. (Bancroft 1845: 248, 260)

Bancroft articulated an already widespread belief: it was men like Jackson who had arisen from the American wilderness as quintessential Americans and should now lead the nation to greatness. Jackson, as Turner would have it half a century later, had "the essential traits of the Kentucky and Tennessee frontier" and was the embodiment of a democracy that "came, stark and strong and full of life, from the American forest" (Turner 1961b: 72).

How are we to explain the nineteenth-century rise of natural manhood and its hegemony in *fin-de-siècle* America? Part of the explanation relies on well substantiated arguments concerning, for instance, changing ideas about nature (wilderness in particular), the material-discursive context of westward expansion, and an ever growing discontent with the advances of "civilization." There is no need to contradict these arguments and I have drawn on them in this essay. I would, however, like to offer an additional perspective relying on insights from the recent field of settler colonial studies. Masculinist narratives of white exceptionalism and an exceptional whiteness originating from American wilderness environments were narratives of destiny that naturalized processes of territorial expansion, indigenous displacement, and large-scale transformations of continental nature, but they were also narratives of origin and belonging that followed a trajectory of white "indigenization" quite typical of settler nations. As studies of settler colonialism have shown, one major discursive strategy evident in settler national narratives is "the suppression or effacement of the indigene [and] the concomitant indigenization of the settler" (Johnston/Lawson 2005: 369). As Patrick Wolfe has convincingly argued, settler colonialism is based on a polymorphic "logic of elimination" that, in the American context, revealed itself in manifestations as diverse as anti-Indian frontier violence, the Indian boarding school system or modern blood quantum criteria (Wolfe 2006). With independence and the rise of American nationalism in the early decades of the nineteenth century, issues of national identity became more pressing, as white Americans tried to both emancipate themselves from their European heritage and assert their authority over the land vis-à-vis Native American "claims" to indigeneity. As in other settler societies, this process of white indigenization is an important element of settler nationalism and "driven by the crucial need to transform an historical tie ('we came here') into a natural one ('the land made us')" (Veracini 2010: 21-2). Earlier settler colonial discourses that were centered on superior Euro-American land use and posited a civilized, settled agrarianism against an imagined "savage nomadism" of Native Americans were enough to legitimize settlement, indigenous displacement, and frontier violence, and also served to explain the rhizomatic expansion of the settler colonies (Finzsch 2008). They were, however, no lasting and sufficient foundation for American national identity.

While the recourse to the superiority of white agriculture remained an important ideological gesture throughout the nineteenth century, a different discourse emerged that was centered on a more direct connection to the continent and continental nature *as such*. In the early 1800s, two strands of (gendered) discourse existed, one expressed chiefly through the work of a scientific masculine elite that was about to merge natural and national history, Jefferson and his refutation of Buffon's theory of degeneration being one prominent example (Dugatkin 2009; Porter 1986).The other, a more popular strand that would diffuse widely into white American society, focused on wilderness and frontier adventures against the background of antebellum expansionism, as was the case with the glorification of Boone. Natural manhood was able to incorporate both of these discursive strands, as evident, for instance, in the figure of the "Hunter-Naturalist," most prominently embodied by the popular Franco-American ornithologist John James Audubon (Nobles 2012). As Daniel Justin Herman has shown, American hunting serves as a good example of such a strategy[6] of white indigenization:

> The image of the nineteenth-century hunter-hero—wearing moccasins and buckskins, carrying a Kentucky rifle, and educated in the school of nature— suggested a new aborigine.This man—the American Native—became the symbolic heir of the American Indian. (Herman 2001: 7)

The indigenizing function of natural manhood was premised on an allegiance to continental nature, pristine and sublime, hence the gradual (though never total) supersession of an agrarian ideal of American masculinity by the *fin-de-siècle* celebration of the frontiersman. Similar to what Philip Deloria has compellingly analyzed as the indigenizing function of a tradition of "Playing Indian," which consisted in a simultaneous appropriation and construction of "Indianness" and

---

6   The term strategy is used here in the Foucauldian sense of a "strategy without strategists" (Dreyfus/Rabinow 1983: 187).

offered white Americans an "authentic" experience of American indigeneity, natural manhood had some commonalities with the turn-of-the-century context of a celebration of "primitive masculinity" (Deloria 1998; Rotundo 1993: 227-32). Natural manhood, however, was defined not by its identification with Native Americans as the last representatives of a primordial Americanness, but rather by its effacement or *replacement* of the Indian by a more appropriately white supremacist version of American "aboriginality" represented by a fraternity of white wilderness heroes.

The Vanishing Wilderness and Masculine Renewal

If 19th-century American discourses of nationhood at times oscillated between "the civilized refinement of the Old World and the wildness of the New" (Nash 2001: 73), by the end of the century white Americans seemed to have picked their side. Hegemonic (i.e. white, Anglo-American, male, middle-class) ideas about nature, nation, race, and gender now interlocked much more tightly and manifested themselves in a whole range of *fin-de-siècle* phenomena, including the growth of hunting clubs and fraternities, an increasing western and far western tourism, the conservation movement, a seemingly omnipresent frontier nostalgia, and the emergence of youth organizations centered on wilderness and frontier ideals. These are disparate phenomena, yet I will argue that they functioned as parts of a strategic assemblage of different discourses and non-discursive elements, forces, and practices in reaction to a historically specific urgency. Michel Foucault addressed such complex historical formations with his concept of the dispositive (*dispositif*), which he described as "the system of relations" that can be established between a variety of heterogeneous and at times disparate or even contradictory elements which in their respective interplay are nonetheless oriented towards a solution for a societal problem. The strategic character of the dispositive does not reflect an overarching master plan, but follows an abstract and distinctly non-subjective intentionality (Foucault 1980: 194–98). In the *fin-de-siècle* United States, the discursive nexus of wilderness/the frontier and masculinity continued to manifest itself in traditional narratives of wilderness conquest in which white Americans took center stage as heroic nation-builders—Roosevelt's bombastic, four-volume work *The Winning of the West* (1889-96) being one prominent example. Another increasingly dominant idea, however, was that of wilderness as a source and space of masculine renewal, and the concomitant perception that such a renewal was necessary not only to retain the vigor of white American manhood but also, and by extension, of the body politic as a whole. While the notion of masculine renewal developed more or less in tandem with narratives of wilderness conquest and thus dates back to antebellum times, it did not gain the same momentum until the last decades of the century.

The focus on what contemporaries understood as the regenerative powers of wilderness constituted a reaction on a broader development in nineteenth-century America that historians of gender have referred to as a "crisis" of white masculinity. In the second half of the century, white middle and upper class Americans felt that American society in general and American manhood in particular were threatened by a perilous development towards "overcivilization." Urbanization and industrialization, changes in the work-place, the transition from entrepreneurial to corporate capitalism, and the increasing presence of women in the public sphere have been identified as reasons for men's sense of insecurity and perceived loss of self-determination (Kimmel 2012: 57; Lears 1981). Somewhat ironically, the manly race that lauded itself for having conquered and subdued the wilderness in the name of civilization was now threatened by the very product of its own heroic deeds. The cure, of course, lay in the call of the wild: not in a general return to the "wilderness condition," but in a temporary immersion into it in those spaces where it still existed. The celebration of a wilderness taming natural manhood and a perceived need for masculine renewal in the wilderness might appear somewhat contradictory at first: while the former rested on the premise that a superior white masculinity was able to withstand and overcome wild nature without "going native," the notion of masculine renewal in the wilderness seemed to suggest the opposite. Here, wilderness served as the prerequisite for the virility of white American masculinity and the vigor of the American race-nation. The former was part of essentially triumphalist, the latter of declensionist narratives, which Mark Seltzer has aptly described as "relentless melodramas of degeneration and devolution" (Seltzer 1992: 74). More importantly, however, and with regard to their ideological effects, not only were triumphalist and declensionist narratives often entangled and mutually reinforced each other, they were also based on the fundamental common assumption of a natural masculine Americanness.

The idea of wilderness as a source of remasculinization for white Americans can be traced back as far as the antebellum period. In his 1835 *A Tour on the Prairies*, Washington Irving, who had only returned to the United States in 1832 after a seventeen-year sojourn in Europe, describes his experiences on the western frontier during a recent travel to the Kansas and Oklahoma territories. Similar to the *fin-de-siècle* rhetoric of figures such as Roosevelt, Irving explains that he

> can conceive nothing more likely to set the youthful blood into a flow, than a wild wood life [...] and the range of a magnificent wilderness, abounding with game, and fruitful of adventure. We send our youth abroad to grow luxurious and effeminate in Europe; it appears to me, that a previous tour on the prairies would be more likely to

produce that manliness, simplicity, and self-dependence, most in unison with our
political institutions. (Irving 1835: 68)

Irving's contemporary Francis Parkman, one of the most renowned historians of
nineteenth-century America and also one of the first to write extensively about
the American West, creates a similar image of a masculinizing frontier
environment in his 1849 book *The Oregon Trail*. An account of his travels
across the Great Plains in 1846, *The Oregon Trail* remains, as Kim Townsend
argues, "one of the American male's most authoritative texts on going West to
prove one's manhood" (Townsend 1986: 106). In his youth, Parkman was of
poor health and sent to live in Massachusetts with his grandfather, who owned a
large tract of undeveloped land. Early on he became "enamored to the woods"
and "his thoughts were always in the forest." He developed a "fondness of
hardships" and boasted about how "sleeping on the earth without a blanket [...]
would harden him into an athlete" (qtd. in Jacobs 1991: 8). Writing to his friend
E. G. Squier in 1850, a few years after his tour on the prairies, Parkman
pronounced his desire to immerse himself once more into a wilderness world
full of "fevers and volcanoes, niggers, Indians and other outcasts of humanity"
(in Seitz 1911: 28). As Frank Meola has argued in his analysis of *The Oregon
Trail*, Parkman's deliberate exposure to the frontier wilderness and his delight in
and gratification of violence against animals involved a desire "both to gain
'strength' from a masculinized landscape defined against 'civilization,' and to
revitalize the male self in that civilization" (Meola 1999: 5). While Parkman's
wilderness adventures did not serve to remake him or enable him to overcome
his illness—a neurological condition never properly diagnosed—, he
nonetheless insisted that the roughness of the out-of-doors provided an antidote
to masculine degeneration and, in his particular case, against a bookwormish,
effeminate, and hence "un-American" type of scholarship:

> If any pale student, glued to his desk, here seek an apology for a way of life whose
> natural fruits is that pallid and emasculate scholarship of which New England has had
> too many examples, it will be far better that this sketch had not been written. For the
> student there is, in its season, no better place than the saddle, and no better companion
> than the rifle or the oar. (qtd. in Farnham 1901: 321-2)

While we might take, as Michael Kimmel does, a work like *The Oregon Trail* as
a "masculinist escape memoir" written by a "[r]uling-class weakling" (Kimmel
2012: 45), such a characterization tends to overlook the broader ideological
double movement these works represent and which cannot be reduced to a white
upper-class perspective alone: the construction of natural manhood as an
original American type, and the simultaneous and increasingly aggressive
refutation of what Ann Douglas has termed the "feminization of American
culture" (Douglas 1977). Only during the second half of the century did both the

appeal of natural manhood and the fear of "overcivilization"—accompanied and reinforced by narratives of a vanishing wilderness—grow strong enough to converge into declensionist narratives of white American masculinity.

In many ways, the discourse of a regenerative wilderness paralleled changing American notions of the human body and, more specifically, its significance for the definition of American masculinity. As Amy Kaplan explains, in the course of the nineteenth century, American notions of masculinity were transformed "from a republican quality of character based on self-control and social responsibility to a corporeal essence identified with the vigor and prowess of the individual male body" (Kaplan 1990: 662).While earlier norms of white middle-class masculinity had valued manly restraint and strictly limited competitiveness and aggressiveness to work life and the economic sphere, after 1850 such traits became an accepted and important part of a new ideal of masculinity increasingly defined in terms of physicality. The notion of "character," already a significant element of conceptions of white middle-class manhood in the early decades of the century, was now conceived not so much as an interior, but as an *embodied* quality that became visible on the surface and in the shape and constitution of the male body (cf. Salazar 2010).The Unitarian minister Thomas Wentworth Higginson, for instance, encouraged white American men to develop a strong masculine physique as well as physical courage, which he saw as indispensable for the development of a manly character. In his view, particularly urban middle-class men, far away from the regenerative powers of raw nature, were degenerating into weaklings without muscles and, accordingly, lacking the determination and willpower required of a manly character. As in other contemporary texts, in Higginson's writing declensionist and triumphalist narratives figure as close and continually embracing companions. Superior American "masculine energy," Higginson feared, was in decline and in order for the race-nation to retain its greatness, white Americans had to "bring up [their] vital and muscular developments into due proportion with [their] nervous energy." Only then would they be "a race of men and women such as the world never saw" (Higginson 1863: 103).

Higginson's apprehensions of decline were bolstered by George Miller Beard's 1869 (re)discovery of "neurasthenia," a nervous ailment which exclusively befell "overcivilized" whites and was supposedly responsible for a whole range of symptoms, including asthma, fatigue, headaches, and nervous exhaustion (Kimmel 2012: 99-100). In an overall context of masculine degeneration, it was the natural man who came to serve as a national ideal of masculinity. As the physician Silas Weir Mitchell, echoing many of his contemporaries, argued:

> The man who lives an outdoor life—who sleeps with the stars visible above him—who wins his bodily subsistence at first-hand from the earth and waters—is a being who defies rain and sun, has a strange sense of elastic strength [...] A few generations

of men living in such fashion store up a capital of vitality which accounts largely for the prodigal activity displayed by their descendants, and made possible only by the sturdy contest with Nature which their ancestors have waged. That such a life is still led by multitudes of our countrymen is what alone serves to keep up our pristine force and energy. (Mitchell 1871: 5-6)

Masculine renewal was not merely an individual endeavor, but a national and racial agenda that was tied to a white American nationalism infused with scientific racist and social Darwinist ideology. Because the triad of nation, race and masculinity constituted a community of fate, masculine renewal was much more than an attempt to reinvigorate white American men, but rather aimed at the strength and vigor of the American race-nation as a whole, reminiscent of the Foucauldian concept of biopolitics as an "*anatomo-politics of the human body*" (Foucault 1978: 139, original emphasis) and a simultaneous attempt to regulate the health of the collective national and racial body. Ideas of "aristocratic" decadence and overcivilized effeminacy, it seems, could no longer be safely projected on the Old World or an overdose of European influence. Instead, the threat of degeneration now had to be addressed within the bounds of the American republic itself, giving rise to a spatial division between an apparently effeminate and feminizing urban East and a masculine and masculinizing "Wild West."

What further spurred *fin-de-siècle* diagnoses of crisis, then, was the widespread perception that the vast spaces of the western frontier, the source of white American exceptionalism and an exceptional whiteness, were now fading into history. In an elegiac preface to the 1892 edition of *The Oregon Trail*, Parkman laments the demise not only of the American wilderness, but also of the American natural man. "He who feared neither bear, Indian, nor devil, the all-daring and all-enduring trapper, belongs to the past, or lives only in a few gray-bearded survivals. In his stead we have the cowboy, and even his star begins to wane" (Parkman 1892: viii–viv). With the frontier vanishing, white Americans nonetheless attempted to preserve its regenerative powers. National parks, created in part by removing Native American and other groups from the "pristine" nature to be enjoyed and protected, wilderness areas, and the vertical frontier of mountaineering were highlighted in contemporary discourse as alternatives to the "real" frontier and a respite from civilized society (Spence 1999; Jacoby 2001; Schrepfer 2005). At the turn of the twentieth century, then, the natural man, conceived as both the natural byproduct and protagonist of westward expansion, had to be (re)produced through performances, practices and institutions of masculine renewal. Individual (auto)biographies of frontier renewal were thus testimonies to both a masculine Americanness embodied by individual white subjects and to the virility of the American race-nation in an era of aggressive expansion to a new, imperial wilderness (Hoganson 1998; Kaplan 1990). Doubtless the most outspoken "symptom" of what David Wrobel has termed "frontier anxiety" (Wrobel 1993), Roosevelt himself personified the performative fabrication of natural manhood: an upper-class Easterner ridiculed by contemporaries as "Jane Dandy," in the 1880s he left for the Dakotas, where he bought a ranch and thoroughly reinvented himself as a rugged frontiersman, hunter, and cowboy, a process copiously documented in a whole number of his books, articles, speeches, and letters. "By wearing the buckskin clothes, by mixing with ranchers, hunters, and savages" as his contemporary Daniel Carter Beard noted, Roosevelt "consciously imbibed the energy, frankness, and fellowship of the wilderness" (qtd. in Rotundo 1993: 228). The "pristine force and energy" that Mitchell identified as the essence of masculine Americanness was thus bound to the fate of the "pristine" American wilderness as both an emblem of national identity and a space of regeneration. As Mark Seltzer has argued regarding turn-of-the-century constructions of masculine Americanness, the "closing" of the frontier entailed a "a relocation of the topography of masculinity to the surrogate frontier of the natural body" and "to the newly invented national parks or 'nature museums'" (Seltzer 1992: 150).

Countermeasures against the seeming double decline of both American nature and American masculinity also materialized in a number of youth programs and organizations like the Woodcraft Indians and the Sons of Daniel Boone, which later merged into the Boy Scouts of America. Essentially, these organizations represented a turn-of-the-century attempt to combine character, body, and nation building by shaping and educating young American males according to wilderness and frontier ideals as well as the requirements of modern patriotic citizenship (Macleod 1983: 45, 175, 253).With regard to the BSA, a "conservationist" agenda is evident in both the organization's efforts to promote the protection of the natural environment as well as in its similar emphasis on a re-empowerment of natural manhood. It is perhaps here, in the general ideology and specific programs of these organizations, that the entanglement of concerns over the future of nature, nation, and white American manhood becomes most visible. The renewal of white masculinity in a modern urbanized and industrialized America that threatened to become ever more effeminate required to "liberate" American boys from the feminizing influences of civilization and to immerse them into a homosocial setting where the wilderness skills of the past could be reinvigorated. As Ernest Thompson Seton explains in the introduction to his widely read Handbook of the Boy Scouts:

> Every American boy, a hundred years ago, had all the practical knowledge that comes from country surroundings; that is, he could ride, shoot, skate, run, swim; he was handy with tools; he knew the woods; he was physically strong, self-reliant, resourceful, well-developed in body and brain [...] and altogether the best material of which a nation could be made. (Seton 1910: xi)

This early twentieth-century focus on natural *boy*hood was already foreshadowed by phenomena such as the first American summer camps developed under the lead of Ernest B. Balch in the 1880s (Paris 2008). However, it also constituted a shift very much in line with the discovery of adolescence, most prominently in the work of G. Stanley Hall, as a distinct and crucial stage of life, which then became the object of regulatory techniques in the social production of American manhood. According to Hall's evolutionary theory, young boys went through a "primitive stage" on their way to adulthood, a stage which required an outlet lest the development into a civilized adult be seriously impaired (cf. Bederman 1995: 77-120). A substantial part of the scouting programs thus relied on an ensemble of material practices usually subsumed under the term "woodcraft"—generally referring to skills of survival and subsistence in the wilderness with minimal or no equipment—, which were in turn closely tied to pioneer history and the natural manhood of the frontiersman.

By means of scouting, the frontier as a space of masculine performativity could be both relocated in a playful and protected environment and adapted to early twentieth-century endeavors of citizenship education. In connection with the advertisement of Everett T. Tomlinson's *Scouting with Daniel Boone*, a story about the adventures of two "pioneer boys" at the side of the great American culture hero, the Boy Scouts magazine *Boys' Life* announced a contest which challenged American boys to write an essay discussing "[t]he qualities of Daniel Boone which made him a good Scout and a valuable citizen, and why those qualities are important in life today" ("Daniel Boone Contest": 4). As Tomlinson himself explains in the introduction to his narrative:

> There never has been a time when the development of a true patriotism was more needed than it is to-day. Our perils and problems are not concerned with savages and wild beasts, but they may be no less dangerous than those which confronted our forefathers. How to meet them, what qualities ought to be strengthened in the life of an American boy, how best to inspire the younger generation with love and devotion for our country, are vital questions of the present. (Tomlinson 1917: vii)

Moreover, the turn-of-the-century national and racial anxieties permeating masculine renewal were exacerbated by what Roosevelt and other Anglo-Americans perceived as the "mighty tide of immigration" (qtd. in Watts 2003: 71). Predominantly Southern and Eastern European immigrants seemingly refused to be "Americanized"—the BSA itself functioned as a major "Americanizing" institution for immigrant boys—and threatened to outbreed native whites with high fertility rates. Along with the ongoing endeavors to keep African Americans in a subordinate position, these anti-immigrant sentiments were part of a defense of an Anglo-American ideal of white Americanness—now interpreted through the conceptual lenses of scientific racism, social Darwinism, and eugenics—endangered by an influx of "undesirable elements."

In this context, the American wilderness had to be protected as both an ideological as well as a material resource. Just like the mythic spaces of the frontier—as a core element of narratives of national origin—had to be protected from unwanted "incursions" by African American "Buffalo Soldiers," who had played a prominent role in post-Civil War frontier history (see, for instance, Bold 2009), the material spaces of the American wilderness were incorporated into a broader project of national and racial regeneration. In the minds of progressive-era white supremacists like Roosevelt, as Patricia Nelson Limerick summarizes,

> the status and security of native-born white Americans were jeopardized by the reproductive power of Blacks and immigrants. Along with exhortations to white women and men to have larger families, the conservation of natural resources and the maintaining of opportunities for outdoors experience found their places in the larger project of protecting the position of white Americans in a rapidly changing world. (Limerick 2002: 339)

*****

By way of its discussion of nature's role in the (trans)formation of nineteenth-century American gender and race relations and conceptions of national identity, this essay has argued for the incorporation of historical perspectives into current debates on environmental education and pedagogy. In its attempt to create environmentally "aware" and responsible individuals for a sustainable future, environmental education should understand historical perspectives as an important part of its programmatic outlook and as a potential corrective. The historical as well as contemporary entanglements of nature with factors such as race and gender require environmental education to be based on what Donna Haraway has termed "politics and epistemologies of location" (Haraway 1988: 589), but also to maintain a perspective that is able to address global issues. This is not an easy task and requires careful negotiation between specific positionalities—reaching down, for instance, to the very (non-)institutional contexts, where environmental education is supposed to take place –, the ways of knowing and seeing attached to them, and, simultaneously, an acceptance of fundamental ecological truths.

This essay has argued that nineteenth-century constructions of white American masculinity were based on specific notions of nature (as wilderness), while, at the same time, perceptions and transformations of the natural environment were, at least in part, accompanied by and related to changing ideals of masculinity. In the context discussed here, discourses of nature were an important element in the construction and perpetuation of a social order based on white hegemony. In a similar way, environmental justice and, more recently, postcolonial environmental perspectives have shown how the material benefits and burdens of a radically transformed natural world have been distributed unequally in accordance with majority interests, reminding us of the "symbiotic link between environmental and social justice, at both the local level and beyond" (Huggan/Tiffin 2010: 115). Historical perspectives addressing the entanglements of race, gender, and other axes of difference and inequality with nature in its discursive and material dimensions should be an important part of a concept of environmental education that understands environmental, sociocultural, and political concerns as closely intertwined. Especially in higher education contexts, a discussion of the complexity of phenomena like the Boy Scouts of America, which, as a sort of materialized zeitgeist, stood (and arguably stand) at an intersection between environmental, gender, race, national and other concerns, may foster an awareness for the intricacies that are bound to seemingly straightforward concepts such as "nature" or "environment" —today no less than yesterday.

Works Cited

Alaimo, Stacy & Susan J. Hekman (eds.). *Material Feminisms*. Bloomington: Indiana UP, 2008.

Anderson, Benedict. *Imagined Communities: Reflections on the Origin and Spread of Nationalism*. London; New York: Verso, [2]2006.

Bancroft, George. *The History of the United States of America* (vol II). Boston: Charles Bowen, 1837.

Bancroft, George. *Memoirs of General Andrew Jackson ... to Which Is Added the Eulogy of Hon. Geo. Bancroft*. Auburn: James C. Derby, 1845.

Bederman, Gail. *Manliness and Civilization: A Cultural History of Gender and Race in the United States, 1880-1917*. Chicago: U of Chicago P, 1995.

Bold, Christine. "Where Did the Black Rough Riders Go?" *Canadian Review of American Studies* 39.3 (2009). 273-97.

Calloway, Colin G. "Neither White nor Red: White Renegades on the American Indian Frontier." *The Western Historical Quarterly* 17.1 (1986). 43-66.

Carroll, Peter N. *Puritanism and the Wilderness: The Intellectual Significance of the New England Frontier 1629-1700*. New York: Columbia UP, 1969.

Carter, Sarah. "Categories and Terrains of Exclusion: Constructing the 'Indian Woman' in the Early Settlement Era in Western Canada." *Great Plains Quarterly* 13.3 (1993). 147-61.

Commoner, Barry. *The Closing Circle: Nature, Man and Technology*. New York: Knopf, 1971.

Connell, R. W. *Masculinities*. Berkeley: University of California Press, [2]2005.

Crèvecoeur, J. Hector St. John de. *Letters from an American Farmer*. New York: E. P. Dutton, 1912.

"The Daniel Boone Contest." *Boys' Life* 4 (June 1914). 4.

Deloria, Philip J. *Playing Indian*. New Haven: Yale UP, 1998.

Douglas, Ann. *The Feminization of American Culture*. New York: Knopf, 1977.

Dreyfus, Hubert L. & Paul Rabinow. *Michel Foucault: Beyond Structuralism and Hermeneutics*. Chicago: U of Chicago P, [2]1983.

Dugatkin, Lee Alan. *Mr. Jefferson and the Giant Moose: Natural History in Early America*. Chicago & London: U of Chicago P, 2009.

Faragher, John Mack. *Daniel Boone: The Life and Legend of an American Pioneer*. New York: Henry Holt, 1992.

Farnham, Charles Haight. *A Life of Francis Parkman*. Boston: Little, Brown, and Company, 1901.

Filson, John. *The Discovery, Settlement, and Present State of Kentucke*. Wilmington: J. Adams, 1784.

Finzsch, Norbert. "'[...] Extirpate or Remove That Vermine': Genocide, Biological Warfare, and Settler Imperialism in the Eighteenth and Early Nineteenth Century." *Journal of Genocide Research* 10.2 (2008). 215-32.

Flint, Timothy. *Indian Wars of the West*. Cincinnati: E. H. Flint, 1833.

Flint, Timothy. *Biographical Memoir of Daniel Boone, the First Settler of Kentucky*. Cincinnati: G. Conclin, 1845.

Foucault, Michel. *Discipline and Punish: The Birth of the Prison*. New York: Vintage, 1977.

— . *The History of Sexuality, Volume 1: An Introduction*. New York: Pantheon, 1978.

— . *Power/Knowledge: Selected Interviews and Other Writings, 1972-1977*. Ed. Colin Gordon. New York: Pantheon Books, 1980.

Garrard, Greg (ed.). *Teaching Ecocriticism and Green Cultural Studies*. Basingstoke & New York: Palgrave Macmillan, 2012.

Greenberg, Amy S. *Manifest Manhood and the Antebellum American Empire*. Cambridge: Cambridge UP, 2005.

Griffen, Clyde. 1990. "Reconstructing Masculinity from the Evangelical Revival to the Waning of Progressivism: A Speculative Synthesis." *Meanings for Manhood: Constructions of Masculinity in Victorian America*. Eds. Mark C. Carnes & Clyde Griffen. Chicago: U of Chicago P. 183-204.

Haraway, Donna J. "Situated Knowledges: The Science Question in Feminism and the Privilege of Partial Perspective." *Feminist Studies* 14.3 (1988). 575-99.

— . *The Companion Species Manifesto: Dogs, People, and Significant Otherness*. Chicago: Prickly Paradigm Press, 2003.

Herman, Daniel Justin. 2001. *Hunting and the American Imagination*. Washington, D.C.: Smithsonian Institution Press, 2001.

Higginson, Thomas Wentworth. "The Murder of the Innocents." *Out-Door Papers*. Boston: Ticknor and Fields, 1863. 79-104.

Hoganson, Kristin L. *Fighting for American Manhood: How Gender Politics Provoked the Spanish-American and Philippine-American Wars*. New Haven: Yale UP, 1998.

Horsman, Reginald. *Race and Manifest Destiny: The Origins of American Racial Anglo-Saxonism*. Cambridge: Harvard UP, 1981.

Huggan, Graham & Helen Tiffin. *Postcolonial Ecocriticism: Literature, Animals, Environment*. London & New York: Routledge, 2010.

Hyde, Anne Farrar. *An American Vision: Far Western Landscape and National Culture, 1820-1920*. New York: New York UP, 1990.

Irving, Washington. *A Tour on the Prairies*. Philadelphia: Carey, Lea, and Blanchard, 1835.

Jacobs, Wilbur R. *Francis Parkman, Historian as Hero: The Formative Years*. Austin: U of Texas P, 1991.

Jacobson, Matthew Frye. *Whiteness of a Different Color: European Immigrants and the Alchemy of Race*. Cambridge: Harvard UP, 1998.

Jacoby, Karl. *Crimes Against Nature: Squatters, Poachers, Thieves, and the Hidden History of American Conservation*. Berkeley: U of California P, 2001.

Jehlen, Myra. *American Incarnation: The Individual, the Nation, and the Continent*. Cambridge: Harvard UP, 1986.

Johnston, Anna & Alan Lawson. "Settler Colonies." *A Companion to Postcolonial Studies*, Eds. Henry Schwarz & Sangeeta Ray. Malden: Blackwell, 2005. 360-76.

Jones, Paula; David Selby & Stephen R. Sterling (eds.). *Sustainability Education: Perspectives and Practice across Higher Education*. London & Washington, D.C.: Earthscan, 2010.

Kann, Mark E. *A Republic of Men: The American Founders, Gendered Language, and Patriarchal Politics*. New York: New York UP, 1998.

Kaplan, Amy. "Romancing the Empire: The Embodiment of American Masculinity in the Popular Historical Novel of the 1890s." *American Literary History* 2.4 (1990). 659-90.

Kasson, John F. *Civilizing the Machine: Technology and Republican Values in America, 1776-1900*. New York: Grossman Publishers, 1976.

Kastor, Peter J. *The Nation's Crucible: The Louisiana Purchase and the Creation of America*. New Haven: Yale UP, 2004.

Kimmel, Michael S. *Manhood in America: A Cultural History*. New York & Oxford: Oxford UP, [3]2012.

Kukla, Jon. *A Wilderness So Immense: The Louisiana Purchase and the Destiny of America.* New York: Knopf, 2003.

Lears, T. J. Jackson. *No Place of Grace: Antimodernism and the Transformation of American Culture, 1880-1920.* New York: Pantheon Books, 1981.

Limerick, Patricia Nelson. "Hoping Against History: Environmental Justice in the Twenty-First Century." *Justice and Natural Resources: Concepts, Strategies, and Applications.* Eds Kathryn M. Mutz; Gary C. Bryner & Douglas S. Kenney. Washington, D.C.: Island Press, 2002. 337-54.

Macleod, David. *Building Character in the American Boy: The Boy Scouts, YMCA, and Their Forerunners, 1870-1920.* Madison: U of Wisconsin P, 1983.

Marx, Leo. *The Machine in the Garden: Technology and the Pastoral Ideal in America.* Oxford & New York: Oxford UP, 1964.

May, Robert E. "Young American Males and Filibustering in the Age of Manifest Destiny: The United States Army as a Cultural Mirror." *The Journal of American History* 78.3 (1991). 857-86.

Meola, Frank M. "A Passage Through 'Indians': Masculinity and Violence in Francis Parkman's *The Oregon Trail.*" *ATQ* 13.1 (1999). 5-25.

Miller, Angela. *The Empire of the Eye: Landscape Representation and American Cultural Politics, 1825-1875.* Ithaca: Cornell UP, 1996.

Miller, Perry. "Nature and the National Ego." *Errand into the Wilderness.* Cambridge: Belknap Press of Harvard UP, 1956. 204-16.

— . "The Responsibility of Mind in a Civilization of Machines." *The American Scholar* 31.1 (1961). 51-69.

— . *Nature's Nation.* Cambridge: The Belknap Press of Harvard UP, 1967.

Mitchell, Lee C. *Witnesses to a Vanishing America: The Nineteenth-Century Response.* Princeton: Princeton UP, 1981.

Mitchell, S. Weir. *Wear and Tear, or, Hints for the Overworked.* Philadelphia: J.B. Lippincott, 1871.

Nash, Roderick Frazier. *Wilderness and the American Mind.* New Haven: Yale UP, [4]2001.

Nobles, Gregory. "John James Audubon, the American 'Hunter-Naturalist'." *Common-Place* 12.2 (2012). http://www.common-place.org/vol-12/no-02/nobles/.

Nye, David E. *America as Second Creation: Technology and Narratives of New Beginnings.* Cambridge: MIT Press, 2003.

O'Sullivan, John L. "The Great Nation of Futurity." *The United States Democratic Review* 6.23 (1839). 426-30.

Onuf, Peter. *Jefferson's Empire: The Language of American Nationhood.* Charlottesville: UP of Virginia, 2000.

Paris, Leslie. *Children's Nature: The Rise of the American Summer Camp.* New York: New York UP, 2008.

Parkman, Francis. *The Oregon Trail: Sketches of Prairie and Rocky Mountain Life.* Boston: Little, Brown, and Company, 1892.

Pearce, Roy Harvey. *Savagism and Civilization: A Study of the Indian and the American Mind.* Berkeley: U of California P, [2]1988.

Porter, Charlotte M. *The Eagle's Nest: Natural History and American Ideas, 1812-1842.* University, AL: U of Alabama P, 1986.

Rome, Adam. "'Political Hermaphrodites': Gender and Environmental Reform in Progressive America." *Environmental History* 11.3 (2006). 440-63.

Rossignol, Marie-Jeanne. *The Nationalist Ferment: The Origins of U.S. Foreign Policy, 1789-1812.* Columbus: Ohio State UP, 2004.

Rotundo, E. Anthony. *American Manhood: Transformations in Masculinity from the Revolution to the Modern Era*. New York: BasicBooks, 1993.

Salazar, James B. *Bodies of Reform: The Rhetoric of Character in Gilded Age America*. New York: New York University Press, 2010.

Schrepfer, Susan R. *Nature's Altars: Mountains, Gender, and American Environmentalism*. Lawrence: UP of Kansas, 2005.

Schrepfer, Susan R. & Douglas Cazaux Sackman. "Gender." *A Companion to American Environmental History*. Ed. Douglas Cazaux Sackman. Chichester: Wiley-Blackwell, 2010. 116-45.

Seitz, Don C. (ed.). *Letters from Francis Parkman to E.G. Squier: With Biographical Notes and a Bibliography of E.G. Squier*. Cedar Rapids: Torch Press, 1911.

Seltzer, Mark. *Bodies and Machines*. New York: Routledge, 1992.

Seton, Ernest Thompson. *Boy Scouts of America: A Handbook of Woodcraft, Scouting, and Life-craft*. New York: Doubleday, Page and Company, 1910.

Slotkin, Richard. *Regeneration Through Violence: The Mythology of the American Frontier, 1600-1860*. Middletown: Wesleyan UP, 1973.

Smith, Henry Nash. *Virgin Land: The American West as Symbol and Myth*. Cambridge: Harvard UP, 1950.

Spence, Mark David. *Dispossessing the Wilderness: Indian Removal and the Making of the National Parks*. New York: Oxford UP, 1999.

Sturgeon, Noël. *Environmentalism in Popular Culture: Gender, Race, Sexuality, and the Politics of the Natural*. Tucson: U of Arizona P, 2009.

Tomlinson, Everett T. *Scouting with Daniel Boone*. Garden City: Doubleday, Page and Company, 1917.

Townsend, Kim. "Francis Parkman and the Male Tradition." *American Quarterly* 38.1 (1986). 97-113.

Van der Tuin, Iris. "'New Feminist Materialisms'." *Women's Studies International Forum* 34.4 (2011). 271-77.

Turner, Frederick Jackson. "Pioneer Ideals and the State University." *The Frontier in American History*. New York: Henry Holt and Co., 1920. 269-89.

— . (1961a). "Contributions of the West to American Democracy." *Frontier and Section: With an Introduction by Ray Allen Billington*. Englewood Cliffs: Prentice-Hall, 1961. 77-97.

— . (1961b). "The Problem of the West." *Frontier and Section: With an Introduction by Ray Allen Billington*. Englewood Cliffs: Prentice-Hall, 1961. 63-76.

— . (1961c). "The Significance of the Frontier in American History." *Frontier and Section: With an Introduction by Ray Allen Billington*. Englewood Cliffs: Prentice-Hall, 1961. 37-62.

UNESCO. *Shaping the Education of Tomorrow*. Paris: United Nations Educational, Scientific and Cultural Organization, 2012.

Vaughan, Alden T. *Roots of American Racism: Essays on the Colonial Experience*. New York & Oxford: Oxford UP, 1995.

Veracini, Lorenzo. *Settler Colonialism: A Theoretical Overview*. Basingstoke & New York: Palgrave Macmillan, 2010.

Watts, Sarah. *Rough Rider in the White House: Theodore Roosevelt and the Politics of Desire*. Chicago: U of Chicago P, 2003.

Webber, Charles Wilkins. *The Hunter-Naturalist: Romance of Sporting; or, Wild Scenes and Wild Hunters*. Philadelphia: Lippincott, Grambo and Co., 1854.

Wolfe, Patrick. "Settler Colonialism and the Elimination of the Native." *Journal of Genocide Research* 8.4 (2006). 387-409.

Wrobel, David M. *The End of American Exceptionalism: Frontier Anxiety from the Old West to the New Deal*. Lawrence: UP of Kansas, 1993.

Yamamoto, Dorothy. *The Boundaries of the Human in Medieval English Literature*. Oxford: Oxford UP, 2000.

Teaching Cultural Ecology
from German Romanticism to the Present
E.T.A. Hoffmann, Gottfried Keller, and W.G. Sebald

Sieglinde Grimm (Cologne)

In Homer's myths we learn about the adventures of Ulysses. Ulysses escapes the cyclop Polyphem by naming himself 'Nobody' and thus hiding his identity (9.365). On another occasion, he asks his seamen to tie him to the ship's mast so that he cannot fall for the sirens' sweet songs (12.160-200). Ulysses' cunning marks the beginning of human self-assertion. He uses reason to control his bodily desires, but this is not to be had for nothing. According to Max Horkheimer and Theodor W. Adorno's reading of *Ulysses*, human nature has since run into a negative dialectics: "Any attempt to break the compulsion of nature by breaking nature only succumbs more deeply to that compulsion. Thus has been the trajectory of European civilization" (Horkheimer & Adorno [1947] 2002: 9). As the debate about ecological crises shows (cf. Riordan 2004: 48; Wanning 2006: 244; Schmidt-Hannisa 2007: 37),[1] this dialectics is still at work today. Cunning and deceit as the inevitable by-products of rationality help man to survive; however, this survival can only be achieved at the expense of the individuality of human nature itself, as Ulysses' self-denial indicates. By calling himself 'Nobody' he erases his individual nature. Literary narratives and poetry often reflect the dialectics of the human desire to control nature and the problematic risks this desire involves for human nature itself. Ecocritical readings, concerned with the numerous relationships between human beings and

---

1   In his ecocritical reading of Sebald's *After Nature*, Colin Riordan refers to Horkheimer and Adorno's *Dialectic of Enlightenment* as follows: "Yet the success of this enlightenment project can only be achieved through an inevitable dialectic of the return of nature [...]. Nature is thus re-created as an object to be feared, leading to ever greater efforts to overcome it." Similarly, Berbeli Wanning uses Adorno's and Horkheimer's observation and argues that a human 'fear of nature' will eventually return in form of what she calls "identity constraint" ("Identitätszwang"). And Hans-Walter Schmidt-Hannisa relates a passage in Sebald's *Rings of Saturn* about the taming of wild horses to "arguments that were developed by Horkheimer and Adorno in *Dialektik der Aufklärung*" regarding the "connection between the subjugation of nature and alienation from it."

nature, can shed new light on this dialectical process as well and thus highlight the role of literary fiction in this respect.

Whereas in an Anglo-American and European context ecocriticism has mostly become an established approach in literary criticism, the academic study of the relation between nature/ecology and literature has been marginalized in Germany by and large.[2] One reason for this could be that for many scholars in German Studies environmental issues seem to be intricately linked to political ideologies that have been excluded from academia ever since the profession of literary studies and criticism had been dominated by 'Blut und Boden' ideologies in the times of the Nazi regime. Moreover, the rise of the political Green Party, the equivalent of which did not gain as much prominence in the Anglo-American world, may have given environmental issues another unwelcome political tendency. Drawing attention to environmental issues in literary criticism—as the term 'green humanities' suggests—is thus almost impossible in Germany and casts the practice of ecocriticism in a dubious light.

Nevertheless, the subject has gained some importance in educational contexts.[3] In an agreement signed in 2007, the *Konferenz der Kultusminister der Länder in der Bundesrepublik Deutschland* (KMK) and the *Deutsche UNESCO-Kommission* (DUK) recommend "education for sustainable development at school."[4] This corresponds with the demands of school curricula on the ability of pupils to participate in cultural and social life. However, ecological concerns so far are only mentioned on primary school level.[5] On the whole, the awareness that future generations should be prepared to cope with ecological challenges can be found in school activities[6] rather than in educational theory.

In my view, two aspects are important for ecocritical pedagogy: first, one has to make sure pupils and students can find a connection between literature and their own life and surroundings (*Lebenswelt*). Before looking at literature as a piece of art consisting of metaphors, plots, narrative structures, or linguistic signs "that relate to each other rather than refer to real things" (Garrard 2012: 10), most children and young adults want to know what a literary text tells them about what is going on in (their) everyday life. In this respect, Kate Soper's

---

2   An exception was the "Deutscher Germanistentag" 2007 in Marburg, focusing on the
     subject "Natur—Kultur."
3   See for instance the recently founded 'Forschungsstelle für Kulturökologie und
     Literaturdidaktik' at Siegen University.
4   Cf. KMK-DUK-Empfehlung (web).
5   Task and aim of schools is to promote "the development of the individual, autonomy in
     the individual's decisions and actions, and a sense of responsibility for public welfare,
     for nature and the environment" (my translation, my emphases). *Grundschule—
     Richtlinien und Lehrpläne* (2008: 11).
6   This was a headmaster's argument, when the 7th and 8th formers of my grammar school
     (in 2009) had to watch a critical report on the American Monsanto-Company in their
     biology lesson.

remark that "it is not language that has a hole in its ozone layer" (Soper 2002: 124) hits the nail on the head because instead of seeing literary texts as self-contained works of art, young learners often understand literary language as inextricably linked to the environment the text is concerned with. Current debates about renewable energy or the explosion of the Fukushima atomic power plant could pave the way for a discussion of ecological aspects in literature. According to the pedagogical maxim that we should 'take the pupils as they come', we could use non-fictional texts such as newspaper articles for an entry into the subject and then deal with the problematic relationship between nature and culture by looking at how it has been dealt with in the history of literature.

My second point concerns a historical and methodological point of view: With the rise of exact experimental and observer-based methods in early 19th-century science, natural philosophy, which traditionally aimed to give orientational knowledge, lost its importance. It was ecological thinking that tried to preserve a holistic view against the methods of the natural sciences (cf. Hofer 2007: 59-61).[7] This coincides with the emergence of biology as a life science directed to counterbalance idealistic, subjectivist views. If we, moreover, bear in mind the origin of poetry from ancient myths and epic narratives, we can argue that literature and poetry have always aimed to provide that very kind of orientational knowledge. Thus, an ecocritical approach to dealing with literature can legitimize a holistic approach that, instead of merely regarding literary art as a texture of signs relating to each other as structuralism and poststructuralism suggest, demands to reestablish the reference of words to things in the real world (cf. Garrard 2012: 9f.; cf. The 'Debate' section in this volume). This shows in Hubert Zapf's recent definition of "cultural ecology [...] as a new paradigm of literary studies which posits the living interrelatedness between culture and nature as a primary source of literary ethics and creativity" (Zapf 2012: 83). Therefore, a theory of teaching the environment should offer a basis to restore the connection between literature and the pupils' lifeworld(s).

In order to achieve these objectives, teaching literary texts should follow three guiding questions:

1) In what way is nature a subject in literary texts? What kind of relationship between nature and man can we find and in which ways is anthropocentrism dealt with?

---

7   Hofer writes: "Today, ecology oscillates [...] so to speak between holistic conceptions of nature following the tradition of natural philosophy and the scientific ideal of the exact natural sciences" (my translation).

2) What is the relationship between naturally and artificially created places including their ecological structures? How are these places modeled in literature?

3) In recourse to the so-called 'first law of ecology',[8] we can ask in which ways literature shows that man is part of nature or part of the environment, e.g. when confronted with natural phenomena or animals so that he develops an idea of his own animality.

By referring to three examples from the 18th century until the present, I will show how these ecocritical concerns can be dealt with in German literature.

E.T.A. Hoffmann: *Der Sandmann* (1817)

In Hoffmann's story *Der Sandmann* ("The Sandman"), the eponymous sandman is represented by the demonic advocate Coppelius. He is introduced to the children as 'Sandman' who'll throw sand into their eyes if they don't want to go to sleep. As a child, Nathanael, the protagonist, witnessed his father's death caused by alchemistic experiments with Coppelius. As a student he believes to recognize Coppelius when he meets the mysterious barometer seller Coppola. When Nathanael buys a pocket telescope from Coppola, his perception changes dramatically: Olimpia, an automaton, built by Spalanzani, a professor of physics, appears to be an attractive and even divine beauty—he addresses her as "himmlische Frau" (SM [1816] 1976: 355) ("heavenly lady," 20),[9] although all she can say is "Ach" ("Ah")—and Nathanael forgets his fiancé Clara. However, Olimpia's eyes reflect nothing but his own romantic 'ego'. When he realizes that Olimpia is just an inanimate doll, Nathanael is driven to insanity and recovers only after he is attended to by Clara. Standing on a tower some time later, he observes the approaching Coppelius through the telescope. When he directs the telescope to Clara (cf. Drux 2012: 197),[10] Nathanael is driven to insanity again and leaps from the tower into the arms of death. The unresolved question within

---

8   "The four Laws of Ecology" were formulated by the physicist and ecologist Barry Commoner. The First Law reads as follows: "Everything is connected to everything else—humans and other species are connected/dependent on a number of other species." Cf. http://emilymorash07.tripod.com/id12.html.

9   E.T.A. Hoffmann's *The Sandmann* is quoted as SM; the translation follows John Oxenford's text (Web).

10   Rudolf Drux argues that Nathanael mistakes Clara for Olimpia.

the logic of the narrative is: What is the reason for Nathanael's death? (Drux: 1986: 83; Liebrand 1996: 104; Engelstein 2003: 187; Lachenmaier 2007: 178).[11]

From an ecocritical perspective, what is at stake in Hoffmann's *Sandman*, namely man's age-old desire to create artificial life, allows to consider contemporary natural philosophy. Stefani Engelstein summarizes what was common sense by mid-eighteenth century thought:

> Only in the context of an increasingly mechanized world could physicians, surgeons, and naturalists begin to recognize the regularity and reciprocal activity of the parts of the living body. Nature was thus, from at least the seventeenth century, irreversibly intertwined with mechanism, and organic function could not be conceived of without reference to machinery. (Engelstein 2003: 176)

With respect to the human desire to create life artificially, the crucial question concerns the extent to which organic (human) life can be explained as a mechanical process, thus offering a possibility of control. Several of E.T.A. Hoffmann's letters give evidence that he actively took part in this discussion. He was, first and foremost, highly critical of the so-called mechanist view, complaining about "machine-men lingering around me uttering nothing but platitudes" (Schnapp 1976: 82; 25 January 1796; my translation) or about "aesthetic cretins with automatic movement bare of inner life" (Winkler 1981: 72; February 1819; my translation). A look at Friedrich Wilhelm Schelling's *Von der Weltseele* (*anima mundi*)[12] will elucidate the interaction of organic functions and mechanism underlying these debates. It is certain that Hoffmann had read this treatise (cf. Schnapp 1976: 403; 26 July 1813).[13]

The problem Schelling deals with is how (human) life comes into being. In his cosmological model, life results from the interaction of organism and mechanism, two energetic forces of nature that follow the principles of cause and effect. 'Organism' is understood as a force of causes and effects streaming

---

11   Literary critics have different views here. For Drux, Nathanael dies because Coppelius has called to Nathanael's mind that he had threatened to throw glowing red grains in Nathanael's eyes when he was a boy. Liebrand states that "the author Nathanael—and poetical absolutism represented by him—execute themselves." Engelstein argues that Nathanael at the end of the story suspects "that he is himself an automaton." In Lachenmaier's opinion Nathanael has his "whole being" and his own self incarnated in the person of Olimpia. The moment he experiences the loss of this love unleashes insanity with suicidal consequences.

12   Schelling's *Von der Weltseele* (1798) can be regarded as a commentary on Plato's cosmology as put forward in the dialogue *Timaios*.

13   While in Dresden, Hoffmann writes to his publisher Carl Friedrich Kunz: "Infinitely I will be obliged to you for instructing Arnold to order Schubert's book [*Ansichten von der Nachtseite der Naturwissenschaften* by Gotthilf Heinrich Schubert]—right now, as I have just finished studying Schelling's *Weltseele*, I'll be able to tackle it" (my translation).

forward in a straight line; this flow is blocked by an exterior force, which is mechanical. As a result, the forward movement turns back to itself in a circle. Thus, 'organism' comprises "a succession that, being enclosed within certain boundaries, flows back to itself" (Schelling [1798] 1907: 445; my translation). Corresponding to this movement, the mechanical force is the negative principle of the organic force, the positive one. However, the organic principle is constitutive. This means that an organism is vital for mechanism, but not vice versa (cf. Engelstein 2003: 175).[14] From a theoretical point of view, therefore, "the separate successions of cause and effect [...] form infinite small straight lines disappearing in the overall organic circle in which the world itself continues to progress" (Schelling [1798] 1907: 446). This kind of progress is based on the interaction of both principles. In other words: 'Life' by mid-eighteenth-century thought depended on what Engelstein calls "the irrevocable bond [...] forged between nature and machine" (Engelstein 2003: 176).

In what way does this help our understanding of Hoffmann's *Sandman*? Engelstein's and Lachenmaier's approaches examine 18th-century natural philosophy, but the connection to Hoffmann's story, in particular Nathanael's desperate urgings towards the doll to 'turn round', remains unclear (cf. Engelstein and Lachenmaier, footnote 11 of this essay). I believe that Nathanael's insanity is reinforced by the extent in which he is defined by mechanism. There are several instances that support this view.

Nathanael comes into contact with mechanism for the first time when his father and Coppelius discover him in his hiding place. Coppelius then pretends to unscrew and rescrew Nathanael's legs. The second contact is through the pocket telescope. Nathanael depends on this technical device, and he can be manipulated by its owner. As a consequence of observing her through the telescope, Nathanael falls in love with Olimpia. His love to Olimpia is the third instance. Nathanael's friends cannot convince him that Olimpia is nothing but an automaton. Instead, he thinks that he has found Olimpia's true mind and temper (*Gemüt*): "Olimpia may appear uncanny to you cold, prosaic men. Only the poetical mind is sensitive to its like in others" (SM 356 [21]). However, Olimpia is nothing but a projection of what Nathanael imagines. She serves as a mirror of his narcissistic ego. This can be seen in a short conversation between Nathanael and Olimpia:

> 'Do you love me, do you love me, Olimpia? Only one word! Do you love me?' whispered Nathaniel; but as she rose Olimpia only sighed, 'Ah—ah!'

---

14   This corresponds with Engelsteins observation of Charles Bonnet's *Betrachtungen über die Natur* (1772): "Bonnet [...] expresses an intense prejudice against mechanical explanations, which leads him to the conclusion that the organism cannot be formed, cannot *become*. The organism is instead astonishingly described as pre-existing the ultimate beginning."

'Yes, my gracious, my beautiful star of love,' said Nathaniel, 'you have risen upon me, and you will shine, for ever lighting my inmost soul.'

'Ah—ah!' replied Olympia, as she departed. Nathaniel followed her [...] (SM 355 [20])

In the end, this development leads to Nathanael's insanity and eventual death. When he learns about Olimpia's true identity, we read that

madness seized Nathaniel in its burning claws, and clutched his very soul, destroying his every sense and thought. 'Ho-ho-ho—a circle of fire! of fire! Spin round, circle! Merrily, merrily! Ho, wooden doll—spin round, pretty doll!' he cried. (SM 359 [24])

Certainly, Nathanael's desperation and death result from his giving way to the overwhelming influence of mechanism. Yet, the decisive argument is that the mechanical principle which defines Olimpia and, in the end, Nathanael as well lacks the capacity to generate life energy on its own.[15] Evidence of this is Nathanael's desperate cry 'Ho wooden doll—spin round, pretty doll', which he repeats again and again in the course of the story. Neither the 'circle of fire' nor the doll have the capacity to move by themselves. If the doll could turn round in circles, this would serve as evidence of the organic principle and of life. But Nathanael, in identifying with the automaton, eventually lacks this principle. This is the actual cause of his death within the logic of the narrative.

Gottfried Keller, *Pankraz der Schmoller* (1856/1873-4)

With Nathanael's hubris in mind, we can now turn to Keller's *Pankraz, der Schmoller*, which translates as *Pankraz, the Sulker*. In this story, we find a similar kind of narcissism. The protagonist is defined by a telling name (Greek 'Pan' translates as 'all' and 'kratos' as 'power') which already denotes the kind of hubris challenged by a critique of anthropocentrism. Moreover, Pankraz is characterized by his sulking attitude; in that respect he represents a kind of post-romantic *Weltschmerz*. Accordingly, Norbert Mecklenburg describes Pankraz as "typically modern: self-centered, addicted to order, lascivious to follow his duties, but evading worldly problems" (2008: 387; my translation). Aged 14,

---

15   Engelstein observes that "Nathanael's terror before [sic!] Clara" when he is looking at her through the telescope at the end of the story "emanates from his suspicion that he is himself an automaton, provoking the cry, 'Holzpüppchen, dreh' dich—Holzpüppchen, dreh' dich'" (2003: 187). However, she gives no explanation concerning the relationship between Nathanael's urging the doll to turn around and the automaton i.e. machine.

Pankraz lives with his mother and sister in the provinical town of Seldwyla. The family live on the widow's pension of the mother and are in constant economic need. Their economic plight is illustrated by a comparison of the butter tub to the cyclical return of natural phenomenon: "This peeping out of the butter tub's green bottom was such a regular phenomenon, just like any celestial phenomena and with the same regularity for a while it changed the family's cool and quietly pitiful contentness to a real discontent" (PS 14).[16] At first sight Pankraz' 'power' seems to rely on a "sense of paramilitary regularity" (PS 16) by which he tries to control his everyday life. Pankraz' pretensions even affect the family's poor meals that consist of a bowl of mashed potatoes and butter, for instance: Each of the family members forms little cavities in the "potato mountain range" ("Kartoffelgebirge") and it is Pankraz who pays attention that "no one took more or less than what was his due, [...] that the milk and the golden butter flowing along within the bowl's sides, would run to equal parts in the prepared cavities" (PS 16f). Pankraz executes power in watching over these kinds of rules and order. At the same time, these rules serve as a protective shield that allow him to withdraw from social responsibility or communicative interaction.

Discontent with his life, he leaves his family, goes out into the world and serves in the British army in India. For Pankraz, the set schedule with regular meals and the income of a soldier offer an almost perfect settlement. Employed as a maid-of-all-work for a commanding officer he can exert his sense of regularity by working as a gardener. The narrator succinctly illustrates this when Pankraz grows a rose grove in which

> the little trees rose up just the height of a person's face and were so closely packed that, if you walked around in it, the roses would touch your nose, which was very nice and comfortable and made the governor laugh, as he didn't have to bow down any more when he wanted to smell at the roses. (PS 51)

Pankraz' gardening work shows that his anthropocentrism is closely linked to the cultivation of wilderness or—if taken as an image in the colonial context—to the domestication of a foreign culture.

Having unhappily fallen in love with the commander's daughter, the beautiful Lydia, who doesn't return his love, he leaves for Africa, where he eventually becomes an officer in the French army. He returns home after many years—accompanied by a range of exotic animals. To his mother and sister, he explains that it was a woman and a wild animal who cured him from sulking. Lydia made him fall in love with her just to test her attractiveness. However, as he was still sulking, he refused to communicate with her. Telling his story at home he realizes what his mistake was: "'This is the outcome of your unhappy sulking' I said to myself. 'Had you only talked to her [...] from the beginning [...], you

---

16   In the following *Pankraz, der Schmoller* is quoted as PS (with my translations).

wouldn't have been deceived so deeply!'" (PS 59). Just as Nathanael's love of Olimpia turns out to be the love of his own romantic ego, Pankraz' love of Lydia is based on nothing but a self-contained obsession with his own subjective idealizations.

The second incident that helps to cure Pankraz happens when he goes lion hunting. Thinking of Lydia, he puts his gun aside to drink water from a creek. Then, he suddenly hears a lion's roar and realizes that the animal is sitting on his gun. Pankraz' position is right in front of the lion, and they both stare into each others' eyes for several hours until help arrives. The animal's gaze is a common theme in ecocriticism and human-animal studies, and in order to analyze the particular relevance of this scene, it is worthwhile to consider what Georges Bataille wrote about this gaze: "Through the animal I'm confronted with a depth which attracts me and which at the same time is something I can trust in. In a certain sense I know all about this depth: it is my own" (Bataille [1974] 1997: 23; my translation). For Pankraz this means that he—vis-à-vis the animal—realizes his creaturely—i.e. 'animal'—life. His character develops not by an operation of consciousness, but by physical experience—or, to quote Jacques Derrida, "by the deranged theatrics of the *wholly other that they call animal.*" (Derrida 2002: 380).[17] Pankraz' description of his bodily condition gives evidence of this: "I felt sweat running down my skin, I was trembling from desperate exhaustion in every fiber of my limbs." And this is what brings about change:

> While I was going through this strain for one long minute after the next, all my anger and bitterness finally disappeared, towards the lion as well, and the weaker I got, the more I felt a pleasant loving patience that I endured all pain patiently and bravely. (PS 68)

Axel Dunker's résumé—"Human peoples and wild animals are indiscriminately set up to stabilize the economy of his [Pankraz'] own psyche" (Dunker 2008: 112)—is still valid, but his assertion that Pankraz was "saved by his immobility which led to a fundamental change of consciousness" (Dunker 2008: 116) cannot explain Pankraz' educational 'turn' (cf. Hoffmann 1999: 291; Pfotenhauer 2000: 180).[18] From an ecocritical point of view, it is rather the experience of his own animality (*Kreatürlichkeit*) to which he owes the cure to his sulking and which breaks his arrogance. And contrary to Dunker's

---

17   This instance resembles Derrida's (2002) discussion of the animal's gaze after he has been looked at by his cat.

18   Nor do other interpretations: Hoffmann observes a "complementary strategy of patient and flexible accommodation, a kind of effemination" in the course of which Pankraz learns to transfer his weakness into strength. According to Helmut Pfotenhauer it was Keller's concept, to have the protagonist "stew speechlessly and sulkingly in the desert's sun until he [was] cured by exaggeration of his own self. Then practical reasoning would overcome illusory imagination" (my translation).

interpretation, this cure is based on Pankraz' very mobility and a change of place. As another statement of Derrida sums up,

> The gaze called 'animal' offers to my sight the abyssal limit of the human: the inhuman or the ahuman, the ends of man [...]. And in these moments of nakedness, under the gaze of the animal, everything can happen to me, I am like a child ready for the apocalypse [...]. (Derrida 2002: 380)

A similar experience of 'nakedness' in the sense of a loss of previous ambitions can be assumed for Pankraz, whose anthropocentric attitude crumbles when faced by the animal. This (change) prepares him to return to Seldwyla and become a valuable citizen.

As far as anthropocentrism is concerned, the conditions for Pankraz' and Nathanael's education are similar. However, there is a remarkable difference as far as the motif of the eye is concerned. Whereas in Hoffmann's *Sandman*, Nathanael finds nothing but a reflection of his own self in Olimpia's dead eyes so that no real exchange can take place, Pankraz, when gazing into the lion's eyes, experiences a dissolution of his hubris, i.e. he becomes aware of his 'other' self. Pankraz experiences a continuity with the more-than-human world that ecocriticism has identified as the crucial basis for ecocentric thinking. It is this sense of interconnection that Nathanael lacks. Moreover, Pankraz' anthropocentrism rests on the assumption of colonial power, which is demonstrated by the 'cultivation' or, rather, 'rationalization' of a natural or wild place. In the end, it is obvious that the very diversity of place linked to a change of circumstances serves as a precondition to undermine Pankraz' hubris.

W. G. Sebald, *After Nature/Nach der Natur* (1988)

As a last example I have chosen a work of contemporary literature: W.G. Sebald's *After Nature*, published in 1988. *After Nature* is a narrative triptych composed of three long poems. The first poem deals with the painter Matthias Grünewald (1480-1528) who created the famous Isenheim altarpiece, which today can be visited in Colmar (Germany). The second and longest poem tells of the life of the natural scientist Georg Wilhelm Steller (1709-1746), who joined Captain Vitus Bering on his second expedition to Alaska and died in Siberia at the age of 37. The third and last part considers the biography of the narrator himself, which in parts is identical with the life of the author Sebald. Thus, *After Nature* comprises a period from the Reformation to Enlightenment and from there to the present time. On the whole, the poem is characterized by an elegiac tone. Except for some distichs, there is no rhyme or meter. It contains passages with long and complicated sentence structures but also stanzas that consist of fragments or separate words only.

Whereas this is lost in the English translation *After Nature*, the German title *Nach der Natur* can be understood as 'according to nature' in the sense that all three characters have a special interest in nature. In the so-called 'Small Cruxifiction' of the Lindenhardt altarpiece, another of his paintings, Grünewald integrated the solar eclipse of 1502 into the crucifixion picture in the form of a small sun above the cross. As the text says, Grünewald "painted / and recalled the catastrophic incursion / of darkness, the last trace of light / flickering from beyond, after nature" (AN 29f. [NN 26]).[19] Following nature in a way similar to Grünewald, Steller, the natural scientist, in his opus *De Bestiis marinis*[20] has tried to present a precise description and classification of sea animals. And the third part aims to give a historically detailed and accurate account of the narrator's biography, beginning from his grandparents' wedding, the wartime experience of his parents' generation up to the period when he writes down his memoirs.

From another perspective, 'after' can also be understood metaphysically in a philosophical sense, referring to questions concerning the confines of human capacity and experience.[21] Sebald's poem recounts numerous experiences that show the limits of human ambition and scientific curiosity. In Grünewald's biography, the crucifixion picture puts forward the question of human suffering, exposing man's finite nature before God. In the middle part of the literary triptych, human suffering surfaces in the form of scurvy when Steller, a doctor, realizes that he can't help a group of dying sailors:

> What does it mean, this *physica*, he asks,
> what is this *iusiurandum Hippocratis*,
> what does surgery mean, what is our
> skill and use when life
> breaks apart and the physician
> has neither might nor means? (AN 64 [57])

Medical science and skill are confronted with their limits. It is particularly through the character of Steller that the scientific spirit is called into question: while his medical, i.e. scientific endeavors lead him to experience frustration and hopelessness during his lifetime, after his death, his "endless inventory, / his zoological masterpiece *De Bestiis Marinis*" turns out to be a "travel chart for hunters, / blueprint for the counting of pelts—" (AN 74 [66]). In the third part of

---

19   The number in angular brackets refers to the German Edition.
20   *Georg Wilhelm Stellers ausführliche Beschreibung von sonderbaren Meeresthieren.* Mit Erläuterungen und nöthigen Kupfern versehen, Halle 1753.
21   'Metaphysics' from Greek 'meta ta physika', in the sense of "after, i.e. beyond the physical world" (cf. Schischkoff 1982: 452).

the text, which focuses on the narrator's biography, the persona's parents confront their impotence and lack of memory in the light of wartime destruction. And, remembering a previous stay in Manchester, in a similarly helpless tone the narrator describes the city's decline, once called "the most wonderful city of modern times, a celestial Jerusalem" by the statesman Disraeli (AN 95 [83]).

After Nature confronts the reader with the limits of human power, especially of the zeal for discovery and exploration. At the same time, 'place' plays an important role within the relationship between man and nature. Already when Steller makes up his mind to leave Danzig for St. Petersburg, he calls his mission "to bring the plan of eternity into the city / born of the terror of the vastness of space" (AN 47 [NN 41]). The main purpose of Bering's expedition was to find a passage between the Arctic Ocean and the Pacific and, thus, to secure territory for the tsar. But one of the expedition's two ships "named after the saints Peter and Paul" (AN 57 [NN 50]) runs aground, and the seamen have to pass the winter in the Arctic, after which half of the crew dies. For the natural scientist Steller, space represents a limit to his ambition. In the end, however, it is more than a mere hindrance: in the vastness of uncultivated and uncultivatable space, Bering, Steller and the seamen lose their lives.

Moreover, just like Keller, Sebald uses the animal's gaze for his argument. On first meeting Bering, who is already in poor health, Steller looks into Bering's tired eyes and experiences a kind of kinship with what could be called the animal aspect of his human fellow:

> It takes an uncannily
> long time, Steller thinks,
> for Bering to open
> his eyes and look
> at him. What is this
> being called human?
> A beast, shrouded
> in deep mourning,
> in a black coat
> lined with
> black fur. (AN 56 [48])[22]

While there is an exchange between human ambition and animality in Keller's *Pankraz, der Schmoller*, the animal's gaze in *After Nature* is used not only to

---

22   In her brilliant reading of Sebald's *After Nature* Claudia Albes shows that Bering's characterization resembles Albrecht Dürer's copper engraving *Melencolia I* which shows a character sitting in a windowless room in deep melancholy amidst utensils used in the science of measuring (2006: 63).

modify human claims but to show their futility and deterioration in the light of bodily decay.[23]

On the whole, the narrative dramaturgy of the text is in itself already 'educational', because it demonstrates the cyclic structure of life. As a writer and artist, the narrator compares his situation to that of Grünewald, who had envisaged possible catastrophes. This is why we learn that Grünewald, with a passionate view of the future, had created

> a planet utterly strange, chalk-coloured
> behind the blackish-blue river.
> Here in an evil state of erosion
> and desolation the heritage of the ruining
> of life that in the end will consume
> even the very stones has been depicted. (AN 31 [27-8])

In a similarly dystopian use of imaginary, the persona's parents could not forget the pictures of the burning cities at the end of the Second World War. Strangely enough, the narrator remembers a painting by Albrecht Altdorfer (1480-1531), depicting *Lot and his Daughters* and the burning city of Sodom in the background: "On the horizon / a terrible conflagration blazes, / devouring a large city" (AN 84 [74]).

Taken as a triptych, the first and the third part of Sebald's poem would correspond to the smaller side-pieces of the altar, which frame the larger episode with Steller and Bering. This middle piece is set in the period of enlightenment, comprising the heyday of anthropocentric self-assurance.[24] The order of the three poems follows the course of history and suggests that history moves in circles of creation and decay. Over and over again, human flights of fancy are cut back by man's physical limitations. However, Sebald's narrator in *After Nature* is not overcome by the impression of destruction,[25] even if he describes the process with particular intensity. As Albes suggests, the three biographies

---

23   The animal's gaze also occurs in Sebald's *Rings of Saturn*. The narrator passes a herd of swine at the cliffs' edge above the sea and approaches one of the heavy, motionlessly sleeping animals: "Slowly, while I was bowing down to it, the animal opened its small eye, skirted by light eyelashes, looking at me questioningly [...]" ([1995] 2011: 85; my translation). Schmidt-Hannisa suggests that this passage alludes to the healing of an obsessed maniac by a herd of swine as told in Mark 5: 1-20, Luke 8: 26-39 and Matthew: 8: 28-34 (2007: 35-6).

24   Georg Braungart decidedly refers to "Anthropozentrismus der Spätaufklärung" (2009: 57).

25   The circular movement of history answers Philipp Schönthaler's question about the "way [in which] Sebald tries to replace the perception of nature as dead matter [as in Alfred Döblin's work] by a concept of an animated nature thus forming a necessary antipole against the dimension of a natural philosophy and a natural history of destruction" (2011: 109; my translation).

seem to be related to each other by way of incarnation, which means "that one and the same soul reincarnates within every 200 years, first as Matthias Grünewald, then as Georg Wilhelm Steller and finally as the narrator W.G. Sebald" (Albes 2006: 52-3; my translation).

This is illustrated for instance by the fact that the protagonists' courses of life meet in the Franconian place of Windsheim (cf. Albes 2006: 51). It is in Windsheim where the narrator's mother learns that she is pregnant on the same day she witnesses the bombing of Nuremberg (cf. NN 74 [84]). Grünewald visited Windsheim in April 1525 (NN 29 [32]) and Steller was born in Windsheim (NN 34 [43]). These kinds of similarities and analogies show the very "connection by association which raises the question of ecocriticism" (Riordan 2004: 46).

In the last passages of the poem, the narrator once more expresses a close emotional relationship to the painter Grünewald. In the monastery of St. Anton, the triptych of the Isenheim altarpiece, with the crucifixion picture in the middle and the painting of Christ's resurrection on the right wing, was supposed to comfort and give hope of recovery to the sick. In a similar way, the last part of his literary triptych, an impression of Altdorfer's painting *Alexanderschlacht*, showing the battle of Arabela between Alexander of Makedonia and the Persian king Darius, ends with a positive view that relies on a bird's perspective:

> Now I know, as with a crane's eye
> one surveys his far-flung realm
> a truly Asiatic spectacle,
> and slowly learns, from the tininess
> of the figures and incomprehensible
> beauty of nature that vaults over them,
> to see that side of life that
> one could not see before. (AN 98 [112])

The narrator's eye wanders over Persian tents, ships approaching Egypt and the Nile Delta, the Red Sea and Africa.

With this brief excursion into almost three centuries of German ecocritical writing, I hope to have shown that what has been said about the dialectical relationship between human individuality and nature in the beginning of this essay constitutes a vital concern for works of literature. While Romantic literature presents the pitfalls of the idealized view, Keller's realist text tries to balance such forms of idealization. Sebald, however, sublates both positions and presents a perspective of humility in the light of our own creaturely being. Reading these literary texts in the light of a critique of anthropocentrism and as counterdiscursive forces that seek to undermine hubristic human ambition suggests that 'teaching the environment'—as Berhard Malkmus points out—has to avoid being stuck only with the "performativity of language [...] imposed on the humanities by the 'linguistic turn'." Instead we should refuse such "a loss of vital openness," which eventually will bring about a "disability to perceive psychological circumstances beyond semiotic categories" (Malkmus 2005: 63; my translation).[26] This is the 'blind spot' which Malkmus detects and criticizes in contemporary (postmodern) literary and cultural theory and which, as he argues, has its roots in the "fear of coming too close to mankind's primary questions" (Malkmus 2005: 73; my translation). In this respect an ecocritical approach to teaching literature helps students and pupils to learn something about our connection to our environments, our histories, and to the planet that we share with numerous non-human beings. Although theories such as F.W.J. Schelling's eighteenth-century natural philosophy can hardly be part of a curriculum for young learners, central issues such as the cyclic structure of growth and decay in nature and the notion of life as a limited amount of time between birth and death can and should be an issue in the teaching of literature.

---

26 To understand Sebald's poem simply as a linguistic or literary answer to the dialectics of negativity as Schönthaler points out (cf. footnote 25 of this essay) not only fails to establish a connection to the 'life-world', but misses the ecocritical idea.

214   Sieglinde Grimm

Works Cited

Albes, Claudia. "Portrait ohne Modell. Bildbeschreibung und autobiographische Reflexion in
    W. G. Sebalds Elementargedicht 'Nach der Natur'." *W.G. Sebald. Politische Archäologie
    und melancholische Bastelei.* Eds. Michael Niehaus & Claudia Öhlschläger. Berlin: Erich
    Schmidt Verlag, 2006. 47-76.
Bataille, Georges. *Theorie der Religion.* Trans. Andreas Knop. Ed. Gerd Bergfleth. München:
    Matthes & Seitz Verlag, 1997 [Paris 1974].
Braungart, Georg. "Poetik der Natur. Literatur und Geologie." *Natur—Kultur. Zur
    Anthropologie von Sprache und Literatur.* Ed. Thomas Anz. Paderborn: Mentis, 2009. 55-
    78.
Derrida, Jacques. "The Animal That Therefore I Am." *Critical Inquiry* 28.2 (2002). 369-418.
Dunker, Axel. *Kontrapunktische Lektüren. Koloniale Strukturen in der deutschsprachigen
    Literatur des 19. Jahrhunderts.* München: Fink, 2008.
Drux, Rudolf. *Marionette Mensch. Ein Metaphernkomplex und sein Kontext von Hoffmann
    bis Büchner.* München: Fink, 1986.
— . "Böse Bürgermädchen. Über den gnadenlosen Weg höherer Töchter zum Ehestand in
    Erzählungen E.T.A. Hoffmanns." *rebellisch verzweifelt infam. Das böse Mädchen als
    ästhetische Figur.* Ed. Renate Möhrmann. Bielefeld: Aisthesis, 2012. 187-98.
Engelstein, Stefani. "Reproductive Machines in E.T.A. Hoffmann." *Body Dialectics in the
    Age of Goethe.* Eds. Marianne Henn & Holger A. Pausch. Amsterdam & New York:
    Rodopi, 2003. 169-94.
Garrard, Greg. *Ecocriticism.* London & New York: Routledge, 2012.
Grundschule—Richtlinien und Lehrpläne. Ed. Ministerium für Schule und Weiterbildung des
    Landes Nordrhein-Westfalen. Frechen: Ritterbach-Verlag, 2008.
Hofer, Stefan. *Die Ökologie der Literatur. Eine systemtheoretische Annäherung.* Bielefeld:
    transcript, 2007.
Hoffmann, E.T.A.: *Der Sandmann.* In: *Fantasie- und Nachtstücke.* München: Winkler, 1976.
    331-63.
— . *Nachlese.* München: Winkler, 1981.
Hoffmann, Volker: "Seldwyla—ein geniales Todesabwehrsystem. Zur anthropologisch-
    ästhetischen Verknüpfung von Einleitung und erster Erzählung 'Pankraz, der Schmoller' in
    Kellers Zyklus 'Die Leute von Seldwyla'." *helle döne schöne. Versammelte Arbeiten zur
    älteren und neueren deutschen Literatur. Festschrift für Wolfgang Walliczek.* Eds. Horst
    Brunner et al. Göppingen: Kümmerle, 1999, 271-94.
Homer: *Odyssee.* Trans. Roland Hampe. Stuttgart: Reclam, 1999.
Horkheimer, Max & Theodor W. Adorno: *Dialectic of Enlightenment.* Stanford UP, 2002.
Keller, Gottfried. *Pankraz, der Schmoller.* In: *Die Leute von Seldwyla.* Frankfurt am Main:
    Insel, 1987. 14-70.
Lachenmaier, Tina. *E.T.A. Hoffmanns Figuren: Imaginative Spielräume der Ich-Identität.
    Die Erscheinungsformen des dissoziierten Ich: Doppelgängertum, Wahnsinn und
    Außenseitertum.* Göttingen: Cuvillier, 2007.
Liebrand, Claudia. *Aporie des Kunstmythos: Die Texte E.T.A. Hoffmanns.* Freiburg im
    Breisgau: Rombach, 1996.
Malkmus, Bernhard. "Ökologie als blinder Fleck der Kultur- und Literaturtheorie." *Natur—
    Kultur—Text. Beiträge zur Ökologie und Literaturwissenschaft.* Eds. Catrin Gersdorff &
    Sylvia Mayer. Heidelberg: Winter, 2005. 53-77.
Mecklenburg, Norbert. *Das Mädchen aus der Fremde. Germanistik als interkulturelle
    Literaturwissenschaft.* München: Iudicium, 2008.

Pfotenhauer, Helmut. *Sprachbilder. Untersuchungen zur Literatur seit dem 18. Jahrhundert.* Würzburg: Königshausen & Neumann 2000.

Riordan, Colin. "Ecocentrism in in Sebald's 'After Nature'." *W. G. Sebald—A Critical Companion.* Eds. J.J. Long & Anne Whitehead. Seattle: U of Washington P 2004, 45-57.

Schelling, Friedrich Wilhelm Joseph. *Von der Weltseele, eine Hypothese der höheren Physik zur Erklärung des allgemeinen Organismus* [1798]. *Vorrede zur ersten Auflage.* In: *Schellings Werke.* Auswahl in drei Bänden. Leipzig: Fritz Eckhardt Verlag 1907 (vol 1). *Schriften zur Naturphilosophie,* 441-49.

Schischkoff, Georgi (ed.). *Philosophisches Wörterbuch.* Stuttgart: Alfred Kröner, [1978] 1982.

Schmidt-Hannisa, Hans-Walter. "Aberration of a Species: On the Relationship between Man and Beast in W.G. Sebald's Works." *W. G. Sebald and Writing History.* Eds. Anne Fuchs & J.J. Jong. Würzburg: Königshausen & Neumann, 2007. 31-44.

Schnapp, Friedrich (ed.). *E.T.A. Hoffmanns Briefwechsel.* Darmstadt: Wiss. Buchgesellschaft, 1967.

Schönthaler, Philipp. *Negative Poetik. Die Figur des Erzählers bei Thomas Bernhard, W.G. Sebald und Imre Kertész.* Bielefeld: transcript, 2011.

Sebald, W.G.. *After Nature.* Trans. Michael Hamburger. London: Penguin, 2002.

— . *Nach der Natur. Ein Elementargedicht.* Frankfurt am Main: Fischer, 2008.

— . *Die Ringe des Saturn.* Frankfurt am Main: Fischer, 2011,

Soper, Kate. "The Idea of Nature." *The Green Studies Reader. From Romanticism to Ecocriticism.* Ed. Laurence Coupe. London & New York: Routledge, 2002. 123-26.

Wanning, Berbeli. "Der Naturbegriff in Literatur und Literaturwissenschaft." *Semantische Kämpfe. Macht und Sprache in den Wissenschaften.* Ed. Ekkehard Felder. Berlin & New York: De Gruyter, 2006. 223-49.

Zapf, Hubert. "Absence and Presence in American Literature." *Literature, Ecology, Ethics. Recent Trends in Ecocriticism.* Eds. Timo Müller & Michael Sauter. Heidelberg: Winter 2012, 83-94.

Internet

Commoner, Barry:
http://emilymorash07.tripod.com/id12.html (17 Jan.2013)

Oxenford, John: E.T.A. Hoffmann: *The Sandman* (1-27):
http://www.fln.vcu.edu/hoffmann/sand_e.html (15 Feb. 2013)

KMK-Empfehlungen:
www.kmk.org/fileadmin/pdf/PresseUndAktuelles/2007/KMK-DUK-Empfehlung.pdf
(17 Feb. 2013)

Forschungsstelle für Kulturökologie und Literaturdidaktik at Siegen University:
http://www.uni-siegen.de/phil/kulturoekologie/index.html (17 Feb. 2013).

I am greatly indebted to Roman Bartosch for inspiring discussions as well as help with the English text.

Debate

The Function of Criticism.
A Response to William Major and Andrew McMurry's Editorial[1]

Roman Bartosch (Cologne) and Greg Garrard (Bath Spa)

It was with what they called "desperate optimism" that William Major and Andrew McMurry assessed the "function of ecocriticism" in the last issue of the *Journal of Ecocriticism* (1). It is with the same desperate optimism that we are writing this short response—coming from two distinct 'branches' of ecocriticism, if you will, but sharing a commitment to debate and dialog, as well as the experience of a recent conference, of which we will speak later. Fortunately, and despite their ostensible dislike for "words upon words" vis-à-vis the more pressing question "What is to be done?" (1), Major and McMurry behave like exemplary humanist scholars in that they self-critically reflect on their field of academic praxis, the relevance of our studies and, as they put it, the connection "between the library cannel and the Greenland ice shield" (1). It is therefore in the same vein that we would like to propose a response. This response will entail

- a reflection on the role of theory and the idea of a linear relation between ecocriticism and the real world (yes, we are saying it, too!)
- a discussion of the potential of ecocriticism once it is released from the pressing apocalypticism of urgency and immediate practicability, and a discussion of the straw specter of the Humanist
- some remarks on the educational implications of these ideas.

One reason for our response is that the Call for Papers that has been cited as a prime example of "humanist boosterism" in the last issue (Major and McMurry 2013: 3) had been sent by one of us (R.B.). In fact, the issues touched upon in Major and McMurry's dismissal were, unsurprisingly, central concerns at the

---

1   This response was first published in the *Journal of Ecocriticism* (5.1) in January 2013. Thanks to Rebecca Raglon for giving us the opportunity to reprint it here. Some of the thoughts presented here also appear in Roman's book *Environmentality – Ecocriticism and the Event of Postcolonial Fiction*, out with Rodopi (2013). For Greg's thoughts on "air travel, climate change and literature," see Garrard 2013.

conference, and we agree that the discussion about the role of criticism, academic environmentalism, humanism and—especially—pedagogy is crucial if ecocriticism wants to be taken seriously, and if it wants seriously to contribute to our dealings with environmental crises.

It is true that ecocriticism developed because ethically-minded or guilt-ridden scholars felt the need to address environmental degradation, species extinction and all the other aspects of our current environmental crises and thus overcome what Major and McMurry identified as "the unstated [requisite] for becoming a scholar:" "that you must, on a professional level, give up the notion that you are working in a biosphere" (2013: 2). Yet, even making allowance for the enjoyable hyperbole of Major and McMurry, we are not sure "nothing much has changed since the time of the Babylonian times" (2)—the role of rhetoric and intellectual labor has changed a lot in the interim, while what early ecocriticism chose to confront was specifically the abstraction and alleged un-worldliness of *postmodernism*. Moreover, the question of the connection between words and world is not new and has been asked repeatedly in ecocriticism. Susie O'Brien, for instance, remarks on various explanations given by prominent ecocritics such as Cheryll Glotfelty, who explains that "as environmental problems compound, work as usual seems unconscionably frivolous" (qtd in O'Brien 2007: 180). She also refers to Glen A. Love, who mentions an ethical and environmentalist consciousness that is commonplace within the English departments and asks, "how are we to account for our general failure to apply any sense of this awareness to our daily work?" (qtd in O'Brien 2007: 180). While these scholars explain their individual, moral motives, O'Brien is not satisfied. She criticizes that Love, like other ecocritics, leaves "unexplained the precise mechanism by which the work of individual scholars, refracted through the profession of literary studies, might effect changes on the political level" (O'Brien 181). But is there such a "precise mechanism?" And, picking up on the other part of the mixed metaphor, is it not inevitable that it will be the prismatic unpredictability of the classroom that will 'refract' our work most beautifully— if anything will?

We tend to agree with Derek Attridge who in *The Singularity of Literature* (2004) claims that

> [t]he effects of the literariness of certain linguistic works [...] are not predictable and do not arise from planning [...]—there can be no guarantee that the alterity brought into the world by a particular literary or other artistic work will be beneficial. (Attridge 60)

Ecocriticism must resist the instrumentalizing of literature *even in its own interests*. Indeed there is, as Attridge goes on to say, no "guarantee that the future will have a place for the literary" (62). But it seems certain that for now, by responding to a literary text *as literature*, "my pleasure and profit come from the experience of an event of referring, from a staging of referentiality, not from any knowledge I acquire" (95-6). To argue otherwise would be to connive with the instrumentalization of knowledge that currently threatens the academic humanities and its ethical promise throughout the western world.

Thus, close readings can help in the environmental context even if they do not make you a better person, as Timothy Morton notes (2012). Why not try to be "slower than thou, in order to outdo the tortoise of close reading" and take part in the "anti-race toward an aesthetic state of meditative calm" (Morton 2007: 12)? It might lead to an environmentally oriented version of what James Wood calls the "dialectical tutoring" of reading: "Literature makes us better noticers of life; we get to practise on life itself; which in turn makes us better readers of detail in literature; which in turn makes us better readers of life" (Wood 2009: 53). Slow reading that conducts the student into a singular and unpredictable encounter with otherness is our business, and it would be foolhardy to pretend to any other.

This sounds as if we had all the time in the world indeed—which we haven't—and it clearly contrasts with the urgency and apocalypticism of Major and McMurry's assessment of the function of ecocriticism. That's not because we think that, politically, we can waste any more time but because we believe that the contribution of ecocriticism is inherently and valuably gradual: making us think anew about the world, nature, and the place of the human animal. Ecocriticism should continue to prompt searching reflection in its institutions and practitioners: successful scholars fly too much (indeed EASLCE's latest conference was in the Canary Islands, accessible only by air), but ASLE-UKI recently voted to make all conference food vegetarian henceforth and there are continuing experiments with Skype lectures and presentation. But twinges of conscience and organizational ethics are not the same as theoretical scholarship with its prerogative for critical and thorough analysis, evidence and argumentative plausibility. If ecocritical practices were simply restricted to transforming scientific findings into environmental activism (as if *those* things always align) we would sell our competences remarkably short, and that is to say nothing, yet, about the responsibilities of being teachers. We should not seek to be the literary wing of the IPCC.

It is because of its authority in questions of thinking things through in new and open ways that the humanities can contribute to comprehending the environmental crisis which is, as Lawrence Buell writes, a "crisis of the imagination" (L. Buell 1995: 2). "I am persuaded," Dana Phillips concludes his discussion of the connection between ecology and criticism, "that the truth of ecology must lie elsewhere, if it lies anywhere at all, in nature-culture, a region where surprising monsters dwell" (Phillips 39). Mapping nature-cultures and dealing with the monsters Phillips talks about is what we can do better than "retrain ourselves as scientific specialists" (see Westling 2012: 82) or sell us short as people who cannot understand the relevance of critical thinking once faced with the urgency of a problem. The task of understanding the "provisional and culturally inflected quality of scientific research at the same time that we acknowledge its indisputable power" (81) is a complicated and maybe even paradoxical one—so there is all reason in the world to think it through properly. As Morton says of deconstruction, part of the task of the environmental humanities is to show that "you don't have to believe everything you think" (Morton 2012: 165).

This already outlines what we believe is the benefit of ecocritical studies once they are freed from apocalypticism and confinement to immediate practical results. We are not saying that ecocritics shouldn't be scientifically literate or keenly interested in action, activism and commitment generally. But at the same time we are cautious of anti-intellectual attempts to play down the relevance of thorough analysis, interrogation, self-critique and constant negotiation of what we mean when we talk about saving the planet. The examples of relevant— practically relevant!—places for that are legion: whether we are looking at postcolonial environments and their struggle with "ecological imperialism" (Crosby), or at the scientific understanding of animals, or at the dangers of exploitation of supposedly easy concepts of the green movement by global capitalist players—think of "sustainable development," for instance—or at what Frederick Buell calls the "culture of hyperexuberance" (F. Buell 2004: 214).

The critical engagement with the complexities of the issues at hand sounds like a traditional humanist enterprise. That is not to say that the humanities have always and only produced wonderful and eternally true wisdom —but neither has any human praxis as far as we know. But they are the place for the discussions that we need if ecocriticism's effectiveness is conceptualized beyond the claim to the immediacy of activism. Peter Singer's animal liberation theses may serve as an illustration here: Singer does not argue from an anti-humanist perspective but sees the concern for sentient creatures in line with an ever-growing expansion of interest in the well-being of "others" (people of color, women and, now, nonhuman animals)—a similar argument to the one brought forward by Aldo Leopold in his land ethic. By contrast, Cary Wolfe says of such moral extensionism that:

> its penchant for the sort of 'pluralism' [...] extends the sphere of consideration (intellectual or ethical) to previously marginalized groups without in the least destabilizing or throwing into question the schema of the human who undertakes such pluralization. (Wolfe 2009: 568)

Is this what Major and McMurry mean by humanism? It's a rather fluid concept: humanism can be defined as the (self-)critical intellectual practice of humans interested in truth of the subjective kind but it is also taken as a phrase that covers hyper-rationality, uncritical anthropocentrism and whatever else have you in the poison cabinet of ecocritical language. Thus Patrick Curry, "reluctantly contradicting" David Ehrenfeld's *The Arrogance of Humanism* (1981), wishes to retain the term for these ontological and ethical entanglements: humanism (Curry 2008: 55). "It is true," he admits,

> that the word and the philosophy have become a hubristic denial of any limits to human self-aggrandisement, and the worship of technology in this pursuit. [...] But humanism also [...] implied almost the opposite of its modern meaning: the need to be humane, including but extending beyond humanity, in order to be fully human. Nor did humanism entail a denial of human limits and fallibility; again, quite the opposite. It is at least possible that in the context of ecocentrism, this original attitude could be recovered. (55)

We would argue for the compatibility, if not the isomorphism, of ontological posthumanism and humane ethics.

Which leads to the third point of our response: how to teach that? The main question of the conference hosted by the University of Cologne, Germany, in September 2012 was not the role of humanism or anti-humanism in the context of a discussion of the effectiveness of literature: "We are looking for contributors to a transdisciplinary symposium on the didactical implementations of ecocriticism, critical animal studies and green cultural studies." We were concerned with the conditions of possibility for ecocritical teachings in a situation where we are grappling with various and highly diverse antagonisms and pedagogical challenges. In their energetic response to the Call for Papers, Major and McMurry approved of "transdisciplinarity" as well as its "didactical implications," but took issue with the warning that teachers should avoid: "breaching the topics' complexity, falling into the mode of environmentalist propaganda or succumbing to warnings and claims to catastrophic urgency which are hard to reconcile with an ethos of critical and democratic pedagogy." What went wrong, or, what turned this "dream come true for ecocritics" (Major and McMurry 2013: 3) into something to be located in the "hallowed halls of humanist boosterism" (3)?

On a very general note, all kinds of inter- or transdisciplinary work requires a great deal of openness to other terminologies and concerns as well as faith in the honesty and accuracy of each other's findings. We cannot be literate in all discourses that are touched upon; so what we needed first was some kind of understanding and trust that enables the historian to talk to the philosopher, and the literature teacher to the biologist. Ecocriticism is maybe *the* field where such an objective is taken seriously; however, unanimous commitment to political or civil activism does not make such trust easier. One of the greatest risks for genuine interdisciplinary ecocritical research is not being taken seriously—not because nobody cares for the environment (although the ratio could be better) but because other academics find it peculiar that ecocritics unashamedly propagate their agendas and personal views and think they can get away with it. It must remain open for the moment whether the cure for that problem lies in rhetorical agnosticism, or more theoretical sophistication—as in Timothy Morton's suggestion to exploit deconstructive theory and language in the service of "ecological humanism" (yes, he said it!): "you need a way of proceeding that is as fast and as smart as the cynicism" because otherwise "you will be laughed at for being anti-intellectual" (Morton 2012: 163) – or in declaring one's partiality and taking it as the basis for debate. Whatever the answer, the tension between teaching and preaching has to be an integral part of a conference dealing with ecocriticism in the curriculum.

John Parham in a provocatively clever essay discusses the last option: open acknowledgement of one's partiality, followed by an invitation to students to "challenge our partiality" (Parham 2006: 17). This is because "a more abstract education in critical thinking might come prior to, even take precedence over, a specific commitment to an education that 'raises environmental awareness'" (19). Yet Parham endorses humanistic education in a posthumanist cause, arguing that critical pedagogy seeks to "enable a democratic classroom practice that encourages free expression" and to foster a "concern to engage students in an oppositional [...] critique of society," even if "environmental pedagogy invariably fails to practice the 'dialogic' approach that it preaches" (7). As teachers, Parham claims, we often address this "tension between the democratic spirit of Academia and the imperative nature of Green thought" (Dominic Wood qtd in Parham 2006: 7), by accumulating what he calls "environmental capital;" analogous to Bourdieu's 'cultural capital', environmental capital means a shelf full of appropriate publications demonstrating environmental consciousness, knowledge of key texts and motifs, and the 'right attitude' to environmentalist action (see Parham 2006: 10).

Yet far from simply applauding the habitus of the activist professor, Parham argues that "the teacher's self-appointed environmental capital creates an unwillingness to entertain dissent which [...] runs the risk of driving a wedge between teacher and student" (11). He quotes John Paul Tassoni who, as an ecofeminist, writes that

> [s]uch impositions reinforce the very sort of monologic, hierarchical relationships that ecofeminists resist. Teachers who force their views on their classes subordinate the interests and concerns of students of their own. Furthermore, such teachers promote passivity in their students. (qtd in Parham 2006: 14)

This impasse was a crucial point on the conference as well, for example in Greg Garrard's paper on the outlines of an 'pedagogy of the unprecedented', which remarkably differs from the didacticism of a David Orr or others who see 'green teaching' as requiring a prescriptive curriculum that will save the world. One delegate, Pamela Swanigan, went so far as to assert that prioritizing preaching over teaching was 'dishonorable'.

Instead of taking these issues as reasons for a bigger dose of gloom, however, we believe that discussing the challenges will make our work better and more effective. And contrary to the beliefs expressed in the last issue of the *Journal of Ecocriticism*, namely that "it takes images of planetary annihilation to motivate people into action after years of sitting idly by watching things slowly decay" and that "even when our images of apocalypse aren't fully accurate, our use of elements of scientifically-established reality reconstructs the surrounding power structures in beneficial ways" (Schatz 2013: 21), we tend to think that, especially in the context of pedagogy, "[e]schatological narrative [...] brings with it philosophical and political problems that seriously compromise its usefulness" (Garrard 2004: 105). Major and McMurry's frenetic prose takes us hurtling, like Thelma and Louise, towards the cliff edge, whereas we prefer less sweaty, if still demanding, journeys, such as Seamus Heaney's 'From the Republic of Conscience':

Fog is a dreaded omen there but lightning
spells universal good and parents hang
swaddled infants in trees during thunderstorms.

...

Their sacred symbol is a stylized boat.
The sail is an ear, the mast a sloping pen,
The hull a mouth-shape, the keel an open eye.

At their inauguration, public leaders
must swear to uphold unwritten law and weep
to atone for their presumption to hold office ... (Heaney 1990)

Heaney's map of an impossible journey exemplifies the reticent, obdurate fragility of literature, to which critics ought to bear patient witness – even to the crack of doom.

If apocalyptic fear is enervating, the optimistic alternative of 'sustainability' is such a distant and elusive destination that education 'for' it can only ever consist in asking students the right sort of questions and then encouraging them in their own search for answers. Such a procedure coheres well with the best traditions of humanistic and democratic education whilst also being the only real preparation imaginable for a risky, exciting and unprecedented future. Which is, after all, where our students will have to live.

Works Cited

Attridge, Derek. *The Singularity of Literature*. London and New York: Routledge, 2004.
Bartosch, Roman. *EnvironMentality—Ecocriticism and the Event of Postcolonial Fiction*. Amsterdam & New York: Rodopi, 2013.
Buell, Frederick. *From Apocalypse to Way of Life*. London & New York: Routledge, 2004.
Buell, Lawrence. *The Environmental Imagination. Thoreau, Nature Writing and the Formation of American Culture*. Cambridge MA: Harvard UP, 1995.
Curry, Patrick. "Nature Post-Nature." *New Formations. A Journal of Culture/Theory/Politics* 26 (2008). 51-64.
Garrard, Greg. *Ecocriticism*. London & New York: Routledge, 2004. Print.
—   .   "A   Novel   Idea: Slow   Reading."   *Times   Higher   Education*. http://www.timeshighereducation.co.uk/story.asp?storycode=412075
—   .   "The   unbearable   lightness   of   green: air   travel,   climate   change   and literature." *Green Letters. Studies in Ecocriticism* 17.2 (2013). 175-88.
Heaney, Seamus. *New Selected Poems: 1966-1987*. London & Boston, 1990.
Major, William and Andrew McMurry. "Introduction: The Function of Ecocriticism; or, Ecocriticism, What Is It Good For?" *Journal of Ecocriticism* 4.2 (2013). 1-7. Online at http://ojs.unbc.ca/index.php/joe/issue/current/showToc
Morton, Timothy. *Ecology without Nature. Rethinking Environmental Aesthetics*. Cambridge: Harvard UP, 2007.
—   .   "Practising   Deconstruction   in   the   Age   of   Ecological   Emergency."   *Teaching Ecocriticism and Green Cultural Studies*. Ed. Greg Garrard. Basingstoke/New York: PalgraveMacmillan, 2012. 156-66.
Parham, John. "The Deficiency of 'Environmental Capital': Why Environmentalism Needs a Reflexive Pedagogy." *Ecodidactic Perspectives on English Language, Literatures and Cultures*. Eds. Sylvia Mayer and Graham Wilson. Trier: Wissenschaftlicher Verlag, 2006. 7-22.
Phillips, Dana. *The Truth of Ecology. Nature, Culture, and Literature in America*. Oxford and New York: Oxford UP, 2003.
Schatz, JL. "The Importance of Apocalypse: The Value of End-of-the-World Politics While Advancing Ecocriticism." *Journal of Ecocriticism* 4.2 (2012). 20-33. Online at http://ojs.unbc.ca/index.php/joe/issue/current/showToc
O'Brien, Susie. "'Back to the World': Reading Ecocriticism in a Postcolonial Context." *Five Emus to the King of Siam: Environment and Empire*. Ed. Helen Tiffin. Amsterdam: Rodopi, 2007. 177-99.
Westling, Louise. "Literature and Ecology." *Teaching Ecocriticism and Green Cultural Studies*. Ed. Greg Garrard. Basingstoke/New York: PalgraveMacmillan, 2012. 75-89.
Wolfe, Cary. "Human, All Too Human: 'Animal Studies' and the Humanities." *PMLA* 124.2 (2009). 564-75.
Wood, James. *How Fiction Works*. London: Vintage, 2009.

Response of William Major and Andrew McMurry[1]

William Major (University of Hartford) and Andrew McMurry (University of Waterloo)

We thank Roman Bartosch and Greg Garrard for their thoughtful and temperate critique of our introduction to a recent special issue of *Journal of Ecocriticism*. Their response contains a number of valuable insights about the roles of ecocriticism, the humanities, and teaching in the present and largely foundering academic archipelago, and we find much to agree with. They would also distance themselves from the discourse of apocalypticism and instead align with the go-slow approach of traditional literary inquiry and the life of the scholar—even the scholar whose watching and waiting has brought her to the unassailable conclusion that her kids and grandkids will not be able to similarly "lean and loaf" at their ease even if they do produce scholarship that fosters the "prismatic unpredictability of the classroom" (Bartosch and Garrard 2) upon which Bartosch and Garrard's cautious optimism teeters. But more on pedagogy later.

First things first. We suspect that what most troubled Bartosch and Garrard was that we threw them—or, rather, their Call for Papers for a conference in Cologne[2]—under the humanist bus. They return the favor,

---

1   [Editors' note: This reponse has first been published in the *Journal of Ecocriticism* 5.1 (2013). We kindly thank the general editor of the journal, Rebecca Raglon, and both authors, William Major and Andrew McMurry, for their permission to reprint it in this context and, thus, add to the dialogue we both are seeking —albeit from afar. It must be noted, however, that the CfP in question has *not* been formulated by Greg Garrard, who had been invited as a keynote speaker for said conference; the language of the CfP that Major and McMurry take issue with and discuss in this paper is therefore entirely in the responsibility of the conference convenors—and not Greg Garrard].

2   Here is the full CFP for "Teaching the Environment: Transdisciplinary Perspectives":
    "We are looking for contributors to a transdisciplinary symposium on the didactical implementations of ecocriticism, critical animal studies and green cultural studies. [With] a special emphasis on transdisciplinary perspectives, we would like to discuss how the tenets of these academic fields can be incorporated into the daily practice of

noting that we ourselves "behave like exemplary humanist scholars." About that bus: these days, not many literary critics wish to be on it, let alone under it. Humanism, this middle ground philosophy that rejects transcendent references as much as it eschews baldly materialist ones, is out of fashion (although, as Bartosch and Garrard remind us, humanism can also embody an admirable notion of the humane and a pointed acknowledgement of our species' fallibility). Some one-time humanists now prefer to style themselves post-humanists, a positionality meant to signal their disavowal of human arrogance, anthropocentrism, and essentialism, among other things. Posthumanists content themselves with a modest claim to plain citizenship in the commonwealth of species.

One unfortunate relic of humanism that we detect in many intellectuals may be said to fall under the rhetorical category of *stance* (Booth) or *attitude* (Burke). What does a humanist stance or attitude look like, intellectually speaking? Gramsci, as an example, suggested that one might do well to espouse a pessimism of the intellect but an optimism of the will. We think Bartosch and Garrard would probably approve of that stance, which we take to be an epitome of the humanist spirit of inquiry. Implicitly, this optative mood is considered upright, courageous, and indispensable.

Where we part ways with all humanisms most decisively is that we have abandoned this disabling rhetoric of the *hopeful spirit*. That is because we think that optimism of the will too often inhibits the operations of the intellect and the move to praxis. No surprise that hope happens: everything in our culture encourages us, as Monty Python had it, to look on the bright side of life. It seems to be one of the articles of secular humanist faith that what man has harmed he can, with a more reasonable, patient application of his intellect and moral compass, unharm. But we think this is just the hopeful spirit working its voodoo, turning vinegar into wine and frowns upside down.

Don't take us wrong: it is not the arrogance of humanism we are talking about here; it's the attitude of humanism. Give engineers a challenge, and they'll roll up their sleeves and say, "let's work the problem." Engineers

---

teaching the humanities and arts—without either breaching the topics' complexity, falling into the mode of environmentalist propaganda or succumbing to warnings and claims to catastrophic urgency which are hard to reconcile with an ethos of critical and democratic pedagogy.
We hope to enable truly transdisciplinary dialogues and therefore, we welcome teachers just as well as theoreticians from academia whose topics may comprise, but do not have to be restricted to, environmental and animal studies, green didactics, eco-composition, posthumanism, the sciences, and related fields. With this broad focus and the variety of topics that it allows, we hope to provide a basis for transdisciplinary connections in an inextricably interconnected world." [note from the editors: a missing word has been added to the footnote].

fervently believe in the techno-fix (what Bill McKibben calls "the defiant reflex"). What do humanists believe in? The dialog-fix. We work the problem through the Socratic circle. In this scheme, there's no time for hand-wringing, only tongue-wagging, which is our kind of *doing*. Now, if we humanists and posthumanists don't like to think of ourselves as can-do pragmatists, that's only because we've been trained to imagine our penchant for *problematizing* and *complicating* signals our commendable skepticism, long-circuit thinking, and inclusivity. We don't panic; we dilate. We are useful eggheads: hard, not soft, boiled. In normal times, we can be quite endearing. But in a crisis, our very strengths may work against us. We become the know-it-all in the cinematic hostage scene who steps up to the gun-wielding villains, saying, "I am a trained negotiator. Let's all just take a deep breath. I'm sure we can work this out." We all know what happens to that guy.

We despair that one day homo academicus will wake up to find that what he thought was wisdom about the current crisis was nothing but willful blindness elevated to virtue. He will realize that he was not just a frog in a pot but a frog in a pot who thought he was St. Jerome in his study. Thus in their CFP Garrard and Bartosch wish to exclude apocalypticism and "environmentalist propaganda" from their cosmopolitan conference just as they would like to exclude it from "the daily practice of teaching the humanities and arts." This preference for the Burkean comic frame is consistent with Garrard's perspective, as announced in his influential primer, *Ecocriticism*. Tragic apocalypticism, he notes, polarizes audiences, plays into the media's preference for sensationalism, eliminates nuance and complexity, promotes villainization, and generally muddies the waters of rational debate. At its worst, the "rhetoric of catastrophism tends to 'produce' the crisis it describes, as in the Malthusian depiction of extreme poverty as 'famine'" (105).

These are important observations, and we go along with them to some extent. But not all the way. We maintain, against Bartosch and Garrard, that discourses of fear, foreboding, and pessimism are appropriate objective correlatives for the whirlwind of terrifying ecological facts we are confronted with daily. These latter must be engaged in their full horror, not blunted in advance by ratiocination. It is thus the safeguarding into reasoned equipoise that we object to, in the university and elsewhere. We believe Bartosch and Garrard are too quick to usher the Other of scholarly ethos and logos out the classroom door, and too ready to assume "catastrophe" is a concept that can be stipulated to and moved past, as if it is merely one more item in the lading-list of apocalyptic misfires, a distraction from the hard work of slow reading and slow thought. We say, "not so fast." Neither democracy or criticism are served by downplaying the palpable, chilling signals of environmental collapse. Granted, we have a long history of unrequited millennial expectations and apocalyptic doomsaying, stemming from a variety of traditions and dispositions. But to what end do we link our current ecological crisis with that kind of thinking? There is vast gulf between the Book of Revelations and 391 ppm of carbon dioxide, and we ecocritics know it. The conflation of ecocatastrophe and end-of-the-worldism has been the rhetorical gambit of right wing denialists and liberal Pollyannas alike; it does not serve ecocriticism well to say, "Tut, tut. Some people always believe the sky is falling; let's not lower ourselves to *that* discussion."

We believe that the stiff-upper-lip, go-slow position costs us immensely. We believe that there is actually much to fear besides fear itself, that the quasi-official stance of optimism has its own risks. We believe that what remained in Pandora's jar after the evils escaped—i.e., *hope*—is no longer our friend but our enemy, a mischief in its own right that lets us lay off hard decisions onto futurity. We caution that the cerebral modulation of unmitigated environmental disaster is a mistake, a kind of preemptive quietism, politically speaking, part and parcel of a culture that overwhelmingly prefers the "feel-good" ending. It is speculated that the tragic frame enervates by overplaying pathos and melodrama, and perhaps it does. But so too does the comic frame, with its glass half-full approach, enervate by overplaying reason and composure.[3]

We turn now to ecocriticism and didactics. Ecocriticism is not special. We perhaps once thought it was special; we perhaps bought into the first wave critique of postmodernism that Bartosch and Garrard (and others) rightly identify as the-then proper response to pomo hyperexuberance. There was a gap, ethical and critical, and ecocritics sought—mostly successfully—to fill it. Yet the fact that ecocritical scholars privileged the biosphere they identified as a neglected area of literary critical intervention did not, we submit, make their work any more useful in terms of addressing the practical problems it raised.

Thus the abstractions of the postmodern, to which Bartosch and Garrard refer, are the real straw men now that early ecocriticism has come and gone and things are getting worse, and there's no way that they are going to get better, if reports from the UN Climate Change summit in Doha, Qatar, are to be believed. As of this writing, greenhouse gases emissions were at an all-

---

3   There is a grim joke that embodies this combination of deferral and denial so typical of contemporary culture: Doctor: I have some very bad news. You have inoperable cancer. Terminal. I estimate you have less than three weeks to live. Patient: I understand. I'll be out of town this summer. Can we schedule the treatments to begin in September?

time high in 2012, over 14 years after the Kyoto Protocol was adopted. But we already know this. We also know there's nothing, practically speaking, we can do about it.

Ecocriticism thinks it is special, and this is a problem. It has set itself up from its earliest days as attending, in ways that previous critical modes had not, to what had been mostly neglected in the Weltanschauung: places, ecologies, non-human others, and so on. It cultivated approaches to texts that thrust these entities into the view of fellow scholars, students, even the wider public in some cases. That ecocriticism has been successful in tending to that garden in the current global context is perhaps in its favor; we can say that although the world is not much less oblivious to its incipient demise since our kind of thing came into being, it could clearly be more so. We have done no harm, in other words, and there are certainly arguments to be made—and Bartosch and Garrard make them—that it's too soon to tell whether we've done some good. We'll just have to wait and see. But the very fact that ecocriticism possesses a *hard kernel*, an ethical center that cannot be overcome, that cannot be out-theorized, that cannot be postmoderned out of existence or rhetorically invalidated, and that center is its animating force…well, because that hard kernel tasks us, dogs us, we suppose we must acknowledge there is a disappointed liberal humanist in both of us, borrowing from Patrick Curry's useful recuperation of humility (qtd. in Bartosch and Garrard (4). And because ecocriticism has failed to live up to our expectations, because it begins to look, twenty years or so in, more or less like just another professional discourse among professional discourses (which it is), routinized into the low-stakes academic poker game, yes, for sure, this gives us pause.

Of course, the failure is in part our own; it is one of those unfulfilled humanist expectations, "how to change the world" and etc., the beliefs we may have had in graduate school about "discourse being practice," and that sort of blather. And we plead guilty to once believing that working out an *explication de texte* was just a step away from manning a barricade. Anyway, we *hoped* it was. We may as well have been New Critics, except that they had an audience. Between then and now, there have been too many conferences, too many papers, too many books, where the so very high stakes of a livable planet came down to "here's a new way to think about this" or "if we learn to talk about objects using these terms, the ones I have derived by running this poem through quantum physics and Lacan, then we might be able to reenchant the world, or heal the circle of life, or get our heads on straight…" Sounds a bit like a fairy tale, doesn't it, when you hear from a few feet back? Or some kind of ersatz New Age religion? Was this how L. Ron Hubbard started? But then he had charisma. To be sure, we like this kind of talk, don't get us wrong, and we've uttered it, too. But where is it going? Does it add up to something? Is it more than whistling past the graveyard? Bartosch and Garrard say, in effect, we're *paying it forward* to our students. Maybe so. We want to know more about how that process works, because if ever there was a time to ponder the question of literary criticism's relevance, it's right now. That is what our special issue was meant to consider.

Which leads us to Bartosch and Garrard's warnings about the downside of the "instrumentalizing of literature (2). We concede the point full in the knowledge that the specters of Stanley Fish and David Horowitz hover behind us every time we bring politics into the classroom. Frankly, we don't know what literature is supposed to do, whether it is supposed to make us better or more ethical people, or whether it does this for our students, who seem to have their own problems. We also admit that it is simply impossible to teach and not preach, at least a little bit, which is why John Parhams's idea to put our cards on the table seems about right, and certainly takes the starch out of the academic guessing game. No one has ever said to either one of us to stop preaching and, anyway, the books themselves, the literature that is not supposed to be instrumentalized, seem to do that quite well. If literature "makes us better noticers of life" (Wood 53, qtd. in Bartosch and Garrard 3) and if books can potentially "bring the student into a singular and unpredictable encounter with otherness" (Bartosch and Garrard 3), then all the better, though we aren't quite sure there aren't other such encounters that will effect the same.

What brings us up short, however, and where we draw the rhetorical line (since there is no other), is in Bartosch and Garrard's position, in citing the invaluable contrast between praxis and criticism, that

> twinges of conscience and organisational ethics are not the same as theoretical scholarship with its prerogative for critical and thorough analysis, evidence and argumentative plausibility. If ecocritical practices were simply restricted to transforming scientific findings into environmental activism (as if those things always align) we would sell our competences remarkably short, and that is to say nothing, yet, about the responsibilities of being teachers. (3)

We think that such "twinges of conscience," such as those referenced by Bartosch and Garrard (ASLE-UKI has gone vegetarian; SKYPE lectures and conference presentations), are actually as necessary as theoretical/critical investments. We think that we need more "twinges of conscience," just as we devoutly acquiesce to the blandishments of "successful scholars[hip]" that whisks us around the globe. What's wrong with conscience and ethics, anyway? "Theoretical scholarship with its prerogative for critical and thorough analysis, evidence and argumentative plausibility" (Bartosch and Garrard 3) is useless without them. No one is suggesting that we not think things through, that we not rigorously examine scientific and humanist claims, that we not utilize all the tools at our disposal in our criticism and teaching. This isn't a Samuel Beckett play; we can do something, and to paraphrase Thoreau, this does not mean we have to do everything. We simply aren't sure we know what to do, and that what we are doing is doing what we think it does. But we do know that more of the same has the potential for more of the same. Which is unacceptable. Which is immoral, too. And ours is hardly an "anti-intellectual attempt to play down the relevance of thorough analysis, interrogation, self-critique and constant negotiation of what we mean when we talk about saving the planet" (Bartosch and Garrard 4); we do not work for the FOX Network. We are, after all, "exemplary humanist scholars."

It is in the realm of teaching that our diverse perspectives converge, and we are aware of the good work that Garrard has done in this realm. The CFP that struck the wrong note with us seemed, however, to immediately cancel the type of dialog we are now having, albeit from afar. As we have explained above, we are little convinced that an apocalyptic consciousness— one tempered, of course, by the good breeding inherent to Doctors of Philosophy—undermines the obvious fealty to intellectual intercourse that ostensibly took place at the conference (though we have been to plenty of conferences in which nothing of the sort occurred). Thinking things through—as good as that makes us feel—hardly obviates what's going on on the ground. Nor does an eye to the ongoing collapse necessarily "breach the topics' complexity," or manifest in "environmentalist propaganda" (Bartosch and Garrard 5). The "ethos of critical and democratic pedagogy" that Bartosch and Garrard undoubtedly support was, regrettably, shut down by the language of the CFP, which was itself an attempt to circumscribe the discourse it wished to enhance. And though we are sympathetic to their aim of not putting off participants from other disciplines who might "find it peculiar that ecocritics unashamedly propagate their agendas and personal views" (5), we can't help but observe that perhaps the more salient point is that ecocritics at least know they have agendas whereas the trouble with some disciplinary scholars is that they naively believe they have none.

What we found, at any rate, was that the language of the CFP worked against the ecocritical discourse, to which we are all volunteers, and against us, as potential contributors, and thus it did damage to that hard ethical kernel that causes us to gravitate together. We suppose that we represent those who have, for good or ill, "fall[en] into the mode of environmentalist propaganda" and "succumb[ed] to warnings and claims to catastrophic urgency" yet who are still wanting to "reconcile with an ethos of critical and democratic pedagogy." We represent those who do not think catastrophic urgency must come to terms with the demands of pedagogy; we think, rather, that pedagogy—and criticism—must come to terms with the urgency of the catastrophe.

Finally, we—Thelma and Louise!—offer this poem by Emily Dickinson to contrast the ecocritical stance of Bartosch and Garrard, as they "bear patient witness—even to the crack of doom," with our own, precarious perch over the cliff's edge:

"Faith" is a fine invention
For Gentlemen who see!
But Microscopes are prudent
In an Emergency!

-Emily Dickinson

Works Cited

Bartosch, Roman and Greg Garrard. "The Function of Criticism. A Response to William Major and Andrew McMurry's Editorial." *Journal of Ecocriticism* 5.1 (2013). 6pp.
Garrard, Greg. *Ecocriticism*. London: Routledge, 2004.

The Case Against Agenda

Pamela Swanigan (Connecticut)

When the organizers of the Cologne symposium on "Teaching the Environment" asked for papers that discussed "how the tenets of [various] academic fields can be incorporated into the daily practice of teaching the humanities and arts— without either breaching the topics' complexity, falling into the mode of environmentalist propaganda or succumbing to warnings and claims to catastrophic urgency which are hard to reconcile with an ethos of critical and democratic pedagogy," they posed, in effect, the same question that John Parham asked 11 years ago in his introduction to *The Environmental Tradition in English Literature*: "[H]ow, pedagogically, do we teach ecocriticism and to what end? [...] Should it be more didactic and aim to teach environmental values?" (xv). Keynote speaker Greg Garrard echoed those questions when he named as a crucial ecocritical task that of identifying the desired outcomes of ecocritical pedagogy.

I feel that we may have moved with too little discussion from the question of "whether" to teach from an environmentalist agenda to the question of "how," with some assumption that the "should we?" part was rhetorical or token. My own answer to Parham's second question would be "No." No, we should not be more didactic and aim to teach "environmental values," whatever those may be. No, we should not entertain the idea that a desired outcome would be, as David Mazel suggests in "Ecocriticism as Praxis," to turn our students into "more thoughtful and effective environmentalists" (3). No, we should not move on to the question of how to effect these ends: not now, not ever.

My reason for rejecting entirely any proposal for agenda-based ecocritical or environmental teaching is threefold: it is dishonorable, it is counterproductive, and it is unnecessary. In this paper I argue mostly for the third point, by providing examples of exercises I have used that allow ecological values and interests to play what I deem a more legitimate part in teaching. However, I would like to touch on the first two points as well.

As to the first point, namely, that this kind of agenda is dishonorable: here I refer to the concept of "honor" by the working definition that I have arrived at over the years (which is rather different than others I have seen)—namely, as meaning "declining to act on a power advantage." In other words, I am referring to the kind of honor that helps us refrain from doing something simply because we can. Since, as is self-evident, this brand of honor quickly becomes a competitive disadvantage to the honorable individual if it is not carried out by a community at large, I believe that when we are in a position to model it from a leadership position, we ought to.

Granted this definition of honor, it follows that taking advantage of our position as teachers to impose upon our students our personal beliefs, however important we deem them, can only be viewed as an act of dishonor. When we give students anything less than a concertedly even-handed set of material, expose them to only the pro-environmentalist sides of an issue, use dysphemistic terms when talking about developers and corporations, and so on, we are telling them that we are willing to take advantage of our authority over them (in the school context) to serve our own interests. Surely this teaches them more about the culture among environmentalists and ecological-minded people than any of the actual material we give them, and what it teaches them is not to our credit.

In the discussion of this point during the symposium, one panel member said that she felt it was dishonest and unrealistic to try to hide her personal values, biases, and activist goals when she was teaching, and therefore she laid them on the table for her students at the start of each course. While I understand her point, it has been my experience that some students, perhaps most students (depending on their stage of education and maturity), will write and say what they think their teachers want to hear, and the more explicit we are about our personal stance on an issue, the more slanted in that direction their own responses become. Many students *assume* in us the dishonorable tendency to mark papers higher if their argument lines up with our opinion; stating that opinion openly will only encourage them in this assumption. As to the notion that impartiality should not be striven for because it cannot be achieved, I am familiar with this kind of thinking from my days as a journalist, and I have noticed that, such arguments notwithstanding, readers and viewers are relieved and gratified when they find a source of information that they can trust to be *relatively* even-handed. There are simple ways to facilitate objectivity in journalism, such as always obtaining and including an even number of comments from representatives on both/all sides of an issue. In an ecocriticism or green studies class, this is easily done: we hardly lack for articulate arguments from advocates of monoculture, genetic engineering, the mining and gas industries, meat-eaters, et cetera. The added benefit of doing this is that our students will not be rhetorically blindsided when they happen to encounter arguments from outside the environmentalist echo chamber.

In another article to which Greg Garrard refers in his abstract, Mike Hulme's "Meet the Humanities," Hulme suggests not only that the humanities should be allowed a greater role in the public and professional discussions of environmental issues such as climate change, but that that role should be something more than the subservient one of translating and popularizing scientific findings, as scientists such as David King contend. Surely this petition for a place at the table is viable only if we adhere to the "ethos of critical and democratic pedagogy" that this symposium's call for papers cited.

Likewise, defenses of the larger humanist tradition vis-à-vis ecocritical approaches, such as Kate Soper's argument that humanism and its priorities are not necessarily inimical or antithetical to what she calls "nature-endorsing" positions (4), can be considered valid only so long as we in the humanities remain accountable to the precepts of academic rigor and honesty. In literary interpretation we teach our students that they must work to some degree of evidentiary standards. For instance, as David Rosenwasser and Jill Stephen tell students in their textbook *Writing Analytically*, they cannot look at the portrait of Whistler's mother and decide that she is an alien and has a third leg hidden under her skirt, because there is simply no textual support for such a reading (77-80). Why then would we abrogate our own efforts at impartiality and use the lectern as a bully pulpit? When and where did we as ecocritical teachers agree that it was acceptable to inject our personal political agenda not only with impunity but with purpose, and to teach to the ends of conversion rather than education? The fact that data overwhelmingly support such events as climate change, environmental degradation, and species extinction makes it all the sillier that we would not provide our students with texts and other materials from climate-change deniers, "cornucopian" thinkers, pro-development lobbyists, etc. To block access to these perspectives, or fail to discuss them in good faith, would suggest that we have something to fear from them.

Agendistic lopsidedness in environmental/green teaching only adds credence to Frederick Crews' already too-accurate observation that many in the academic humanities "subscribe to a two-tiered conception of truth. They make a token bow to empirically grounded knowledge, but they deem it too pedestrian for mapping the labyrinth of the soul or for doing justice to the emotional currents coursing between interacting persons. Instead of merely avowing that the subjective realm is elusive, however, they then advance their own preferred theory, which is typically sweeping, absolute, and bristling with partisanship" (9). I would say that so long as we feel free to introduce our personal biases, convictions, and political stances into our teaching, and to teach tendentiously to outcomes related to these personal politics, we saw off our own branch from a number of angles. We widen rather than bridge the gap between us and the so-called positivist disciplines. We contribute to our own discrediting and our own increasing irrelevance in important debates. And—most inexcusably, to my mind—we traduce and terminally vitiate the purpose of pedagogy.

I disagree with the suggestion that there might be any "effectiveness" in introducing a mandate for ecocritical teaching separate from that of pedagogy at large. A crucial part of that pedagogical mandate, as I have always understood it, is to make our students more resistant to brainwashing by helping them develop their critical faculties and independent judgement. To participate ourselves in the process of indoctrination—whether by lobbying from behind the lectern for personal causes such as vegetarianism, environmental activism, "green" living, and animal rights or by presenting as unassailable theories such as evolution, climate change, and biophilia—seems to me both professionally unconscionable and pragmatically self-defeating. To the extent that these causes and theories are legitimate, they will stand up to any amount of evidence and rhetoric from opposing sides; therefore, we can only benefit by presenting these issues as open debates, providing our students with plenty of opposing material, and encouraging them to subject all evidence and assertions equally to rigorous, reality-based critical thinking. If elements of our pet causes and beliefs alter or even fall under this process, then the intellectually honest and honorable thing to do is to let this happen and to admit it. We may have the right to dogma as individuals, but I do not believe we have that right as professionals with significant advantages of positional power and knowledge over a group of other people.

As to my second reason for rejecting the teaching of ecocriticism from a stance of personal political bias, namely, that it is counterproductive: this follows from the first point in a self-evident way. If we have taught our students, as surely is incumbent upon us to do, the critical-thinking techniques of examining propositions and information for bias, hidden assumptions, and vested interest, then they will fail to accept—as they *should* fail to accept—our propagandizing. I can't think of a greater disservice we can do to our beliefs and causes than to yoke them, in our students' minds, to hypocrisy and a lack of integrity.

As to my third point: what would make a corruption of our pedagogical mandate all the more tragic is that, in my experience of teaching first-year university-level English, doing so is entirely unnecessary. We are an alarmist species by nature. Although I understand that multi-volume sets have been written on how close to the surface our biophilic instincts are and how easily they are triggered, if indeed they exist at all, it is both my experience and my conviction that most people have residing within them numerous perceptual gauges telling them that things are not okay, and even the most urbanized surely have some number of conscious perceptions to the same effect. To consider it necessary to actively proselytize for environmentalism is to betray a fundamental conviction that humans are not, after all, animals—or at least that they are not animal enough to have a network of evolutionary responses that can be and will be triggered by a pedagogically legitimate exposure to ecological and environmental issues and information. This conviction is a common one, perhaps the prevailing one, within the academic humanities, but from what I have seen in my years of teaching, it is incorrect. Whenever I presented my students with a data set that warned them of peril and another that assured them in equally authoritative terms of safety (for instance, in the case of the plastic additive bisphenol A), almost all of them believed the former over the latter.

In support of my contention that environmentalist views do not have to be imposed, I will briefly describe a number of assignments and activities that I used in my first-year English course at a university-college in the Vancouver area. My interest in nature and the sciences led me to use these themes as vehicles for my mandated task of teaching analysis, reasoning, critical reading, and literary interpretation. On assessing their effectiveness to these subordinate roles, I noticed that at no point did I have to thrust my own conclusions on my students. Most of them developed an interest and a sense of urgency entirely of their own accord, upon simply being exposed to the ideas and information. If they didn't, I left it alone: to my mind, it is no more my prerogative to tell students how to feel than it is to tell them what to think.

I say "I left it alone" blithely enough, but there were many times, especially in my early years of teaching, when I found it almost impossible not to try to sway my students' views. Initially my fix for this was to take that exercise or debate out of the curriculum, so that I wouldn't be tempted. However, once I had come to trust the processes of analysis and critical thinking—and, as importantly, my ability to teach these skills effectively—I realized that the better route would be to introduce stronger arguments from other perspectives, and to discuss these at greater length and always in good faith, so that my students felt safe in adopting perspectives that differed from or conflicted with what they sensed to be mine.

The first activity I will describe is a question that I asked my students in order to facilitate analysis, "Why is anger?" Most of my students were quite oblivious to the idea of emotions as an animalistic, primal-stem response to survival situations, universal across cultures and history. Here I should say that in a typical class of 25 students, I would usually have something like 10 from mainland China and Hong Kong, six or seven from Pakistan and India, a couple of Persians and Afghanis, a smattering of Eastern Europeans and perhaps five European-descended British Columbians. This meant that reflexive Judeo-Christian answers rarely arose, and any culture-specific answer would show itself to be inadequate. The analysis therefore went by necessity to the level of what I now recognize as evolutionary psychology, though I didn't know such a field existed at the time. Living in the multicultural region they did, my students expressed a great deal of interest and relief at the way these species-level analyses provided clarity and order to human patterns that any culture-level analysis would have rendered even more chaotic.

In light of a question that Greg Garrard asked me after my presentation, "Do you consider Darwinism an ideology?", I want to clarify that I was not teaching Darwinism, or even evolution, as such. We were simply trying to find an analytical approach and level that would make sense of human emotional responses. Far from trying to indoctrinate my students into believing in evolutionary theory, I was discussing with them various ways in which we might explain the universal existence of emotions such as anger. As it happened, no religious or psychological concepts that the students offered accounted for the existence and cross-culturally consistent application of human emotion. The only explanation that held up, in the face of my students' remarkably diverse backgrounds and perspectives, was that emotional responses reside and function at a physical, animal level, and that the "negative" emotions such as anger worked to spur individuals and groups into defensive action. I want to clarify also that the courses I taught were first-year English composition and literature courses, and that our analyses were therefore fairly rudimentary in terms of their ecocritical and scientific content. (On the one occasion when I taught a special section to a group of Animal Science majors, we were able to have more nuanced and rigorous debates about ideas such as biophilia, evolutionary ethics, and so on.)

When we moved on to reasoning through propositions, we arrived at similarly evolution-based conclusions—again, without any indoctrination or agenda on my part, but simply through rational discussion. One proposition that I asked my students to assess was a statement made in my first or second semester of teaching by a young fellow named Bashir. He said, with great firmness, "All men are hard-wired to prefer women with larger breasts over ones with smaller breasts." He insisted that this was "a scientific fact."

When I used this instance as an analytical exercise in subsequent years, we would start by examining the key terms. I would ask what "hard-wired" meant, and we would agree that it meant inborn, not learned. Then I would ask what kinds of traits and responses were "inborn," generally speaking. After students had mentioned things like crying when hungry or hurt, screaming when afraid, wanting to mate, et cetera, we would conclude that hard-wired traits went to survival.

I would then ask, "If this is generally true, then the next question is whether, and if so how, larger breasts would confer a survival advantage." I would ask if having larger breasts reduced the infant's or mother's mortality at childbirth. The students usually agreed that it did not. I would ask if women with smaller breasts produced less milk, and at this usually a significant number of students would say "Yes." This would trigger some usually lively discussion about what breasts are about, and how the colloquial term "jugs" didn't actually mean that larger-breasted women are toting milk about on our chests, but just that our fat placement is different than for women with smaller breasts.

Finally, I would ask if anyone could think of *any* way in which having larger breasts conferred a survival advantage. Sometimes someone would talk about sexual selection, but a student or I would point out that only in some parts of the world, and only fairly recently in any longer-term sense, were female breasts sexualized. So we would declare Bashir's assertion to be generally without merit. At this point, I would ask if anyone could think of a less laborious way to arrive at the same conclusion with a similar degree of confidence, and usually a student would say, "Yeah, well, if men were really hard-wired this way, there would be no small-breasted women left."

As with the question about anger, I was always fascinated and gratified to see how alive to analysis, to thinking, to reasoning through their perceptions students became as we approached an animal-level explanation that seemed to make sense of otherwise inconsistent or conflicting perceptions. As I said earlier, because we were in such a multicultural setting, any explanations given on a cultural, racial, linguistic, tribal, religious, or political level simply did not hold up under scrutiny. The only level of analysis that bore out across the class group or the Vancouver-area population as a whole was this evolutionary/ species level, and I saw many times the relief of clarity, of important basic things making sense, that this part of the course gave my students. Interestingly, one of my students recently sent me an email inviting me to join an Evolutionary Ethics group on the social website LinkedIn. At the time that I was teaching this fellow, I had no idea such a field existed, and this student had little or no orientation toward this area: he was a very science-minded German-Israeli planning on an engineering career. I was both gratified and rather envious to see that he had found and joined a social group of evolutionary ethicists.

For critical reading, I often used a column from the *Guardian* by George Monbiot, about genetically modified food, called "Starved of the Truth." My initial reason for using it was that it was the only short piece of writing I could find that contained explicit examples of chain reasoning exposing rhetorical fallacies such as faulty syllogisms and false synonymies. To give one example of such a passage:

> It is true that some [GM] trials . . . are succeeding. Despite the best efforts of the industry's boosters to confuse the two ideas, however, this does not equate to feeding the world. The world has a surplus of food, but still people go hungry. They go hungry because they cannot afford to buy it. They cannot afford to buy it because the sources of wealth have been bought up by landowners and corporations. The purpose of the biotech industry is to further monopolise these sources, by creating and then patenting seeds that do not reproduce themselves, and thus must be bought for money–from the biotech firms themselves.

As I started using the essay to teach more aspects of reading, thinking and composition purposes, I began to feel uneasy about spending so much time with this one side of the GM argument. I therefore created a research assignment in which the students had to find, read, and summarize a letter by Lord Taverne that Monbiot rebuts in his essay. I recognize now that this section of the course was quite slanted; if I were to teach it again, I would include much more pro–genetic-engineering material.

A fourth incidentally ecocritical exercise was one intended to give my students practice at reading at the university level. This meant learning to re-read, make marginal notes, identify key claims, stay with complex concepts and passages until they genuinely understood them, and so on. I used an article from *Harper's* magazine called "Unraveling the DNA Myth," by geneticist and author Barry Commoner. In this article, Commoner points out that both the scientific and journalistic communities were underplaying, not to say deliberately disregarding, the implications of recent findings in genetics that overturned Francis Crick's "central dogma" of a 1:1 ratio between genes and proteins, along with the "fact" that genetic information travels only in one direction, from the gene to the site of protein synthesis, and never the other way.

I found this text to be at exactly the right level of difficulty. To begin with, the thesis was clearly stated but unexpectedly placed, so that the students needed to be able to identify it for real rather than by rote. As well, although as a former magazine editor I suspect Commoner thought he had simplified the science in his article enough for the average *Harper's* reader to understand, in reality it required a considerable amount of time with the text and mental effort to become conversant with the scientific part of the argument. I would have my students come up to the board or the overhead projector and diagram out the conventional wisdom on how "messenger RNA" worked and how the relatively recent discovery of "alternative splicing"—the rearrangement of genetic information at the site of protein synthesis—differed from it. My students needed to be absolutely clear on the process of alternative splicing if they were going to understand Commoner's argument and the implications of recent genetic findings from the Human Genome Project and other studies.

I sometimes asked the students who were taking biology at the same time to go to their biology professors and ask how their scientific understanding and/or syllabus had been changed by the partial overthrow of Crick's Central Dogma. And as with the Monbiot article, I usually required my students to read some of the many impassioned refutations of Commoner's piece, including one in *Nature Genetics* magazine called "Wag the Dogma," which takes Commoner to task for misrepresenting Crick's original proposition and for suggesting that geneticists themselves hold simplistic views of their very complex field.

Another way I used Commoner's text was in an in-class reading exam. In this exam, my students had to put the Commoner essay, an essay by Andrew Nikiforuk on bacteria, and a chapter from Ronald Wright's book *A Short History of Progress* into "conversation" and say which two texts were saying the closest to the same thing. This required them to distinguish between conservationist and deep ecological perspectives, arguments based on biological time from those based on evolutionary time, and so on.

All of this, along with many other uses of this one text, had many incidentally "green studies" effects beyond making stronger readers out of my students. It addressed scientific illiteracy. It introduced them to the concept of knowledge asymmetry and showed them one way to mitigate it, namely by finding credible sources of scientific popularizing. It helped them integrate the science and humanities sides of their coursework. And it did all of this without my needing to promote my own beliefs, depart from my mandate to teach analysis and objective reasoning, stifle dissenting opinion, or present student with a lopsided set of data and viewpoints.

I could go on endlessly about the number of different texts, questions, propositions and activities of a nature-oriented, scientific or environmentally focused nature that I used in my first-year English course over the decade that I taught at this particular university-college. But I want to mention one final text I used, for literature courses, and that is R. K. Narayan's novel *The Man-Eater of Malgudi*. Again, my motives for choosing this text were pure. I loved it, I thought my students would love it (and I never heard of one who didn't), and its combination of wit, suspense, lively pacing, and plot twists made the novel "teach" better at the first-year level than any other I have found before or since.

In *The Man-Eater of Malgudi*, Nataraj, a devoutly pacifist Hindu printing-press owner, has his life disrupted when Vasu, a violent, profane, and immensely strong taxidermist, installs himself in the printing-shop attic. This plot premise makes it not only legitimate but imperative to ask students to analyze differing attitudes toward nature. Of particular use is the book's use of the Hindu concept of the *rakshasa*, or monster-demon, whose immense powers make him impossible to overthrow but inevitably become the instrument of his destruction in the end. Naturally this invites a discussion of whether the human species at large can be considered a *rakshasa*, as well as of whether this concept encourages passivity—on the grounds that a) we can't do anything about these major world problems and b) the monster-demon will eventually self-destruct anyway—or if Narayan is suggesting that we intervene even knowing that it is futile and may be counterproductive. For example, Nataraj decides near the end of the novel that he must keep Vasu from shooting the temple elephant even if it means abandoning his own pacifist beliefs and trying to kill Vasu himself; he is diverted from this only by finding Vasu dead in his chair, rifle in hand. I ask, as an exam-essay question, "If Vasu had not already been dead, *would* Nataraj have shot him?" This requires students to analyze not only the textual evidence of characterization, irony, etc., but also the author's implied stance on intervention versus faith in an ultimately self-regulating dispensation.

These are just a few of the dozens of ways I have, to quote the call for papers, "incorporate[d] ecocritical tenets into the daily practice of teaching the humanities [...] without breaching the topics' complexity or falling into the mode of environmentalist propaganda." In my view, it is easily done. If we follow our interests in terms of content, and follow the principles of unbiased teaching, human nature does the rest.

Works Cited

Crews, Frederick. *Follies of the Wise: Dissenting Essays*. Emeryville, CA: Shoemaker
    Hoard, 2006.
Garrard, Greg. "Evaluating the Pedagogies of Ecocriticism and Environmental Writing."
    Symposium program draft, Aug. 2012. Abstract
Hulme, Mike. "Meet the Humanities." *Nature Climate Change* 1.1 (July 2011). 177-9.
Mazel, David. "Ecocriticism as Praxis."In *Teaching North American Environmental
    Literature*. Eds. Laird Christensen, Mark C. Long and Fred Waage. New York: MLA,
    2008. 37-43.
Parham, John. *The Environmental Tradition in English Literature*. Aldershot.: Ashgate, 2002.
Rosenwasser, David, and Jill Stephen. *Writing Analytically*. 2nded. New York: Heinle, 2003.
Soper, Kate. *What is Nature? Culture, Politics and the Non-Human*. Oxford and Cambridge,
    MA: Blackwell, 1995.

Ecodidactics? A German Perspective

Sieglinde Grimm (Cologne)

When writing the CfP for the symposium "Teaching the Environment," Roman Bartosch could not foresee what kind of reactions his words would arouse. The call was for contributions that dealt with ecocritical pedagogy "without [...] falling into the mode of environmentalist propaganda" or "succumbing to warnings and claims to catastrophic urgency which are hard to reconcile with an ethos of critical and democratic pedagogy" (cited in Major & McMurry 2012: 3). This has obviously been far too modest for William Major and Andrew McMurry, who accused the CfP of "humanist boosterism" and proposed that ecocriticism instead employ the argument of "catastrophic urgency" (3). [1] Their reproach of "humanist boosterism" implied that author and conference hide within the ivory tower of academia instead of seeking a confrontation with the "terrifying ecological facts" (2)—thus disregarding, as it were, the 'real thing' in favor of theory and abstraction.

In their reply, Bartosch and Greg Garrard, who had been invited as the keynote speaker for this conference, defended their position by insisting on two arguments: firstly, that ecocriticism must resist the instrumentalization of literature in its own interest and secondly, that ecocriticism should not "play down the relevance of thorough analysis, interrogation, self-critique and constant negotiation of what we mean when we talk about saving the planet" (Bartosch & Garrard 2013: 3). [2] Before I outline yet two other aspects that are both related to issues of pedagogical praxis, I'd like to add a few remarks that will hopefully help to shed some light on the dispute of theory versus practical urgency, which obviously seems to be a fundamental problem of ecocriticism in general and ecocritical pedagogy in particular.

---

1   Mayor and McMurry's piece has been reprinted in this publication—see their response for a detailed account of their arguments.

2   Their essay has been reprinted in this publication as well.

A Meta-Perspective: German Neohumanism

Major and McMurry are two American ecocritics writing about an ecocritical conference organized by the English Department II of the University of Cologne in Germany. In order to understand why this should be a relevant observation, one has to see that the position of ecocriticism in the Anglophone world is not the same as the one in Germany. In the U.S., for instance, ecocriticism has become a reasonably established approach within the humanities, and "an ethical and environmentalist consciousness [...] is commonplace within the English departments," as Bartosch and Garrard point out in reference to Glen A. Love (Bartosch & Garrard 2013: 1). This, however, is by no means the case within English departments in Germany and even less in German departments in this country. What are the reasons for this?

On a rather superficial level, one could argue that whereas in the Anglo-American world "green issues" have entered the discourse of the humanities because they could not make it into politics, in Germany, green issues have influenced mainstream politics indeed—and therefore "could not make it" into the humanities. Political agenda and scholarly inquiry rarely meet in German literary studies departments, and maybe for good reasons.

It is therefore worthwhile to look at the historical development of what we now call the humanities. And indeed, 'humanism' itself, or, rather, 'neohumanism', with its peak in early 19th-century thought, plays an important role in the debate between the conference organizers and the ecocritical colleagues from the U.S. In Germany, neohumanism refers to poets and scholars such as Friedrich Schiller, Wilhelm von Humboldt, and Georg Wilhelm Friedrich Hegel. 'Education' or, to be more precise, the German *Bildung* competed against the revolutionary power which had taken shape in France in 1789. Both were nourished by Enlightenment ideas, aiming to form politically educated, free, and mature citizens who would be able to create a democratic basis for a new republican state. This is why in *On the Aesthetic Education of Man in a Series of Letters* (1794), for instance in the 27th letter, Schiller argues that a society fostering free citizens in a republic can come to life only in an "aesthetic state" (Schiller: 1794/1975: 406). This vision of *Bildung* and education as a necessary prerequisite for engendering an autonomous subject, which has since been referred to as *"deutscher Sonderweg,"* was further elaborated in the Hegelian concept of *Geist*. In his speech closing the school year of 1809, Hegel, then a principal of the royal *Gymnasialanstalt* at Nuremberg, claimed:

> not each so-called useful subject matter—this sensuous matter finds its way into the child's imagination unprecedentedly—but only *spiritual* content, which has value and interest in

and for itself, can strengthen the soul and can provide a stability without exterior aid [...] (Hegel 1986: 319; my translation)[3]

Humboldt adapts the Hegelian 'spirit' (as 'consciousness') for his concept of *Bildung,* which he defines as a "connection of our self with the world" ("Verknüpfung unseres Ich mit der Welt"), in the course of which the self has "to press its spirit's form onto the material objects in order to make both of them become more similar" ("dem Stoff die Gestalt seines Geistes aufdrücken und beide einander ähnlicher machen"; Humboldt, c. 1793/1980, vol. I, 236; my translation). According to these ideals, objects of education are "spiritualized" ("vergeistigt"); this includes a subordination of matter as opposed to 'spirit' or 'form'. In his philosophy of language, Humboldt transfers this ambition onto language, thus using language as a means for the consciousness to communicate. In doing so, he opposes theories demonstrating the origin of language from natural sounds.[4] According to Humboldt, language serves as a "forming organ of consciousness" ("bildendes Organ des Gedankens") in the process of which an "intellectual activity, definitely spiritual and definitely interior" is turned outward by "the sound of speech" (Humboldt 1830-35/1996: 426).

In the history of human consciousness, Hegel's concept of *Geist* was constitutive for the idea of the 'subject' in German Idealism at the peak of neohumanism. Berbeli Wanning has pointed out that the rise of the subject was accompanied by a general "desubstantialization of nature" ("Entkernung der Natur"), which implied a "sublimation of the feeling for nature" in early Romanticism (Wanning 2006: 234; my translation). This shows in Humboldt's idea of education—*Bildung*—as something "superior and more interior" ("als etwas Höheres und mehr Innerliches"), which refers to the Hegelian *Geist* as well (Humboldt 1830-35/1996: 401). In other words, the reverse of the humanist medal called *Bildung* shows in the repression of practical and applicable knowledge as well as of interaction with the exterior world and the environment.

Thus, the *deutsche Sonderweg* brought about a difference within Western European ideas of Enlightenment *Bildung* and education. Education in the sense of late 18th-century philanthropist Johann Bernhard Basedow, who in his *Elementarlehre* emphasized practical knowledge of life such as nature study, knowledge of animals, or of different practical professions, became obsolete. As Georg Bollenbeck outlines in his brilliant study on *Bildung und Kultur. Glanz und Elend eines Deutungsmusters* ("Education and Culture. Glory and Misery of a German Paradigm"), "within a few years only" the German intelligentsia of

---

3   The original reads: "nicht jeder sogenannte nützliche Stoff, jene sinnliche Materiatur, wie sie unmittelbar in die Vorstellungsweise des Kindes fällt, nur der geistige Inhalt, welcher Wert und Interesse in und für sich selbst hat, stärkt die Seele und verschafft diesen unabhängigen Halt."

4   These theories were put forward, for instance, by Jean-Jacques Rousseau and Étienne Bonnot de Condillac.

the late 18th century rejected "economy, utility, professional education, and technology" in favor of an "ideal of a purpose-free (*zweckfrei*) spiritual kind of *Bildung*" (Bollenbeck 1996: 99; my translation). Whereas during the mid-18th century *Bildung* and education both still comprised practical fields such as the study of finance, economy, and politics in Germany, Great Britain, and France alike, those areas that aimed at applicable knowledge or practicability and the material world—nature!—were increasingly disregarded in Germany. With the intention to achieve cultural predominance in Western Europe, the philosopher Max Scheler, for instance, criticized Darwinian biology for the way it mixed up environment *(Umwelt)* and world *(Welt)*, pointing out that the utilitarian "subordination of noble virtues under utility" (Scheler 1915: 43f) could be taken as evidence of British depravity.[5]

Although this rather abstract and, after all, also elitist concept of neohumanist *Bildung* crumbled in the light of 19th-century industrialization, the rise of the social democrats, and the influence of the natural sciences with their own methodologies, it still served the ideals of the German *Bildungsbürgertum*. In order to point out the consequences for German humanism, one might as well quote Thomas Mann, who in his *Betrachtungen eines Unpolitischen*, published in 1918, argued that "German humanism resists politics from its very roots" ("die deutsche Humanität widerstrebt der Politisierung von Grund auf"). He emphasizes that "Spirit [*Geist*] is *not* politics; [...] German identity means culture, soul, freedom, art, and *not* civilization, society, the right to vote, literature" ("Geist ist *nicht* Politik: [...] Deutschtum, das ist Kultur, Seele, Freiheit, Kunst und *nicht* Zivilisation, Gesellschaft, Stimmrecht, Literatur") (Mann 2002: 52; my translation).

As Bollenbeck argues, the bourgeois desire for education and refinement fell prey to early National Socialist claims to restoring the ambitions associated with *Bildung*[6] in an idealist and neohumanist context. In the course of this development, during the Nazi-Regime the works of many writers and poets were usurped and misused. As a consequence, after 1945, political concerns were curtailed drastically within the newly established humanities. As Elisabeth K. Paefgen, Professor of the Didactics of German Literature, writes:

> In the decade following the National Socialist dictatorship, German literature was not an undisputed object of teaching. Literature even gained special recognition, because it could be dealt with as a valuable, ideally educational but at the same time neutral object. Far

---

5   See my essay "Braucht der gebildete Mensch die Ökonomie? Eine europäische Perspektive." *Didaktik Deutsch* 31 (2011). 11-21.

6   Hitler flattered the educational ideal of the bourgeoisie, although later on he disavowed it: supposedly, "a nation's general education has to be an ideal one. Primarily it should relate to humanist subjects:" In his words, "[muss] die allgemeine Bildung einer Nation [...] stets eine ideale sein. Sie soll mehr den humanistischen Fächern entsprechen" (Hitler 1925/27 and 1945: 469).

from showing any political implications, which the teaching of literature had been encumbered with throughout the first half of the 20th century, German literary critics and teachers of German located literature in an area without historical connotations, trying instead to obtain from literature liberating answers to general challenges of life. (Paefgen 2006: 16; my translation).

I agree with Paefgen's observations but maintain that these consequences are still relevant today—especially the tendency to avoid political and also environmental aspects not only in literary pedagogy but also in criticism.

And indeed, after 1945 this development was promoted by critical approaches such as Wolfgang Kayser's idea of literature and poetry in *Das sprachliche Kunstwerk* (1948) or Emil Staiger's "werkimmanente Literaturwissenschaft," which he developed in *Die Kunst der Interpretation* (1955), both of which can be seen as German equivalents of the New Criticism, and Hans Kügler's "Lesendes Erschließen auf strukturaler Basis" (1971), which tried to adopt Barthesian structuralism.

Throughout the 1970s, there was a strong impact of linguistic theory which focused on teaching literature primarily as a linguistic artifice; this continued with poststructuralism. Both approaches, as Greg Garrard puts it, "have emphasized the linguistic function of signs that relate to each other rather than refer to real things" (Garrard 2012: 9-10) and thus led to an exclusion of notions of applicable knowledge.

The consequences of the impact of structuralist and poststructuralist theory have been analyzed by Bernhard Malkmus in his essay "Ökologie als blinder Fleck der Kultur- und Literaturtheorie" (2005) ("Ecology as the blind spot of cultural and literary theory"). Just like Garrard, Malkmus points to the fact that by merely relying on a realm of signs, the human self feels "unbound from the area of signified" realities. Moreover, Malkmus accuses literary criticism following the "linguistic turn" (as structuralism and poststructuralism do) of an "incapability to perceive psychological realities beyond semiotic categories" (Malkmus 2005: 63; my translation).[7]

In contemporary debates on education—*Bildung*—in Germany, political, economic, and also environmental implications are still marginalized, if not excluded. In the words of the expert on *Bildung,* the scholar of classical literature Manfred Fuhrmann, writing in 2004, "[t]he term 'Bildung' [refers] to the totality of culture—to a totality within which [questions of] industry, technology, and economy"—and, one might add, environmental issues—"can be disregarded" (Fuhrmann 2004: 222; my translation).

Similar observations can be made in the teaching of (German) literature and literacy theories. Christine Garbe, Professor of Literacy and Didactics of

---

7   Malkmus demonstrates this by his reading of Thomas Pynchon's parable *The Crying of Lot 49* in which he shows that poststructuralist approaches miss its satirical intention.

German Literature, observes a difference between fictional and non-fictional, i.e. expository, texts: whereas reading fictional texts on a personal level is "related to the development of the imagination, the strengthening of empathy and of moral consciousness, and the development of a life-affirming ("lebensthematisch") identity as well as recognition of foreign cultures," only non-fictional texts relate to "the ability to communicate, to form political opinions, cognitive orientation, and an increase of (cognitive) knowledge." From a social perspective, according to Garbe, fictional texts "foster the development of 'cultural memory'," whereas non-fictional, expository texts promote "an understanding of social structures and social change" (Garbe 2009: 18; my translation). With similar categories in mind and allegedly defending the case of literature, Klaus Maiwald, Professor of Teaching German Language and Literature, pleads to choose the subjects of expository texts from the field of German language and literature teaching only in order to deny "oneself to participate in this common-or-garden affront more decisively: our objects are language and literature, not automobile and environment" (2004: 44).

> Obviously, there is a strong tendency to divest teaching humanist subjects from social or political relevance, from practical concerns of life, and partly even from cognitive understanding. In contrast to the alliance of literature with social criticism, civilization, and politics (as Mann suggested), the teaching of literature is uncoupled from practical interests; a practice which, in my view, still echoes German neohumanist ideals. With Humboldt's theory of language in mind, one can moreover assume that his hypostatic vision of language paved the way for those linguistic theories that considered language and, consequentially, literature for their own sake only and independent of environmental implications.

Compared to literature departments in the Anglophone world, this marks a difference in the atmosphere of teaching and of research; the gap between the American critics Major and McMurry and Bartosch's CfP owes to these differences. Had the call for papers made use of a confrontation with "terrifying ecological facts," as Major and McMurry suggest, most German literary critics would probably not have considered the CfP to be of any concern to them. Rather, they would have thought that this was a pamphlet of the Green Party inviting its members to return to their early days of fundamentalist debates.

Pedagogical Implications

The restrictions of historical differences notwithstanding, the development of an ecocritical pedagogy in Germany could perhaps be a mutually beneficial experience. Although it seems as if teaching cultural ecology or, as it were,

"Teaching Environments" in Germany is a challenge to teaching traditions per se, I would like to outline some pedagogical opportunities for ecocriticism in the light of post-PISA didactics. With this I come to the second point of my argument. Irrespective of the above-mentioned differences between the humanities in the Anglophone world and both literary criticism and pedagogy in Germany, there seem to be some opportunities right now, linked to the Bologna Process and to the introduction of 'competence'-oriented curricula. In the following, I want to concentrate on this change, which has called forth a lot of debates among educators and teachers of literature.

As a basis for my argument I will use Franz E. Weinert's well-known definition of 'competence', which is often referred to in discussions about literary pedagogy after the so-called PISA-shock: according to Weinert, competence comprises

> the cognitive capabilities and practical skills which are available to or can be learned by individuals to solve given problems and the corresponding motivational, volitional, and social willingness to make use of the solutions in variable situations in a successful and responsible way. (Weinert 2002: 27-8; my translation)

In the light of this definition, competence is diametrically opposed to the idea of *Bildung* as it was discussed by Hegel and Humboldt during the 19th century. Competence refers to applied knowledge and must have reference to practical orientation, whereas the ideal of *Bildung*, discussed above, serves its own purposes entirely and does not aim at external or practical purposes in any utilitarian sense. Moreover, if we look at Thomas Mann's observation about the degradation of "civilization, society, the right to vote, and literature" as opposed to "culture, soul, freedom, and art," we see that the very claims which are not appropriate for the noble idealist thought are rehabilitated by what competence represents. In idealist educational thinking, social capabilities remain subject to inner and moral claims; and 'volitional' readiness and stamina, which can be associated with the right to vote (in the sense of adopting an attitude) and politics, are contrasted with the idea of 'freedom' connected to an idealist 'spirit'. In contrast to idealistic and pietistic *Bildung*, 'civilization' refers to technical progress and work-sharing economy, which can be linked to successful problem-solving and utility. Literature here is to be understood in its social critical function as opposed to an ideal of art based on Romantic universalisms or pietistic introspection.

Compared to the abstract and elitist concept of *Bildung* introduced by neohumanism, competence allows us to include areas of experience, practical knowledge, and the fundamental processes of comprehension associated with it. In doing so, it not only challenges the traditional 18th-century idea of *Bildung* but also allows ecological thinking to be incorporated into the field of education.

I will, in my last point, explain this idea in more detail. Just as the neohumanist concept of *Bildung* focused on the subject and its consciousness, and reduced the natural world to serving as the spirit's object comprising materialism, economy, and the environment alike, PISA and the focus on competences offer a chance for environmental concerns to be integrated in the educational context of the humanities. This already shows in Ernst Haeckel's famous definition of ecology:

> By *ecology* we understand the overall *science/study of the relationships of the organism with the environment*, including all further *conditions of existence*. These are partly of organic, partly of anorganic nature. [...] As organic conditions of existence we consider all relationships of the organism with all other organisms that it touches, most of which are either useful or harmful to it. (Haeckel 1866: 286; my translation)[8]

It is notable that the concept of ecology emphasizes the existence and relevance of numerous references of science (or scholarship) to the exterior world/environment. This means that a focus on environments is able to call into question some humanist pretensions and to revise the noble concepts of neohumanist idealism focusing, in Humboldt and Hegel's parlance, on *Bildung* or *Geist*. An ecological view abstains from examining inward-looking thoughts or interior subjective realms. It examines the relations of organisms in and with the outside world, as many place-centered approaches within ecocriticism show, not their relations to or within the realm of ideas. This is underlined by the fact that ecology predisposes Darwinian biology and evolutionary theory, which can be taken as a critique of idealist thought as such. Evidence of this can be found in Haeckel's letter to Darwin from 1879, congratulating him on the occasion of his 70th birthday on having elevated biology (as a natural science) and thus having "overturned the anthropocentric fable."[9]

As a consequence for any practice of "Teaching Environments," one has to look at what we understand by "environment" or, rather, nature as such, as well as man's interrelations with it. In his study *Die Ökologie der Literatur* ("The Ecology of Nature") (2007), Stefan Hofer suggests different concepts of nature in order to make explicit which idea of 'nature' any ecocritical approach follows. In his view, 'nature' so far has been understood in a threefold way. First, within the natural sciences, natural phenomena were observed and

---

8   The original reads: "Unter *Oecologie* verstehen wir die gesammte *Wissenschaft von den Beziehungen des Organismus zur umgebenden Aussenwelt*, wohin wir im weiteren Sinne alle '*Existenz-Bedingungen*' rechnen können. Diese sind theils organischer, theils anorganischer Natur; [...] Als organische Existenz-Bedingungen betrachten wir die sämmtlichen Verhältnisse des Organismus zu allen übrigen Organismen, mit denen er in Berührung kommt, und von denen die meisten entweder zu seinem Nutzen oder zu seinem Schaden beitragen."

9   Letter to Charles Darwin from 9 February 1879, cited in Uschmann 1984: 156.

classified; a second approach consisted in experimental examination in laboratories, aiming to explain findings with laws and regularities (*Gesetzmäßigkeiten*); the third approach towards nature consisted in a holistic natural philosophy as it was passed on from ancient philosophy; its purpose being to provide orientation.[10] Hofer points out that experimental and observer-based natural sciences increasingly produced *Herrschaftswissen* (hegemonic knowledge), leaving behind any form of philosophy of nature:

> Ultimately, the development of the natural sciences has led to favoring experimental and observer-based approaches and their efforts to create 'intervening' and 'dominating' knowledge. In contrast, natural philosophy, the interest of which primarily is to offer orientational knowledge, has been pushed back to a great extent. (Hofer 2007: 59; my translation)[11]

In the course of this development, Hofer explains, exact natural sciences not only uncoupled ethics, moral and religious knowledge; their priority also influenced the concept of ecology, which is now oscillating between a "holistic idea of nature in the tradition of natural philosophy and the scientific ideal of exact natural sciences" (Hofer 2007: 61).

Hofer's ideas correspond to Niklas Luhmann's argument concerning the lack of "action-guided" values as a result of having defined 'nature' only through the natural sciences after its post-Enlightenment desacralization: "Nature could and had to be left to natural sciences. [...] According to Stoic and Christian doctrine, non-human nature had to be left to man to be made use of" (Luhmann 2008: 10; my translation).[12]

According to Luhmann, much of what was deemed to have been given by nature or through divine order had to be redefined in the wake of Enlightenment: "The consequence is that a lot of what was experienced as 'nature' before now requires a decision and falls under the pressure of reasoning" (Hofer 2007: 68/Luhmann 2008: 139; my translation)

As Luhmann points out, orientational knowledge can give an idea of how to cope with the (sometimes dubious) outcome of *Herrschaftswissen* (as provided, for instance, by the natural sciences). With this in mind, we can conclude a new

---

10   Cf. Kate Soper's "Ecological Discourses of Nature," where Soper discusses the "multiple roles" of 'nature' in ecological discourse "as the 'metaphysical', the 'realist' and the 'lay' (or 'surface') ideas of nature" (Soper 1995: 125).

11   The original reads: "Die weitere Entwicklung der Naturwissenschaften hat schliesslich zu einer deutlichen Favorisierung von experientell-beobachtenden Ansätzen und ihrem Streben nach einem 'Eingreif- und Herrschafts-Wissen' geführt. Das naturphilosophische Denken, dessen Interesse eher im Bereich des 'Orientierungswissens' liegt, ist demgegenüber stark in den Hintergrund getreten."

12   The original reads: "Die Natur konnte und musste den Naturwissenschaften überlassen bleiben. [...] Die außermenschliche Natur blieb nach stoischer wie nach christlicher Lehre dem Menschen zur Nutzung überlassen."

understanding of "Teaching Environments": ecocriticism and ecocritical pedagogy have to focus on the relationship between man and nature as it is shown in literary texts. "Teaching environments," as we understand it, can and should provide this kind of orientational knowledge. As it were, literary pedagogy can resume the ancient task of literature, poetry, and art: to explain the position of man on this planet, and to provide forms of explanation that cannot be provided by the natural sciences. Teaching literature can give these kinds of explanation; it cannot, however, prescribe action in the light of "catastrophic urgency" or offer 'safe' solutions. Instead, the alternative to "humanist boosterism" or to neohumanism is to show in how far human existence depends on man's relationship to the exterior—or: non-human—world. In order to show this, when teaching literature we cannot restrict ourselves to looking at a literary text as a linguistic artifice only.

The second outcome lies in the field of literary criticism, which in a way serves as a prerequisite for teaching. As I have tried to show in my essay "Teaching Cultural Ecology" in this volume—where I emphasize the literary engagement with the relationship between man and nature, the meaning of place and the question of the extent to which man is connected and even subject(ed) to organisms outside his self—ecocriticism and cultural ecology can shed new light even on canonical texts. Thus, what is at stake when "Teaching Environments" is more than adding just another perspective to literary discourse. An ecocritical approach can come closer to what literature is at its core: a demonstration of basic cultural patterns of what we experience in our lives. Notably, this objective is found in current school curricula as "tasks of teaching literature"

> Discovering and dealing with literature—also in its different historical and social relationships—is to arouse an interest and pleasure in reading, and is to motivate a more general appreciation of literature. Reading literature allows us to learn about basic patterns of human experience and it helps to develop one's own positions and attitudes. (*Kernlehrplan*, 2007: 11; my translation)[13]

---

13   The original reads: "Die Begegnung und Auseinandersetzung mit Literatur—auch in ihren unterschiedlichen historischen und gesellschaftlichen Bezügen—soll Leseinteresse wie Lesevergnügen wecken und zur Lektüre von Literatur anregen. Sie ermöglicht es, Grundmuster menschlicher Erfahrungen kennen zu lernen und trägt dazu bei, eigene Positionen und Werthaltungen zu entwickeln."

Conclusion

Let me briefly sum up my arguments: the differences between Bartosch's CfP and Major & McMurry are caused by different traditions of teaching literary texts and of research in Germany and the Anglophone world. In the course of the *deutsche Sonderweg*, neohumanist thought developed a hypostasis of *Geist*, language, and art, the effect of which was less palpable in the U.S. and Great Britain, both of which had been strongly influenced by utilitarian thought in the 18th and throughout the 19th century. Right now, however, post-PISA literature pedagogy offers a chance for ecocritical pedagogy to gain ground in Germany; aiming at applied knowledge, problem solving, and social competence, it transcends the subject as it was formed in early 19th-century idealism.

Our approach to "Teaching Environments" is far from "humanist boosterism" in the sense of anthropocentrism. Quite the contrary, it shows the way in which mankind's existence depends on its relationship to the natural and non-human world rather than on inward, merely mental speculation. This does not imply a dismissal of cognitive knowledge but rather an analysis of these very relationships in the sense of the Heideggerian "In-der-Welt-sein" which defines the human being by its environmental settlement.

With this perspective, we can reform the practice of teaching literature—almost in terms of what Aristotle, one of the first 'critics' to be interested in a functional poetics, had to say about poetry: looking at his text, we find that teaching literary texts offers orientational knowledge. As Aristotle points out, human beings "find pleasure in the consideration of [poetic] imagery, because in the course of this they can learn something and find out what the images mean" (Aristoteles: 1448b; my translation). Making literary texts accessible is what we do when we teach literature. Poetry, to Aristotle, is a representation of what is happening in the world and in the environment of everyone. This dimension of literature is still valid today. To reveal this dimension to the pupils is the task of the teaching of literature.

Works Cited

Aristoteles. *Poetik*. Stuttgart: Reclam, 1987.
Bartosch, Roman & Greg Garrard. "The Function of Criticism: A Response to William Major and Andrew McMurry's Editorial." *The Journal of Ecocriticism* 5.1. (2013). 1-6.
Bollenbeck, Georg. *Bildung und Kultur. Glanz und Elend eines deutschen Deutungsmusters.* Frankfurt/M.: Suhrkamp, 1996.
Fritzsch, Theodor (ed.). *J. B. Basedows Elementarwerk mit den Kupfertafeln Chodowieckis u.a.* 3 vols. Leipzig: Verlag Ernst Wiegand, [1774] 1909.
Fuhrmann, Manfred. *Der europäische Bildungskanon*. Frankfurt/M. /Leipzig: Insel, 2004.
Garbe, Christine. "Lesekompetenz." *Texte lesen. Textverstehen. Lesedidaktik. Lesesozialisation.* Eds. Christine Garbe, Karl Holle & Tatjana Jesch. Paderborn et al.: Schöningh/UTB, 2009. 13-38.
Garrard, Greg. *Ecocriticism*. 2nd ed. London & New York: Routledge, 2012.
Grimm, Sieglinde. "Braucht der gebildete Mensch die Ökonomie? Zum Verhältnis von Bildung und Kompetenz nach PISA—eine europäische Perspektive." *Didaktik Deutsch* 31 (2011) 11-21.
Haeckel, Ernst. *Generelle Morphologie der Organismen. Allgemeine Grundzüge der organischen Formen-Wissenschaft, mechanisch begründet durch die von Charles Darwin reformirte Descendenz-Theorie.* Berlin: Verlag von Georg Reimer, 1866.
Hegel, Georg Wilhelm Friedrich. "Rede zum Schuljahrabschluß am 29. September 1809." *Werke in 20 Bänden* (20 vols.). Eds. Eva Moldenhauer und Karl Markus Michel. Vol. 4. *Nürnberger und Heidelberger Schriften 1808-1817.* Frankfurt/M.: Suhrkamp, 1986. 312-26.
Hitler, Adolf. *Mein Kampf*. München, [1925/27] 1945.
Hofer, Stefan. *Die Ökologie der Literatur. Eine systemtheoretische Annäherung. Mit einer Studie zu Werken Peter Handkes.* Bielefeld: transcript, 2007.
Humboldt, Wilhelm von. "Theorie der Bildung des Menschen." *Werke in fünf Bänden.* Eds. Andreas Flitner & Klaus Giel. 3rd ed. Vol 1. *Schriften zur Anthropologie und Geschichte.* Darmstadt: Wissenschaftliche Buchgesellschaft, 1980-1996. 234-40.
— . "Über die Verschiedenheit des menschlichen Sprachbaues und ihren Einfluss auf die geistige Entwicklung des Menschengeschlechts." *Werke in fünf Bänden.* Eds. Andreas Flitner & Klaus Giel. 8th ed. Vol. 3. *Schriften zur Sprachphilosophie.* Darmstadt: Wissenschaftliche Buchgesellschaft, 1996. 368-756.
Kayser, Wolfgang. *Das sprachliche Kunstwerk. Eine Einführung in die Literaturwissenschaft.* Bern: Francke, 1948.
Kernlehrplan für den verkürzten Bildungsgang des Gymnasiums—Sekundarstufe I (G 8) in NRW. Deutsch. Ed. Ministerium für Schule, Jugend und Kinder des Landes Nordrhein-Westfalen. Frechen: Ritterbach Verlag, 2007.
Kügler, Hans. *Literatur und Kommunikation. Ein Beitrag zur didaktischen Theorie und methodischen Praxis.* Stuttgart: Klett, 1971.
Luhmann, Niklas. *Ökologische Kommunikation. Kann die Moderne Gesellschaft sich auf ökologische Gefährdungen einstellen?* 5th ed. Wiesbaden: Verlag für Sozialwissenschaften, 2008.
Maiwald, Klaus. "Neue Kleider für den Kaiser, oder alte Hüte? Zur schwierigen Verwebung von Textverstehen und Testaufgaben." *Aufgabenkultur und Lesekompetenz. Deutschdidaktische Positionen.* Eds. Juliane Köster, Will Lütgert & Jürgen Creutzburg: Frankfurt/M. et al.: Peter Lang, 2004. 43-50.

Major, William & Andrew McMurry. "Introduction: The Function of Ecocriticism; or, Ecocriticism, What Is It Good For?". *The Journal of Ecocriticism* 4.2 (2012). 1-7.

— . "Response of William Major and Andrew McMurry." *The Journal of Ecocriticism* 5.1 (2013). 1-5.

Malkmus, Bernhard. "Ökologie als blinder Fleck der Kultur- und Literaturtheorie." *Natur— Kultur—Text. Beiträge zu Ökologie und Literaturwissenschaft.* Eds. Catrin Gersdorf & Sylvia Mayer. Heidelberg: Winter, 2005. 53-78.

Mann, Thomas: *Betrachtungen eines Unpolitischen.* Frankfurt/M.: Fischer, [1983] 2002.

Paefgen, Elisabeth K. *Einführung in die Literaturdidaktik.* 2nd ed. Stuttgart & Weimar: Metzler, 2006.

Scheler, Max: *Der Genius des Krieges und der Deutsche Krieg.* Leipzig: Verlag der Weißen Bücher, 1915.

Schiller, Friedrich. "Über die ästhetische Erziehung des Menschen in einer Reihe von Briefen." *Friedrich Schiller. Sämtliche Werke in 5 Bänden.* Vol. 5. München: Winkler-Verlag, 1975. 311-408.

Soper, Kate. "The Idea of Nature." *The Green Studies Reader. From Romanticism to Ecocriticism.* Ed. Laurence Coupe. London & New York: De Gruyter, 2006. 223-49.

Staiger, Emil. *Die Kunst der Interpretation. Studien zur deutschen Literaturgeschichte.* Zürich: Atlantis Verlag, 1955.

Uschmann, Georg. *Ernst Haeckel. Biographie in Briefen.* Gütersloh: Prisma-Verlag, 1984.

Wanning, Berbeli. "Der Naturbegriff in Literatur und Literaturwissenschaft." *Semantische Kämpfe. Macht und Sprache in den Wissenschaften.* Ed. Ekkehard Felder. Berlin & New York: De Gruyter, 2006. 223-49.

Weinert, Franz E. "Vergleichende Leistungsmessung in Schulen—eine umstrittene Selbstverständlichkeit." *Leistungsmessungen in Schulen.* Ed. Franz E. Weinert. Weinheim & Basel: Beltz-Verlag, 2. Aufl., 2002. 17-31.

List of Illustrations

p. 45: Cover illustration of the book *Alien Invaders*. Reprinted with kind permission © Raven Tree Press (www.raventreepress.com).

p. 47: Illustration from the book *Alien Invaders*. Reprinted with kind permission © Raven Tree Press (www.raventreepress.com).

p. 65: Illustration from the book *The Rabbits* by John Marsden and Shaun Tan, Lothian Children's Books, an imprint of Hachette Australia, 1998. Reprinted with kind permission (©).

p. 66: Illustration from the book *The Rabbits* by John Marsden and Shaun Tan, Lothian Children's Books, an imprint of Hachette Australia, 1998. Reprinted with kind permission (©).

p. 67: Illustration from the book *The Rabbits* by John Marsden and Shaun Tan, Lothian Children's Books, an imprint of Hachette Australia, 1998. Reprinted with kind permission (©).

p. 80: Illustration from the book *The Stranger* by Chris Van Allsburg © (1986). Used by permission of Houghton Mifflin Harcourt Publishing Company. All rights reserved.

p. 83: Cover illustration from the book *The Rough Face Girl* by Rafe Martin © (1992), illustrated by David Shannon. Used with permission of Puffin Books, a division of Penguin Group (USA) Inc.

p. 87: Illustration from the book *Zoo* by Anthony Browne © (1992). Reprinted by permission of Farrar Straus and Giroux Books for Young Readers and The Random House Group UK Limited. All rights reserved.

p. 89: Illustration from the book *We're going on a Bear Hunt Babies* by Michael Rosen © (1989), illustrated by Helen Oxenbury © (1989). Reproduced by permission of Walker Books Ltd, London SE11 5HJ.

p. 90: Illustration from the book *Flotsam* by David Wiesner © (2006) Used by permission of Clarion Books, an imprint of Houghton Mifflin Harcourt Publishing Company. All rights reserved.

p. 92: Cover illustration from the book *The Savage* by David Almond © (2008), illustrated by Dave McKean© (2008). Reproduced by permission of Walker Books Ltd, London SE11 5HJ.

is currently working on his dissertation about "Wilderness and Transformations of Masculinity in Nineteenth-Century America."

Adrian Rainbow teaches literature, media and cultural studies in the English Department at the University of Zürich. He holds a PhD in English (University of Exeter), an MA in Critical Theory (University of Exeter), and a BA Double Major in English Literature and Philosophy (University of British Columbia). He has published in gender theory, literary theory, and the aesthetics of violence, and is currently working on his *Habilitation* project (postdoctoral project) on ecopedagogy and critical ecoliteracy, examining the pedagogical and political function of contemporary literature. In addition to ecocriticism, his other research interests include gender studies, and literary and cultural theory

Pamela Swanigan is a PhD student (ABD), specializing in ecocriticism and children's literature, at the University of Connecticut. She has taught for 10 years at a polytechnic university near Vancouver, British Columbia, and before that worked as a magazine writer and editor, singer, and horse-trainer. She lives in Nova Scotia.

Haiko Wandhoff is *Privatdozent* at the Institute for German Literature, Humboldt University, Berlin. His research focuses on Medieval epic and lyric, word and image, ekphrasis, heraldry and the history of media and communication. He is the author of *Ekphrasis. Kunstbeschreibungen und virtuelle Räume in der Literatur des Mittelalters* (2003) and *Der epische Blick. Eine mediengeschichtliche Studie zur höfischen Literatur* (1996). Wandhoff is the editor of *Zur Bildlichkeit mittelalterlicher Texte*, a special issue of *Das Mittelalter* (2008). He has taught at Duke University and at the Universities of Göttingen, Munich, Zürich and North Carolina.

List of Contributors

Roman Bartosch teaches English literatures at the University of Cologne. He has published on postcolonial and posthumanist theory and in his research focuses on literary theories, especially new formalism, reception aesthetics and hermeneutics. When he is not engaged in not-understanding literary animals, he thinks about literary canonicity, literary quality and questions of ethical criticism. His book *EnvironMentality—Ecocriticism and the Event of Postcolonial Fiction* was released with Rodopi in 2013.

Born in Greater London, **Janice Bland** initially gathered extensive experience in teaching English at all levels from primary school to adult education—mostly in Germany. After completing her PhD in 2012 (University of Jena), Janice joined the Department of English and American Studies at the University of Paderborn. Her interests are Children's Literature in Language Education, TEFL, Drama and Creative Writing. Janice has published widely, including a monograph and edited volume with Bloomsbury Academic, textbooks with Macmillan and Schroedel, and four collections of plays for schools with Players Press. Janice co-edits the new international peer-reviewed and open-access CLELEjournal: Children's Literature in English Language Education.

Celestine Caruso studied English and Biology at the University of Cologne, where she graduated in 2006. She then studied at the Department of English and Comparative Literary Studies and the Centre for Applied Linguistics at Warwick University (2006-7). From 2006 to 2009, she worked at the department of Biology Didactics at the University of Cologne where she is currently writing her PhD-thesis. Since 2009, she has also been teaching English literature and culture at the English Department (Cologne).

Kylie Crane is *Juniorprofessor* for Anglophone Literatures and Cultures at the University of Mainz (Germersheim). Her first book *Myths of Wilderness in Contemporary Narratives: Environmental Postcolonialism in Australia and Canada* was published with Palgrave Macmillan in 2012. She has also presented and published on ecocriticism, food studies, postcolonial studies, indigenous writing (esp. in Australia), and cultural geography. Currently Kylie is working on a book project with the working title *Concrete and Plastic*, engaging with affect, aesthetics and material worlds.

Sieglinde Grimm studied German and English Philology, Philosophy and Sport at the University of Regenburg, the University of Munich and the University of Warwick. She graduated in 1990/91 ("Erstes Staatsexamen" and MA) and received her PhD from the University of Munich in 1995. She has taught at the University of Cologne (1992-2001), the University of Prague (1996), at Cambridge University (1998) and at the University of Frankfurt (2002-3). In 2006, she has received her *Zweites Staatsexamen*, and she has taught at a Gymnasium in Bonn from 2006 to 2009. She is now Professor of German at the University of Cologne and works on German literature of the 18th century (Hölderlin), on literary Modernism (Kafka and Rilke) as well as on pedagogy, intercultural learning and cultural ecology from a didactical perspective. She is currently co-editing a book on cultural ecology and the teaching of literature.

In February 2013, **Uwe Küchler** was appointed *Juniorprofessor* for the Teaching of English as a Foreign Language (TEFL) at Rheinische Friedrich-Wilhelms-Universität Bonn. He studied at Berlin's Humboldt-Universität (Germany), the University of London's Goldsmiths' College (Great Britain) and at Georgetown University in Washington DC (USA). Küchler was a Hans-Böckler-Scholar and member of a Postgraduate College at the Technische Universität Dortmund. He has worked as Assistant Professor at the Universität Halle-Wittenberg and taught English at a Secondary School (*Gymnasium*). Küchler's research interests comprise skills/multiple literacies as well as the teaching of literature, film and media in EFL. In his doctoral dissertation he pursued questions of intercultural learning and teaching in the context of higher education (*Interkulturelle Hochschullehre*, 2007). Currently, he is working on a book project that explores ecological issues in TEFL teaching.

Bettina Kümmerling-Meibauer is Professor in the German Department at the University of Tübingen, Germany. In 2010 she held the guest professorship in memory of Astrid Lindgren at the Linnaeus University, Kalmar/Växjö, Sweden, and in 2011 she was guest professor for children's literature at the University of Vienna. She is co-editor of the book series "Children's Literature, Culture, and Cognition" (John Benjamins, Amsterdam), and chair of the research project "Children's Literature and European Avant-Garde," funded by the European Science Foundation. Her research interests are international children's literature, interfaces between children's and adult literature, canon formations in children's literature, and the relationship between literacy studies, cognitive studies and children's literature.

Dominik Ohrem teaches Anglo-American history at the University of Cologne. In his research and teaching he focuses on US-histories of gender and race, the histories of African and Native Americans as well as environmental history. He